TOURISM:
the human perspective

RICHARD VOASE

Hodder & Stoughton

A MEMBER OF THE HODDER HEADLINE GROUP

British Library Cataloguing in Publication Data
A catalogue record for this title is available from The British
Library

ISBN 0 340 62067 6

First impression 1995
Impression number   10 9 8 7 6 5 4 3 2 1
Year   1999 1998 1997 1996 1995

Typeset by Litho Link Ltd, Welshpool, Powys, Wales.
Printed in Great Britain for Hodder & Stoughton Educational,
a division of Hodder Headline Plc, 338 Euston Road, London
NW1 3BH by Bath Press, Bath, Avon.

To Eileen and Neville, my parents

Contents

Acknowledgements

I am immensely grateful to my friend and colleague Vivienne Cuthill for her comments on the text. I am also grateful to Charlie Cooper, Mick Finn, John Hall and Kevin Meethan for their comments on particular chapters. Tim Bahaire, Martin Elliot-White, Alison Lewis, Roger Oldham and Stuart Wilks have assisted through the provision of specific sources and items of information, for which I thank them. I also acknowledge a debt to a host of friends and colleagues past and present who, throughout the progress of a career, have educated me and ultimately made possible a work such as this.

List of tables

Chapter 1

Introduction

The hospitality instinct

The inspiration for this book arose from one of those occasions when, for a moment, time appeared to stand still. As I gazed out over an English resort beach on a splendid summer's day, it seemed there was not one sad face to be seen. Young parents with young children, many also accompanied by grandparents, were rediscovering the pleasures of the family and the extended family. The heat of the sun reflected upwards from the white sand. Similarly, it seemed that the pleasure experienced by these people in each others' company also radiated upwards. Their joy was almost palpable. What became powerfully evident, in that timeless moment, was that the satisfactions of the holiday that these people were spending together would be largely derived from this experience of being together. No doubt the sandy beach, the blue sea and the fine weather made it easier; but these things were facilitators, means to an end, rather than ends in themselves.

With reflection came the thought that much of the rhyme and rhetoric of what has been labelled *the tourism industry* risks missing the point of what people are actually looking for in a tourist trip. They are wooed with talk of value for money, activities and facilities, but what they seek is more akin to a rediscovery of themselves. After all, a holiday is no normal purchase. It is *the* occasion in the year when the holiday-maker personally sets the agenda and determines what he or she shall do, uninhibited by the demands of paid employment and domesticity. The responsibilities of working in the tourism industry and delivering that dream are great, as are the satisfactions of a job well done. For a person working in tourism, understanding the depth and potential of those responsibilities is important, if the dream is to be delivered to the customer and the rewards of a job well done are to be known, experienced and enjoyed. It means acquiring and nurturing a passion for service, so that delivering the dream becomes instinctive, almost second nature. The term coined to describe this, and which makes frequent appearances in this text, is the *hospitality instinct.*

There are three theses that underpin the content of this book: first, that tourism is, Christopher Holloway's words, *largely psychological in its attractions* (1989, p. 11); secondly, that the psychology of the attractiveness of tourism is determined by the evolving culture and mores of the society which generates it; and thirdly, that competitive advantage in serving the tourist consumer of the future, whom Martin and Mason (1993, p. 37) have described as 'the thoughtful consumer' and whom the Henley Centre for Forecasting (1992, p. 56) have described as 'added-value' seekers, will be gained not by quality assurance systems alone, but by an instinctive passion for service which is as psychological in its nature as are the satisfactions of the tourist it serves.

The business writer Charles Handy (1991, p. 20) refers to the work of an American author Donald Schon who argued that applying concepts from one area of life to another was a good way of acquiring new insights. Schon's idea, termed 'displacement of concepts', is used to some considerable extent in this book in pursuit of fresh insights into the nature of the tourist experience. Moreover, if the character of tourism is indeed determined more by culture and mores than by accessibility and opportunity, as shall be argued during the course of this text, then these 'displaced concepts' may be at least as instrumental in determining tourist behaviour, or in explaining it, as more straightforward cause-and-effect rationales. As such, the approach which has been adopted is eclectic; but tourism as a phenomenon, and as a subject of study, and the consumer society which generates it, is by its very nature eclectic.

The 'resort-at-the-turning-point' is a theme which recurs throughout the book. This is partly due to the nature of the practitioner experience brought to the work, but mainly because of its generic importance. The destination is the essence of tourism, the foundation upon which other industry sectors form the superstructure. Carriers and tour operators can simply move on when times become hard, as when Sovereign Holidays, faced with declining interest in the Costa del Sol, removed the region from their UK brochure (Bunting 1990). The tour operator simply transfers their operation to some other more fashionable sun-spot but the destination, like an old oak, remains rooted in the ground. The development, evolution and mid-life crises of the destination can variously attract and repel their markets; and it will be argued that their success or otherwise in managing their evolution has a determining influence on the patterns of the industry.

The intended role of the book is as a companion volume to the standard reference texts. Its purpose is to provide a commentary, rooted in practitioner experience, and with the aim of offering a human perspective on tourism. The expansion of the industry and the proliferation of tourism study opportunities over recent years has given rise to a need for new textual material and further definition, exploration and understanding of the subject. What follows are the assembled notes of one explorer's journey so far.

Tourism in an economic context

There is a symbiotic relationship between social change and economic change and for that reason, by way of introduction, it is useful to place tourism in its economic context. Tourism is reckoned to be the world's largest industry. In 1987, it was considered to generate over 101 million jobs, representing one in every 16 jobs in the worldwide economy, and gross sales of over $2 trillion (Ritchie and Hawkins (eds.) 1991, p. 72). Tourism is also a growth industry. Predictions are that world tourism could grow by up to 4.5 per cent per annum by the turn of the century, providing between 38 million and 55 million additional jobs in the process (WTCC 1992, p. 3; Ritchie and Hawkins (eds.) 1991, p. 74). Within the United Kingdom, from which much of the material and most of the examples in this book are drawn, spending by UK residents on tourism was estimated in 1991 at £22 billion (English Tourist Board 1992b, p. 3), comparable with the total amount spent on education by all local authorities, the total amount spent by all domestic consumers on household goods and services, and the equivalent of 60 per cent of the Government's total expenditure on the National Health Service (Central Statistical Office 1994a, pp. 44, 249 and 45). Inbound tourism to the UK, that is, tourist visitors from overseas, brought £7.8 billion into the country in the year 1990 (English Tourist Board 1991), making the industry the second-largest generator of invisible export earnings, after financial services (Central Statistical Office 1994a, p. 235).

Not only is tourism a growth industry, but it is considered to offer a low-cost way of creating jobs in comparison with the capital-intensive require-ments of job creation in manufacturing industry. UK research quoted by Battersby (1990) estimated the cost of creating one job in tourism as £5,000, compared with £35,000 in a manufacturing concern. Research in the USA, quoted in Ritchie and Hawkins (eds.) (1991, p. 72), suggested that £1bn. of sales in tourism supports 5,000 jobs, whereas similar sales in the chemical industry support fewer than 300 jobs. The expanding nature of tourism has not gone unnoticed by governments in developing countries when seeking to diversify their economies and to find new and rapid ways of generating foreign currency earnings. In countries with mature economies, city governments faced with the contraction of their traditional manufacturing industries, and a shift to service industries, have used tourism development as a tool in their strategies for regeneration. The education sector has not been slow to recognise the potential of tourism as a growing provider of jobs, and there has been an explosion of courses available at both Further Education and Higher Education level. Between the years 1985 and 1993, the number of undergraduate tourism degree courses in the UK expanded from 0 to 17 (Tourism Society 1993).

And yet there is the need to be constructively critical of this picture of apparent growth. Statistics can be deceptive: the compilation of tourism statistics, in particular, can present an array of problems:

[There is] . . . The need to identify and separate 'tourism' activities and expenditures from other recreational and business activities of individuals, and to identify the tourism receipts from other receipts in establishments or service organisations which provide services both to tourists and others, such as local residents. (Bar-On 1989, p. 6)

How exactly can it be determined whether a job is in the tourism industry or not? For example, the chances of a barperson in a historic city serving exclusively tourists during an evening are remote, to say the least. Jobs created in public houses, restaurants, retail outlets etc., which may indeed contribute to the servicing of tourists, can equally be regarded as part of the general service industry structure. Wright (1994), reviewing a report produced by the Council for the Protection of Rural England, quotes its observation that the 1.5 million people which the English Tourist Board claimed to be employed in tourism included all persons working in libraries, sports, public houses and cafés. Wright concluded that a person can, apparently, work in tourism without realising it.

Another feature of tourism which has been known to attract criticism is that many tourism-related jobs are low paid and require low levels of skills, and may be part time or seasonal. Such jobs do not, it is said, offer the stability and opportunities for self-betterment which other kinds of job afford. Whether tourism jobs are good or bad depends very much on the perspective of the commentator. It has been argued that such jobs offer a positive 'entry-point' into work for ethnic minorities and women who otherwise, in some localities, would find it difficult to secure paid employment (Ritchie and Hawkins (eds.) 1991, p. 74). Equally, the same phenomenon could be regarded as an imprisonment of such

minorities in low-skilled roles. It can be argued that the increased availability of part-time and seasonal work can meet a genuine need in society: over recent years, there has been a considerable increase in the percentage of UK women active in the job market, the proportion having increased from 49.6 per cent in 1986 to 52.6 per cent in 1992, and projected to reach 56.6 per cent by the year 2006. Although many of these additional women took full-time employment, the biggest increase was seen in part-time work, and in comparison with other European countries, UK women have a distinct predilection for part-time employment (Central Statistical Office 1994b). Also, the numbers of students in higher education has increased significantly over recent years and these form a useful reservoir of seasonal labour for tourism-related jobs within the UK and abroad.

Tourism in a political context

Public authorities, and the publics who elect them, can have very mixed attitudes towards tourism. Paradoxically, it is in those locations where tourism is a significant contributor to the local economy that ambivalence can become outright hostility, for example in 'tourist historic' cities and seaside communities. This conundrum is discussed in Chapters 12 and 13. Suffice it to say for the moment that ambivalence about tourism reaches right to the top: the UK Government announced, in 1992, a cut in government support to the English Tourist Board (ETB), whose responsibility is to develop tourism in England and market domestic tourist opportunities to British people, from £13.9m. in 1993/94 to £9m. in 1995/96 (Smithers 1992). The rationale was that the infrastructure of domestic tourism development and promotion was now in place and that the level of central government support could be reduced. Over the preceding years the balance of payments on the tourism account, which was even in 1985, had drifted into a £2.7bn. deficit by 1992. It is not unreasonable to suggest that some of the tourist expenditure which went abroad could have been retained within the UK, given the right domestic product and adequate promotion. Arguably an increase in an investment of £13.9m.

in the activities of the ETB would have been a small price to pay in an attempt to reduce a trading deficit of £2.7bn. It will be argued in this book that public bodies bear a significant responsibility for developing and sustaining the tourism industry, and that degrees of success or failure can be linked with the vigour or otherwise with which public bodies have discharged their responsibilities.

Definition of a tourist

Burkart and Medlik (1981, p. 320) suggest that tourists 'are people who travel to destinations outside the places where they normally live and work with a view to returning within a few days, weeks or months' and point out that tourists can be classified in accordance with various other criteria relating to type and nature of trip. Various definitions are discussed at length in the principal texts (e.g. Burkart and Medlik 1981, pp. 42–3; Mathieson and Wall 1982, pp. 10–13) and it is not proposed to duplicate those discussions here, save to emphasise that a tourist is not defined so much by having vacational intentions, but by being away from his or her home and home area for reasons of pleasure, business, visiting friends and relatives, or one of a range of other reasons. This coincides with the definitions favoured by the statutory tourist authorities within the United Kingdom, such as the British Tourist Authority (BTA) and ETB. It is useful to consider that for many laypeople, tourism is equated with holidaymaking, whereas a businessperson, a conference delegate, a person staying with a relative, all fall within the definition of being a tourist. The failure of the public to understand this can lead to problems when specific types of tourist are viewed by the public as some kind of a nuisance or hazard. For example, in some resorts in the south of England, the arrival of overseas students in large numbers for language tuition can be perceived by local residents as a nuisance, but the reality is that such tourists can contribute more to local economies than regular vacational tourists (see Batchelor 1992). Two qualifications need to be appended to the definition of a tourist: first, there is a point at which a tourist becomes a resident. A simple way of determining residency

or otherwise may be to consider whether the tourist is paying that country's taxes. If the tourist is liable to taxation, then the tourist has probably become a resident. For example, the United Kingdom Inland Revenue considers that a person resident in the UK for six months or longer becomes liable to UK taxation. Similarly, an elderly person staying in hotel accommodation in Spain from the UK from November until March may be regarded as a long-stay tourist rather than a resident. There are also special cases: for example, a British person taking up residence in the Isle of Man for tax avoidance purposes must spend no more than 26 days per year in mainland UK if tax avoidance is to be maintained.

The second qualification of the definition is potentially more problematic because it concerns day-trippers or *excursionists*. Technically, day-visitors are not tourists because their trip does not include an overnight stay. However, some sectors of the tourist infrastructure of a country or region are heavily or even entirely dependent upon the excursionist market. Theme parks are such an example, Disneyland Paris being an exception with its associated hotel accommodation. Certain museums, retail centres, and theatrical quarters such as the West End of London are dependent in varying degrees on visits from excursionists. One could take the view that theme parks and the other facilities mentioned are simply part of the *leisure* infrastructure and as such are not tourist facilities, nor are the excursionists tourists. But the reality is that in terms of *perception* these facilities are part of the tourist product and in terms of *revenues*, day-tripper spend is significant: in 1988/89, UK residents made over 630 million day trips and spent over £5bn., the equivalent of nearly half of the domestic tourism spend for the same year (Central Statistical Office 1993, p. 149). For these reasons it is useful to regard day-tripping as tourist activity but to bear in mind that some tourist destinations would not exist in their present form if they had to depend entirely on day-visitor revenues: resorts, as opposed to theme parks and tourist cities, would be unable to sustain themselves. A resort which attracts only day-visitors needs no hotel base. This implies a denuded resident population, an erosion of the local tax base, no staying-visitor support for evening theatrical entertainments, in short the resort would cease to exist as the place which presently makes it enjoyable to visit, whether for a day-trip or a holiday. There are examples of resorts which for local reasons, such as the presence of an amusement park in the central seafront such as at Margate, attract high-spending day-visitors: the day-visitor spend in Margate in 1991 was a signficant £18.40 per head, representing around 65 per cent of the daily spend for a staying visitor which was £28, about average for a seaside resort in that year (Thanet District Council 1991a, p. 37). On the other hand, a day-visitor to Bridlington in 1979 spent only £3.19, the equivalent of only 44 per cent of the staying-visitor spend of £7.29 (East Yorkshire Borough Council 1980a, pp. 18, 35).

Tourism and the host community

The impact of tourism on host communities has been the subject of considerable academic attention, not least because of the global diversity of contemporary destinations and the individuality of the outcomes in terms of social, economic and cultural effects. Of principal focus in this text is the response of host communities in mature destinations within the developed world, both resorts and cities, to tourism and its impact on their economies and lifestyles. Such responses, as alluded to earlier and discussed in the coming chapters, can range from unqualified enthusiasm to acute scepticism. It is suggested that the key to understanding this may lie in the perspective taken. From one perspective, tourism is an *activity*: the tourist visits a destination for vacation or business purposes as a means to an end. The tourist is not consciously consuming, but simply exercising his or her leisure or business life in a different location. Where the host regards tourism as an activity, the individual tourist may be welcomed, perhaps with considerable enthusiasm, as a valued guest. When the tourist arrives in large numbers and is perceived to create inconvenience in the life of the community, the welcome may be less enthusiastic. Either way, the *activity perspective* determines the nature of the welcome.

Producers, that is those who work in tourism, are more likely to take an *industry perspective*. Producers make their living from tourism and are conscious of being part of a collection of industry sectors concerned with transport, accommodation, visitor attractions, destination marketing, catering, retailing, and others, which interlink in order to deliver what is termed the 'tourist product'. Some of these sectors, such as the restaurant trade, may be only partly dependent on tourism. A sector such as accommodation is by definition almost wholly dependent on tourism, with the possible exception of those hotels, such as some of the major London hotels, which offer long-term residence opportunities as a limited ancillary service. The dependency of visitor attractions on tourists is either 100 per cent or zero, depending on the chosen definition of what constitutes a tourist, and the link between retailing and tourism depends very largely on local circumstances. The manager of a resort branch of a well-known chain of department stores suggested, in conversation a few years ago, that the continued presence of his employer in that town was dependent upon the additional revenues yielded by the annual influx of tourists. The store's viability, if required to sustain itself purely from residential business, was questionable. Paradoxically, this was at a time when the local authority in that particular town was questioning its role and responsibility for marketing the resort as a tourist destination.

Although it is primarily the producer who thinks in terms of the industry perspective, it is also possible for tourists to do the same and view the purchase of holidays as active consumption, rather than as an extension of their leisure lives. This could be said to have a lot to do with the phenomenon of package holidays, which are marketed very vigorously in terms which are not at all dissimilar from those adopted for fast-moving consumer goods. For example, in the summer of 1994, UK travel agencies and tour operators engaged in a price war in the launch of the 1995 range of brochures. Discounts of up to 13 per cent and 'children go free' incentives were offered, and the Consumers' Association was reported to have warned potential customers that the special deals on offer were 'simply advertising gimmicks to persuade people to make bookings' (*Yorkshire Post* 1994a, p. 4). Where both the tourist producer and tourist consumer are agreed that the objective of the transaction is to secure a good financial deal, and there are many buyers and sellers, a vigorous market is the result. It will be suggested in Chapter 6 that this conspicuous consumption belies the real satisfactions which people seek from holidays.

Misunderstandings and conflict seem to arise when the two perspectives, of *activity* and *industry*, become confused. Hostility to tourism from the host community may result from genuine misunderstanding of the economic contribution made by tourism. For example, tourism in a historic city may support a range of retail shopping opportunities which, without the visitor base, would not be available to the host community. But residents, regarding tourism as an *activity*, regard parking problems and an excess of people on the streets as an intrusion into the normal life of the city. Alternatively, hostility may arise from partial understanding: the resident realises that tourism brings money into the town, but has concluded that the revenues remain in the pockets of direct recipients such as hoteliers, not appreciating that tourism income trickles down through the community as hoteliers employ staff, buy provisions and make other purchases, and that tourist spending is actually amplified through the *multiplier effect*: that is, that tourism expenditure actually raises the whole level of economic activity in the locality (see Mathieson and Wall 1982, ch. 3 for a discussion of the multiplier effect). One consequence of this amplification of economic activity is that the total number of jobs created by tourism exceeds those directly created by the industry: for example, one piece of research has suggested that for each job created by tourism developments which were supported by the ETB, two extra jobs were created (Battersby 1990).

The third explanation is that residents are fully aware of and understand all the economic benefits that tourism can bring, but are insulated from the need for a prosperous local economy. Retired people with an occupational pension and investment income may have little personal interest in the health of local businesses and may simply not wish to share the locality with tourists. This is a particular problem in destinations which have passed their peak, whose tourism business is contracting, and which become favoured locations for retirement. The problem is encapsulated in this statement from a resident of the Yorkshire resort of Bridlington, collected by a school student during a geography fieldwork project in 1985:

I don't like the 'season' when all the holidaymakers come here. Bridlington is far better during the winter when it's quiet. That's when I like to walk my dog along the beach. During the summer I won't go near the beach or the harbour. It's too messy. I know the visitors spend a lot of money here but, since I'm on my own now since my husband died and I've got a good income, it really doesn't affect me . . . (Atkinson et al. 1985, p. B25)

Translated into voting habits, such attitudes can undermine the destination's ability to maintain and sustain its appeal. So, is tourism an activity or an industry? In truth, it is both at one and the same time. It is a mobile leisure activity in which tourists consciously make use of the facilities of someone else's territory, and pay for the privilege. It is also an industry, equipped with professional associations, specialist education and training provision, and in most countries is covered by some legislative framework. In the UK, for example, an Act of Parliament (the Development of Tourism Act 1969) instituted the statutory tourist boards for England, Scotland and Wales, and the BTA whose responsibility is the marketing of Britain as a destination abroad.

Responsibilities and rewards

The process of selling holidays has often been compared with the selling of dreams. Working in tourism is easily viewed from the outside as a glamorous option, but the reality is that delivering other people's dreams involves a lot of meticulous and, to be frank, humdrum work. Norman (1989), writing about employment and training in tourism, observed that a customer will judge a £20 million investment in a hotel by whether a cup of coffee is available at ten o'clock in the evening. Williams and Shaw, writing in Cooper (ed.) (1990, ch. 4), report on research which was undertaken in England's West Country. The research concerned the business performance of people retiring from first careers elsewhere in the country in order to acquire and operate tourism businesses, in a region in which they themselves had formerly enjoyed being tourists. Once there, the level of service they wish to provide is unexceptional because of their non-economic motivations, and their low level of hospitality management skills. The discovery that working in paradise means being at the beck and call of visitors at all hours of the day and night can be a rude awakening. Basil Fawlty, the caricature created by John Cleese and apparently modelled on a real hotel proprietor encountered somewhere in the south-west of England, is so unnervingly funny because facets of his character are, in the experience of many people, unnervingly real.

The responsibility of working in tourism is greater than in many other consumer industries, because the customer entrusts the provider with his or her very being. The provider must accommodate, feed and reassure the customer in surroundings which may be unfamiliar and, for some, a little frightening. The customer is, and feels, vulnerable. That is why shabby treatment on holiday hurts so much. If a customer feels wronged, he or she is unable to resolve the matter as he or she may do, if slighted in a shop at home, by simply walking out. Withdrawing from a situation when flying at 30 thousand feet over the Atlantic Ocean, or when pre-booked and pre-paid into a hotel in a foreign country, presents difficulties. Moreover, the injury will affect, and maybe take place in front of, spouses and children. That is why understanding the vulnerability of the customer, and their expectations of their precious saved-for and long-anticipated holiday, has to be rooted in something more than a commitment to fulfilling the requirements of a quality assurance manual. What is needed is an authentic passion for service, an instinct for hospitality which communicates itself to the customers and convinces that even when things go wrong, as they inevitably do from time to time, they are being looked after and their needs are receiving the highest priority. Thomas Cook understood and practised the hospitality instinct (see Chapter 2 and Brendon 1991); so did Sir Billy Butlin, and arguably so does Richard Branson, as the following observations from a biographer seem to indicate:

To most people, a man who can answer two hundred letters within a few days of nearly losing his life in a car accident has an unusual dedication to his work. Branson does not see it that way. He feels a responsibility to his employees, and to his customers . . . The truth is of course that Richard Branson loves his work for its own sake, and finds the principal fulfilment of his life in it. (Jackson 1994, pp. 359–60)

Major tour operators go to great pains to convince us that they, as organisations, possess and practise the hospitality instinct. Sample this strapline from a 1994 Thomsons television advertisement: 'We spend fifty-two weeks a year making your two weeks perfect'. Consider this from Airtours: 'Working hard to make you happy from beginning to end'. A graduate trainee with Thomsons or Airtours will not be a professional recliner-on-a-sunbed. What is promised is a job of work with the commission to create, as nearly as possible, two weeks of consistent bliss for other people. Therein lie the responsibilities, and the rewards.

Chapter 2

Being hospitable

Delivering the dream to tourist customers involves more than a personal passion for service. It involves teams of people working together who strive to ensure, for example, that Thomsons' clients enjoy the two perfect weeks which that company's advertising message promises. People like teams. They warm to the air of confidence and mutual trust which a good team enjoys. That, no doubt, is why a television advertising campaign for British Petroleum (BP), screened in early 1995, sought to emphasise the claimed aptitude for teamwork of employees of that company. It portrayed the fictional frustration of a television journalist and film crew who, travelling the world to find a BP employee who would claim credit for a particular achievement, is constantly referred to colleagues in other parts of the globe. At each juncture the journalist is told that, without others' co-operation, the achievement would not have been possible. If the dream is to be delivered through other people, then those people need to share in the passion for service. Insight is needed into how managements can create an organisational culture which facilitates the practice of the hospitality instinct.

Motivation in the workplace has been extensively discussed in management literature and a useful starting point may be Handy's (1993) *Understanding Organisations*, and its chapter-by-chapter bibliographies, and whose summaries of the common body of motivational theory have contributed to the content of this chapter. The purpose of this chapter is to consider some of the most widely discussed theories and concepts relating to management, motivation and leadership and relate them to the context of a service industry such as tourism, and in particular to the creation of an instinctive passion for service in its employees.

Inspiration

A group of students once agreed to conduct a little *ad hoc* research in preparation for a seminar. Each was to interview a person working in the tourism and leisure industries and gather some information on the rewards of the job, levels of motivation, remuneration levels and the like. The results, although based on a very small sample size and limited to particular people who were accessible to the students during the course of a week, were interesting. It seemed that people in managerial roles in these industries found their work prestigious and rewarding, and that these rewards outweighed the perceived disadvantages of unsocial hours. One of their greatest frustrations was the difficulty in instilling a similar sense of mission into their employees who were part time or seasonal, working unsocial hours for a flate rate of low pay. And yet, under certain conditions, this seasonal work-force could not only be highly motivated, but consider itself highly rewarded. One student reported on the rewards of working for a company organising camping holidays in the south of France: the pay was not high, but contact with fellow seasonal workers gave rise to an excellent social life, and the location was exotic. Knowing that such work is temporary had a lot to do with levels of motivation. A waiter who regularly works the ski resorts of the French alps in winter and the hotels of the Riviera in summer can soon become accustomed to and possibly bored by the rhythm of the job, just as surely as a businessperson who is compelled to fly to Hong Kong twice per month will begin to regard such trips as a burden rather than a novelty. Seasonal or part-time work in the tourism and leisure industries tends to be low paid and bereft of employee benefits such as pension schemes, and consequently compares unfavourably with employment in some other fields. There are two key observations which, together, issue a challenge to managements in these industries.

1   *The operational employees are the interface with the customer*   Being an adept and highly motivated manager is not of itself useful when it is the staff, rather than the manager, who are dealing with customers. In common with most service industries, the 'product' is a service which is consumed as it is delivered and success depends not just on whether, for example, a cup of coffee is hot rather than tepid, but on the manner in which it is served. This is an issue which simply does not arise in the manufacturing sector. An employee working on a production line in a factory packing frozen peas has to observe certain standards of dress and conduct in order to comply with laws relating to food hygiene and health and safety at work, but essentially is not on public view and standards of appearance, language and deportment are secondary to the need to get the peas packed. That worker, buying back his or her own products in a supermarket, may serve him- or herself alongside another customer who has no idea of his or her role in providing that product. In the café, the waiter or waitress and the cup of coffee are inseparable parts of the same product. They are one and the same thing, part of the *service*. Arguably, the employee is the major partner in this service. Customers are generally ready to forgive tepid coffee if it is replaced swiftly and courteously; the best cup of coffee, served after a ten-minute wait with ill grace, is unlikely to satisfy.

2   *The purchase has great importance to the customer*   Just how important a holiday can be has been illustrated in the conclusion to Chapter 1. Thomsons' and Airtours' promises about spending all year to make your two weeks perfect, and working hard to make you happy from beginning to end, are indicative not just of the customer's anticipation and expectation of a good time, but of the amount of the household budget involved. After a house and a car, holidays can be the third most significant purchase. What is of equal importance is that, whether an expensive holiday or a cup of coffee while on a day-trip, often the service will be delivered to the customer in the presence of his or her relatives, friends or colleagues. This adds another dimension to the level of expectation: an office argument in the course of one's work is to be expected from time to time, but being treated badly by a waiter in the presence of family and friends is quite another. The customer is relaxed, unprepared for conflict; is reluctant to initiate conflict because of the presence of family and friends, and other customers nearby; yet is highly affronted by the treatment received. Whether the customer chooses fight or flight, the end result will be the unlikeliness of a repeat visit and the relating of the tale to third parties, creating a 'reputation' for the establishment concerned. It has to be said, too, that on occasions a minority of customers will take advantage of problem situations to belittle staff in the presence of onlookers. This could happen to any tourism or hospitality staff, but observation suggests that a special burden is borne by employees of public-sector organisations such as railways.

The challenge to the manager is to make people feel good about themselves to the extent that good customer service comes naturally. We all know that this is possible: some hotels, some restaurants, some airlines just seem to have a feel about them which communicates itself to the customer; we know that we, as customers, are at the centre of the operation, and *believe* that if a problem should arise, it will be dealt with effectively. It is a positive pleasure to be their customer. We use them again, and tell our friends. The discussion which follows will be framed by the thesis that success requires *both management and leadership*. The two are not the same thing. For example, the management of a hotel may install impeccable systems for service delivery including intensive training in reception and waiting duties, specifications for room cleaning, a portfolio of information to deal with guest queries, and a complete Staff Manual containing written synopses of the systems and expectations. Making sure that such arrangements are in place, operating, maintained and amended when necessary is the essence of *operational management*. However, this of itself is not enough. The most impeccable operational systems may be part of what is required to make employees feel equipped and empowered to do the job, but a real passion for service requires inspiration from some other source. There are some people for whom serving people, helping them to enjoy their stay, is inspiration and a reward in itself. This kind of self-motivation is of particular importance in the professions such as Law and Education where employees are relied upon to maintain, of their own volition, standards set by peer agreement.

Some larger organisations are apt to expect their statements of purpose, or mission statements, to inspire work-forces to a vision of the future. This can sometimes pose a problem, not merely because, as Kotler and Armstrong (1991, pp. 30–1) observe, these statements are not always well worded, but they are by definition a specific rather than a shared vision: no matter how much consultation takes place before the final version of such a statement is produced, each person's vision of his or her personal commitment to their work, what motivates, inspires and rewards them, will be as individual as their own personalities. This is not to say that people cannot draw inspiration from ideals, but very often there is a bland quality to committee-designed statements of purpose and a concomitant risk of alienating staff by outlining expectations in coded 'management-speak' rather than straightforward language. Freemantle comments as follows:

The difference between a conventional objective and a vision of success is a passionate conviction about what has to be achieved . . . Ownership of the vision throughout the organisation is crucial. That can never be accomplished by a mechanistic MBO [management by objectives] process. (1992 pp. 31–2)

So, impersonal company pronouncements may be an improbable basis for creating a passion for service. However, many employees can find themselves moved and inspired by the example of *other people*. The theatricality of an American sales conference is the most vivid application of this principle. Consumer durables such as (for example) vacuum cleaners have in themselves limited inspirational value, but in the hands of a trainer equipped with evangelistic presentational techniques and a gospel-durable belief in the product, a salesperson can go home from a sales convention in no doubt of the contribution of these vacuum cleaners to life, the universe and everything. And in a very real sense, such a belief is not ill founded: those who work in tourism may consider the importance of the holiday in the lives of their customers to be a powerful reward, but the world needs vacuum cleaners as it needs holidays. Feeling inspired about one's job need not just be the prerogative of those whose work the world regards as glamorous. But it is the example of *other inspired people* which helps this vision become real.

To put it another way: just suppose a person has a neighbour whose passion is for collecting stamps, a passion which he or she does not share. Yet, because of the neighbour's passion for the pursuit, that person looks in philatelists' shop windows in case any of the examples about which the neighbour is currently enthusing are there; on trips abroad, the person seeks out stamp shops, even becoming a minor expert in his or her own right. The person does all this, not out of an enthusiasm for stamps, but out of respect and admiration for the enthusiasm of the neighbour, and feels rewarded when able to contribute to the neighbour's hobby. In the same way, parents share in their children's interests, spouses seek to understand and contribute to each other's special interests, colleagues of this author have graciously offered references and pieces of information for the preparation of this book. The situation could be summarised in terms of three principles:

- enthusiasm is *earned*, rather than *demanded*
- enthusiasm is *inspired by personal example*
- enthusiasm is *infectious*, travelling from person to person

The ability to motivate others through example, to inspire rather than prescribe, to evoke an enthusiasm in employees whose share of the financial and other rewards may be minimal but who are simply pleased to be part of something which is good, is to do with style rather than technique, with personality rather than knowledge. This goes beyond management; it is *leadership*, a term and a concept which is now making a welcome return to the body of management theory. Just as 'marketing' is at one and the same time a philosophy of business and a promotional process, 'management' is at one and the same time a set of techniques *and* the application of a set of personal qualities whose use empowers people for success. Managers who successfully combine the two roles have an understanding of the importance of both. Consider the following from Sir John Harvey-Jones:

I have always believed that management is an art rather than a science. The artistry lies in the combination of skills, perceptions, intuitions and combined experiences which are brought to bear on problems which are continually different and almost invariably unique. Management is ultimately about people, and thankfully, there are endless differences between people. People change dramatically from day to day ... the fact that no management problem is ever the same as the other, that each solution is a unique one, does not however mean that there is nothing in management which requires learning. (1994, Introduction, p. 1)

These words evoke a picture of a manager whose success in motivating staff relies on inspiration rather than coercion. Management demands a range of intuitive and personality skills in addition to expertise and techniques. Knowing that management is an art means understanding that differences between people are not inconveniences to be dealt with through corporate homogenisation; those differences are assets which are to be positively celebrated: after all, any organisation which does not encourage self-examination and internal debate will find itself being less than the sum of its parts. And although to some extent managers are born rather than made, much can be learned through thought, reflection and the application of theoretical models which have proved themselves elsewhere. For the rest of this chapter, a body of theory surrounding motivation and leadership will be surveyed, and the implications for the practice of the hospitality instinct considered.

Motivation in the workplace

Successful military leaders such as Admiral Lord Nelson placed the most hazardous and unpleasant demands on those in their charge, and yet his seamen loved him, and wept when he died. A seasonal worker, finding himself or herself working in a hotel restaurant for a manager who genuinely cares not only about the quality of the service to customers but about the well-being of employees, may work better than ever before simply because he or she feels comfortable and supported, and is confident of being dealt with fairly. This may occur even if the senior management of the hotel are mediocre. Alternatively, another worker's response in identical circumstances could be very different: unimpressed by one middle-manager's attempt to work well for mediocre senior management, the worker may turn in an indifferent performance in spite of the supportive nature of his or her immediate circumstances. In this sense we must invoke Harvey-Jones's observation that 'no management problem is ever the same' but can examine various theories to see what insights they can afford into the human personality in the workplace.

There are a number of commonly known theories by which motivation in the workplace can be understood. McGregor (1960) advanced what is known as his X and Y theory. He suggested under theory X that workers were inherently unmotivated and would perform in anticipation of financial reward. His preference was for his theory Y which held that workers are by nature creative and, if encouraged to set their own goals, can demonstrate a reservoir of potential which under theory X would remain untapped. In other words, theory Y argues for participative rather than authoritarian management. In a stable employment situation this sounds the more attractive of the two propositions, but in the case of a manager recruiting cleaning staff for a summer season at a hotel, one wonders if the time, occasion and circumstance are conducive to the application of such a principle. The short duration of the engagement combined with limited opportunities for creativity suggest theory X may have more to offer in such circumstances than theory Y. Herzberg's (1968) motivation-hygiene theory suggested, with the benefit of having been researched and tested, that there were two separate sets of factors which motivated people in the workplace. He pointed to what he termed *hygiene factors* such as salary, working environment and company policy, which did not of themselves motivate but which would act as demotivators if they were not pitched correctly. The real *motivators*, as identified by Herzberg, were of a more aspirational nature and included such things as responsibility, the opportunity to achieve and advance and job satisfaction. Such elements as salary had to be right, but were not prime motivators.

At this point it may be useful to refer to a topical and disputed innovation of the present day, that is, *performance-related pay* (PRP), which in the view of the author poses a threat to the development of a passion for service within an organisational culture. In a western world whose political and economic culture is far more market orientated than it was, say, 15 years ago, the notion of linking pay to performance makes superficial sense. After all, people want higher salaries when seeking promotion, so why not reward them with extra remuneration for performing well in their present jobs? The first point to be made in considering this issue is that salary is regarded, in Herzberg's terms, as a *hygiene* rather than a *motivational* factor. Recent research quoted by Handy showed that young urban professionals in the USA valued independence, gratifying work and contribution to the public good, more highly than money as factors in the job. In the UK, a 1989 survey documented the greater importance attached to job quality, security and a feeling of doing something worthwhile amongst a sample of 1,063 workers (Handy 1993, p. 32). Admittedly in a parallel survey in the USA quoted by Handy, a sample of all workers narrowly rated money as most important, followed by the other factors. But it is amongst the managerial and professional classes, rather than general workers, that PRP schemes (as opposed to traditional bonus

schemes) are being introduced, precisely amongst those for whom, the evidence suggests, the motivators of work are not primarily financial.

At the time of writing, PRP is being introduced across a range of public and private organisations in the UK, just at the same time as its problems are being perceived on the other side of the Atlantic. The problem caused by PRP is not so much the financial reward, but that it is used by employees as a measure of comparison, or, in Handy's terms, 'equity' (1993, p. 52). Pay levels are the barometer of the relative value that the organisation sets on certain jobs and certain people. Opponents of PRP argue that, given that organisations are organic by nature, itemising the contribution of any one employee toward specific achievements can never be entirely objective; think of the hypothetical example, quoted earlier, of the effective restaurant manager compensating for the mediocrity of the hotel's senior management. Who is responsible for that achievement? The restaurant manager, whose achievement it was, or the general manager, who hired him? PRP has been the subject of documentary examination (BBC Radio 4 1993) and attracted contrasting views from various industry contributors. The problems associated with such schemes appeared to be concerned not so much with staff appraisal, but with the difficulty of administering the schemes objectively, employing 'equity'. The chairman of Northern Foods described PRP as 'a second-best to good hands-on management' and it was noted that an enormous scheme in the USA, involving 160,000 federal employees, had recently been abandoned. The management consultant David Freemantle has emphatic views on the subject:

You may as well call it carrot pay. It is one of the wildest examples of how organisations corrupt their culture . . . it is impossible to differentiate fairly between the performance of all individuals in a team . . . By introducing carrot pay, top bosses opt out of the essential leadership role of inspiring their people to achieve great things. (1992, pp. 199–200)

The essence of the threat posed by PRP is that it encourages organisational introspection. 'Performance' and 'service' are not necessarily the same thing, and employees who are subject to a

PRP regime may become more concerned with the internal appearance of their results as measured by the PRP scheme, than with the external reality as experienced by customers. Freemantle's recommended alternative is to select the best people, pay them a good salary and 'work flat out to help them achieve great results', not dissimiliar from the principle proposed by the chairman of Northern Foods and arguably in keeping with the need to create a passion for service which is the hallmark of the hospitality instinct. In many ways the debate over PRP encapsulates the tension of management versus leadership. A manager who is unsure of the nature of leadership may think, mistakenly, that financial incentives have a generic capacity to make staff perform. Managers who understand leadership know that inspiration and example can achieve a great deal more.

Concluding this brief survey, it is useful to consider the work of the psychologist Abraham Maslow and his theoretical 'hierarchy of needs'. This was outlined in his book *Motivation and Personality* (1970) in which he argued that human behaviour could be understood as an effort to satisfy a series of needs of progressive complexity, starting with basic needs such as food, shelter and security, and then seeking love, a sense of belonging, aesthetic pleasure and so on. This theory has been used extensively in Chapter 6 in an examination of tourist motivations. Various writers have applied Maslow's theory to motivation in the workplace whereby the basic needs, which the employee regards as prerequisites or in Maslow's terminology *prepotent*, can be regarded as salary, office accommodation, pension scheme, safe working environment and so on. Once these are satisfied, rapport with colleagues, positive appreciation from superiors, meaningful work and career development opportunities can be regarded as 'higher needs' which, the lower needs having been satisfied, command the attention of employees. Applying Maslow to workplace motivation has its uses in that the basic or lower needs are in some ways comparable with Herzberg's *hygiene factors* and the higher needs comparable with his *motivators*. Maslow himself stated that his theory should be applied to analyse any single act of an individual in terms of all the needs of the hierarchy (Maslow 1970, p. 55) and it is important

to remember, bearing in mind Herzberg's theory and the observations about leadership made above, that actual *motivation* only begins when the higher needs of the Maslow hierarchy are being satisfied.

Leadership qualities

If Sir John Harvey-Jones is right about management being more an art than a science, then defining the qualities of a good leader may be as difficult as defining good art. Leadership is one of life's vitally important abstractions, such as freedom, love and inspiration. By common consent these things are known to exist, are observed and experienced, but describing or ascribing them is difficult. Presumably, in the same way as good art communicates effectively with its intended audience, a good leader inspires his or her subordinates. Yet some works of art, while revered by experts, do not communicate easily with a general audience. This can only mean that the audience is ignorant, the work is not art, or the art and its audience are mutually alien to one another. Leadership involves, as a pivotal quality, the ability to establish effective communication. Reasons for the effective communication as listed by Freemantle include the need for feedback on progress, understanding the real nature of problems encountered by the organisation, the need to know how their own performance can improve, and an opportunity to raise both professional and personal concerns secure in the knowledge that their manager is interested in them (1992, p. 17).

Styles of leadership have been variously described as varying between the democratic and the authoritarian, which leads to questions about the choice of methods used to achieve results. Is a manager good because he or she achieves particular *ends*, or are the *means* just as important? Admiral Lord Nelson, mentioned earlier, had the remarkable ability to plan meticulously, so that his captains knew exactly what was expected of them. Added to this, he had the talent to seize opportunities when they presented themselves, which was all the more impressive because such was his relationship with his captains that they knew how his mind would work when events took an unexpected turn. His strategies could be highly unorthodox, as at the Battle of Trafalgar. He could also be disobedient to his own superiors when the opportunity suited, as at the Battle of Copenhagen when, ignoring a signal from his senior admiral, Nelson held a telescope to his blind eye and declared 'I see no ships'. Nelson was uniquely possessed of the twin talents of planning and opportunism. This contrasts with, for example, Lawrence of Arabia, whose successes were the product of a more chaotic temperament and who must have been, in some measure, difficult to work for.

As with motivation, there are various theories as to what makes a good leader. *Trait theories* suggest that leadership qualities are traits which are inherent to the personality, either inherited or acquired in early childhood while the personality is being formed. A trait theorist would suggest that there is such a thing as a 'born leader', and that attempts to create leaders out of people who are not in possession of the right traits are unlikely to succeed. Trait theories have a lot to be said for them: it is certainly true that some people are endowed with a degree of intelligence, self-assurance and extroversion which makes them effective leaders. Recruitment to the officer training programmes of the British armed forces does not aim to instil such qualities into people, but to identify their presence and develop them so that their owners become effective officers. There are, however, a number of problems associated with trait theories. A person who is intelligent, extrovert and self-assured does not necessarily become a good leader: experience shows that there are many people who possess all of these talents and more, but who are unable to harness them to the motivation and empowerment of other people. What is more, having the right traits for leadership in certain situations does not necessarily mean that the leader is effective in all situations. For example, a person may be a highly effective leader and manager in the workplace, thriving on the responsibility and authority enjoyed over people who are to some extent distant; but in the home, he or she may be less adequate in meeting the more intimate motivational needs of a spouse and family.

Also, different cultures have different ideas of what a leader should be. Within western society,

research by Hofstede quoted by Handy suggests that different countries have different expectations with respect to the degree of remoteness, termed 'power distance', which leaders should adopt, implying that the effectiveness of a management style is in part determined by cultural attitudes to authoritarianism or consensuality. Countries such as France and Italy are said to be more comfortable with large power distances, Scandinavian countries with narrow power distances, Anglo-Saxon countries lying somewhere in the middle (1993, p. 109). 'Born leaders' along the lines of Lord Nelson may be less welcome in collectivist cultures such as Japan where, as Handy (1993, p. 117) points out, the language has no word for 'leadership'.

Style theories take a different, in some ways opposite, position to trait theories. They maintain that success is achieved not by having the right personality traits, but by adopting the appropriate style. This usually boils down to a balance between authoritarianism and consensuality, to be modified in accordance with the culture of operation as noted above. The authoritarian style is what could be termed a 'top-down' approach whereby the manager decides and the employees implement. The ultimate consensual style is a 'bottom-up' approach whereby employees are heavily involved in consultation, and decisions represent the sum total of collective wisdom. Not surprisingly, theorists educated in western liberal democracies favour consensual styles and it is true that the work of motivational theorists such as Herzberg suggest that this style is more likely to be effective. But even within a western liberal democracy, the choice of style must differ in accordance with the needs of the organisation. An army on active service, for example, is unlikely to afford itself the luxury of consensual decision-making for reasons which will be obvious. In tourism, which as an industry draws on a variety of industry sectors each with their own characteristics, some variety of style is obviously necessary. A tour operator putting together and selling holiday packages may give its product managers guidelines to work to in negotiation with accommodation providers and airlines, but needs to rely on these product managers to contribute their own views on the development of the overall product. They, after all, are the ones who visit the contractor. Similarly, the tour operator representative actually handling the holidays on site is the person closest to the customer and whose views and reports will be valuable in framing future policy. Authoritarian supervision over such people would be almost impossible; they have to be trusted. Not so with seasonally recruited employees to operate a hotel: there is the potential for closer supervision, and arguably the need to set clear ground-rules as to expectations and standards and to exert discipline if these standards are not maintained.

In the real world, each management situation is unique, and interpretation through trait and style theories alone may be inappropriate. *Contingency theories* seek to recognise this and, adopting a situational approach, place the unique character of each situation at the centre. The variables involved may include:

- the relationship between the leader and the employees
- the nature of the task(s) involved
- the familiarity of the employees with the task(s)
- the familiarity of the leader with the task(s)
- differences in familiarity and experience amongst the employees

Contingency theory would suggest a different style for each situation, but it is important to observe the principle of equity among staff. For example, a manager knowing a lot about brochure production but little about negotiations with carriers may be ill advised to adopt a directive style with the staff working in brochure production, and a consultative style with those involved in negotiations with carriers. The staff who are skilled in brochure production may have as many ideas about improving their own effectiveness as those in carrier negotiation, and would feel considerably slighted if denied the opportunity to contribute to the furtherance of their own work, especially if staff in another department are given such an opportunity. Different styles also need to be applied to different employees in accordance with their length of service with the organisation. Even the most experienced person is a novice on the first day in a new job: basic information such as the location of the cloakroom is unknown to this

person. The 'learning curve' of a new employee, that is, the time required until the employee gets used to the job and becomes an asset rather than a burden to the organisation, can vary from a few days to many months, depending on the level and complexity of the job. Managers who adopt an authoritarian approach may favour a sink-or-swim attitude toward new staff in the belief that it does them good. Of course, it is only through doing, and possibly making mistakes, that the new employee will learn. But the need for challenge needs to be balanced against the need for support during the induction period.

Managerial qualities

It is beyond the capability of any one person to calculate the variables involved in any management or leadership situation on each and every occasion that a new problem or issue is faced. To that extent, being an effective manager has to be an art rather than a science, as Harvey-Jones suggested. To practise this art effectively, four maxims are offered here, which all derive from the supposition that it is as well to treat people the way you yourself would like to be treated. Loving your neighbour does not mean necessarily liking them, and it is a very rare circumstance that a manager finds himself or herself actually *liking* all of his or her subordinates, and vice versa. But very effective working relationships can be established by acting toward staff in a way which is respectful, and demonstrative of having their best interests, as well as those of the organisation, at heart. Also, having a healthy and honest view of one's own strengths and weaknesses is an essential part of this equation. Everyone has within him- or herself the template for behaviour toward others: quite simply, we know what it takes to make us feel comfortable, inspired, equipped and confident in our work, and the challenge is to create those same conditions for others in the workplace. There are people whose personal make-up creates difficulties in attaining this ideal: for example, someone who has suffered under the attentions of a poor manager early in his or her career may find it difficult to be generous with his or her own subordinates when he or she achieves managerial status. 'It wasn't easy for me, why should it be easy for them?' may be the view espoused. This is not only unpleasant but short-sighted, because it serves to perpetuate the original wrong. Maslow observes that aggressive behaviour in human beings, which he identified with an 'authoritarian' view of life, seems to be rooted in the perception of life as a jungle. While the well-balanced person welcomes newcomers as potential friends and allies unless or until they prove unworthy, the insecure person sees threats everywhere and regards other people as either those whom he or she can dominate, or those who will dominate him or her. Arising out of this can be a bifurcation of behaviour, pandering to people who have power and domineering those who are subordinate (1970, p. 126). But presumably both the well-balanced and the insecure person share the common human desire for comfort, support and a sense of direction. What both need, and this could form the first maxim, is to **nurture the courage to treat staff reasonably**, even when this runs contrary to personal inclination, or in the face of the perception, real or imagined, that good treatment is not deserved.

Freemantle's prescription for success in his book *Incredible Bosses* (1992, p. xiii) is '*credibility* as a reflection of *integrity*' (Freemantle's italics). Having credibility and integrity as a manager means being consistent in word and deed so that, in the best of cases as with Lord Nelson, subordinates *know* the mind of their manager and what he or she would be likely to do in certain situations. Managers who restrict the flow of information in an organisation as a means of maintaining personal power, or whose decisions are habitually guided by personal or political motives, may find it difficult to retain integrity in the eyes of subordinates. Maintaining credibility is vital in an organisation, especially when occasional hard and unpopular decisions need to be taken. For example, employees can show an astonishing willingness to respond to the demands of a crisis, as long as they are confident that the demands placed on them are genuine. For example, a manager who is known for habitual procrastination may find it less easy to mobilise staff to deal with unexpected exigencies, because the staff will suspect that the erisis need not have happened. The credible manager actually

strengthens his relationship with his or her staff through tackling crisis: the mutual trust which has already been built up is further tested and refined through the successful tackling of the unexpected. The second maxim could thus be to **demonstrate consistency of word and deed**, even if the cost is to spend more time than comes naturally in communicating with the staff.

One of the major issues facing a manager is how to handle competition between different members of staff in the workplace. Particularly in Anglo-American business cultures where promotion and advancement are in theory based on merit, ambitious employees will seek to perform in a way which either (a) is effective or (b) gets them noticed. Of course, it is possible to be effective *and* be noticed, but the two are not necessarily the same thing. Some managers think that, by actively encouraging competition amongst their subordinates, they create a form of conflict which enhances the general performance of the organisation. A degree of natural competition is inevitable and it is important that employees with the talent and determination to excel be encouraged to do so; however, to manufacture a culture of competitiveness encourages a kind of attention-seeking which diverts effort away from longer-term objectives and into ephemeral and possibly wasteful activities. This is a respect in which German business cultures have an advantage over those prevalent in the UK and USA. German employees are encouraged to work for the well-being of the whole company, and personality cults are discouraged (Appleton 1991). Where competition is encouraged, extreme cases of internecine competition may not stop at simple attention-seeking; staff may seek actively to destroy each other's efforts in the race to keep ahead. An alternative strategy is for the manager to take an interest in the *absolute* achievements, as opposed to *relative* achievements, of staff. By this is meant taking a detailed interest in their aspirations, qualifications and personal and professional objectives. Appraisal systems can be a useful way of formalising this, though real success would involve demonstrating an authentic interest outside official systems. Training opportunities, and genuine words of encouragement and appreciation, can mean a great deal in terms of employee motivation; and

employees encouraged to seek absolute improvements in their performance and preparedness for
the job may well exceed the standards needed just
to keep ahead of colleagues in a culture of
competitive free-for-all. But by all means,
encourage competition with other teams. Other
operators in the market-place are the real
competitors; internal competition is a mis-
direction of effort. The third maxim is therefore
this: **compete with your competitors, not with
each other**.

Handy refers to research suggesting that
successful senior managers are *self*-centred, in
terms of having a strong sense of their own
identity, and yet to have progressed to the senior
echelons must have operated at middle-manager
level where the demands of the role tend to be
organisation-centred (1993, p. 65). By this it is
meant that a middle-management role is tactical
and operational, rather than strategic, with a job
purpose whose focus is implementing rather than
determining the policies of the organisation. This
leads Handy to conclude that at some stage in their
careers, these managers must endure some *role
incompatibility*. Nelson's disobedience toward his
senior admiral, mentioned earlier in the chapter,
may be an example of a nascent high-flyer
resolving a role-incompatibility situation through
outright disobedience. How, for example, does the
gifted restaurant manager in the earlier example
react toward senior managers who quite possibly
are less gifted than he or she? Whom is he or she
serving: management, staff, or customers? This is
the dilemma which has framed the plot for many
films and television programmes: a common
formula is the hero hands-on cop being impeded in
his or her effectiveness by pen-pushing superiors.
In the film *Star Trek IV*, Admiral James T Kirk, by
common consent an effective if fictional leader,
was demoted to the rank of Captain (albeit with
his own and everyone else's approval) for having
commandeered a starship in the previous film in
order to recover his loyal lieutenant, Spock.

The dilemma of true loyalty has frequently
intrigued dramatists. In Shakespeare's *King Lear*,
the Duke of Kent issues a plain-spoken reprimand
to his king over a self-evident act of folly, and is
banished for his pains (Act I, Scene i). When the
preoccupations of senior management are more
concerned with internal politics than the
effectiveness of the organisation, middle
managers can find themselves in a quandary.
Freemantle's robust advice is to confront such
bosses, speak out rather than keep silent and
refuse to succumb to bad practices (1992, p. 63).
Managers acting on such advice could find
themselves, like Lear's Duke of Kent, making a
rapid unscheduled exit, leaving the job open to a
substitute who may be more willing to comply
with the *status quo*. One way of preventing such
confrontations is for the employee to make it clear
at an early stage, consistently and with good
grace, of the principles on which he or she can
comfortably operate, and his or her willingness to
apply these within the wider organisation. That
way, it may be possible to form what Handy
termed a 'psychological contract' with senior
managers (1993, p. 45). Insecure superiors may
still feel threatened, but at least it will be known
whether or not the employee's preferred way of
doing things has any place in the organisation, and
personal intentions for the long term can be
planned accordingly. The fourth maxim could
therefore be to **seek to harmonise your
loyalties and principles**.

Observing motivations in other lives

A biographer's observations on Richard Branson
were quoted at the end of Chapter 1. Four
examples follow, two from tourism and two from
general business. Biographies and interviews can
be a useful source of mentorship, in that the
purpose of a biographer or interviewer is to get to
the heart of what motivates his or her subject.

Lord Hanson, Chairman of Hanson plc, whose
conglomerate company grew by acquisition to
become one of the success stories of the 1980s,
attributed his success to 'relentless cost-cutting
coupled with excellent service'. Giving an
interview to the local newspaper of his original
home town of Huddersfield, he attributed his
success to 'Yorkshire values', in particular toward
costs and sticking to his word. Quoting an
occasion when he considered his promises were
not believed by a third party, he is apparently still
angered by the incident, saying that 'My word is
one of the greatest assets I have got in business'.

Speaking of his early introduction to business in the family firm, he talks of 'early mentors in the company' who helped him to learn about business. At the conclusion of the article, when asked for his advice to anyone wishing to emulate him, he mentions determination plus, again, the usefulness of a mentor (Woodward 1993). The appearance is of a man who, like Freemantle, values 'credibility as a reflection of integrity' and acknowledges a debt to older and wiser people who early in his career were prepared to act as trusted and experienced advisers.

The late American oil magnate **John Paul Getty** wrote a series of magazine articles in the 1960s which were published in paperback form in the 1970s (Getty 1971). Although he was writing for a world which has changed somewhat in the intervening decades, two of his observations in particular are of interest. First, he is an advocate of what he described as a 'liberal arts' college education for young people who aspire to become executives, and is worried by what he sees as an 'overspecialisation' in education:

However, I regard as disheartening the growing trend toward specialisation, toward one-track orientation among young executives, especially in their education. It seems that many young men [sic] are devoting an inordinately large portion of their academic lives to the study of the 'useful disciplines', while ignoring those subjects that aid an individual in developing into a multidimensional human being. (1971, p. 71)

And he, like Lord Hanson, appears concerned about standards of credibility and integrity:

As far as I am concerned, nothing eliminates an individual from consideration for promotion faster than the knowledge that he [sic] is a buck passer. And the higher a man rises in the organisational lineup, the more essential it is for him to be an individual of absolute integrity. If he does not stand by his decisions, accept his responsibilities, where necessary admit his mistakes and otherwise prove his honesty, an executive cannot move up; he can, at best, only remain where he is or – even better, from the company's standpoint, move out. (1971, p. 99)

The second quotation from Getty is interesting inasmuch as it concludes on a note of tolerance which seems faintly surprising in view of Getty's aversion to the type of character involved. Summary dismissal without warning does not seem to be on the cards; giving the person a chance to mend his or her ways, while identifying the alternative, is suggested. More intriguing is Getty's scepticism toward vocational training and advocacy of the splendidly described *multi-dimensional human being.*

Thomas Cook ran his first excursion in 1841. It was a temperance outing by train from Leicester to Loughborough, and signalled the beginning of 'Cook's Tours' which expanded to include Continental excursions and ultimately into the present-day tour operator and travel agent that still bears his name. He was later to say in his company publication *Cook's Excursionist* in 1856 (Brendon 1991, p. 5) that 'That moment . . . was the starting point of a career of labour and pleasure which has expanded into . . . a mission of good-will and benevolence on a large scale'. It was evident that it was the enjoyment of the business as well as its means of earning him a living that motivated Cook:

Cook's profit margins were always tiny. But the real trouble was, as John [his son] pointed out, that his father liked to sacrifice commerce to altruism . . . tourists often became friends. This is not to suggest that Cook was an incompetent entrepreneur, merely that he was not just an entrepreneur. (Brendon 1991, p. 99)

Brendon also quotes Cook's son, John, criticising his father's mixing of business and pleasure, pointing out that 'I have *never* allowed my family or private matters to affect my business labours or duties for one hour'. This is an interesting contrast: a picture of a man, Cook, who is endowed with the hospitality instinct to the brim and beyond, and a son whose aversion to mixing business and pleasure might cause him some difficulties if he were to work in the tourism and hospitality industries of today. What can be concluded is that, for Thomas Cook, tourism was not just a convenient job option: this man was on a mission. Cook's credibility lay in his willingness to, quite literally, travel the distance with his customers. Brendon also records a vote of thanks recorded by some guests on a trip to Switzerland, wherein the proposer reported that he 'never enjoyed a journey better and this was in great measure to be attributed to Mr Cook's supervision and general management' (1991, pp. 99–100). There is still a role for this kind of hospitality in contemporary tourism. A really effective courier can attract a valediction of that kind, and stories of remarkable hospitality in rural bed and breakfast establishments are examples of the same.

Lord Forte, interviewed in the mid-1980s had an essentially 1980s business philosophy which is comparable with that of Lord Hanson:

Essentially I believe that business is business. One is here to make money. I have a duty to our shareholders, to our staff and to our customers. Without profit I would not be in business. (Torkildsen 1986)

Yet he claims, like Hanson, an ethical framework. Torkildsen's own summation of Forte's approach was this:

A strong philosophy, pride of achievement, sound business principles and the 'old-fashioned', traditional virtues of duty and citizenship have carried Charles Forte through the commercial jungle with conviction, belief and commitment.

When we compare all four leaders, the preoccupation of the two 1980s contemporaries with cost control is not surprising given the particularly competitive business climate of that era. Thomas Cook's philanthropy would not have helped him survive in such a climate; and Getty

would probably by now be recruiting vocationally trained specialists to cope with the enormous new complexities created by information technology, globalisation of business and tighter legislative frameworks. Nevertheless, Getty's affection for a broad-based education is interesting, and the issues of credibility through integrity, passion for service and human values appear to be common to all four. In present times, it is easy to believe, with the support of repeated evidence in the newspapers, that the presence of human values in business practice has diminished. Perhaps such values never disappeared from business culture, but have been temporarily eclipsed in the mistaken belief that the balance sheet is the supreme moral arbiter. Hutton, arguing for a reform of contemporary UK society, saw shortcomings in an economy in which 'the only admissable objective is the maximisation of shareholder value', and made the following observation on the nature of the enterprise in a free-market economy:

the firms that are its life-blood are social as well as economic organisations. They are formed by human beings with human as well as contractual claims upon each other, and behind this social world lies the moral domain. (1995)

The example of Richard Branson (see Chapter 1) who apparently combines success in business with a recognition of the moral obligations which bind together management, staff and customers, offers evidence that it is possible for a new balance of values to assert itself amongst a new generation of entrepreneurs.

Chapter 3

Accommodation and transport

The purpose of this chapter is to undertake a select examination of accommodation and transport in the context of Holloway's suggestion, set out in Chapter 1, that tourism is *largely psychological in its attractions*. Accommodation and transport, and tourism, enjoy a symbiotic relationship. Both exist in a state of mutual dependency. Axiomatic to any tourist trip is the need to travel, and be accommodated at the destination, and in some cases *en route* as well. The exercise of choice in travel may involve stylistic statements imbued with encoded messages, to which the term 'symbolic consumption' may be applied. The tourist's expectations of his or her accommodation may involve securing some features comparable with the physical environment of home, and, less visibly, some of the psychological apparatus of the home environment; what could be termed 'covert comforts'. What needs to be considered is the extent to which the nature of accommodation, and the means of travel, form part of the psychological product. The basis of the chosen approach is to examine accommodation from a perspective of environmental psychology, and transport from a perspective of semiology.

Expectations of accommodation

The role of accommodation can be superficially simple. It is a means of staying in a particular destination, the enjoyment of which is the primary purpose of the trip. Viewed in this light, accommodation is secondary to and ancillary to the primary purpose. In some kinds of tourist trip, accommodation takes centre stage. Lundberg and Lundberg observe that 'hotels are integral to the international travel experience; for some people, they are the *raison d'être* for a trip' (1993, p. 97). Bayley argues that hotels, in particular, are representations of the civilisation which produces them, and compares what he describes as the 'grim, joyless people-processing homogeneity of Hilton or Marriot' to the Fordist means of industrial mass production which were, until very recently, dominant features in the economies of advanced societies. Bayley also identifies a contemporary trend, reflected through the media, to rediscover the virtues of smaller hotels whose character is redolent of an age gone by. An example quoted by Bayley is London's Stafford which in reality, he claims, is not a re-creation of the past but had simply never changed since the earlier decades of the century (1994). This is arguably an example of contemporary society seeking inspiration from the past rather than the present or future, and an indication of a cultural condition which has been described as *post-modern* and which is discussed in Chapter 7.

But essentially, the role of accommodation is to fulfil the basic needs of sleep, eating and personal grooming. The tourist's expectations of it may be little more than this, just as a night flight on a charter jet to a Mediterranean resort area offers nothing more than a quick and rapid transfer to sought-after sunny climes. Tourist accommodation needs to be set in a context of contemporary choice and expectation and examined in terms of the attachment to the concept of 'home' and how such attachments may accompany the tourist on a trip. After all, the transport element of any tourist trip will be, with very few exceptions, a minor element in the total duration of the tourist trip; so too will be a visit to a particular visitor attraction. By contrast, the tourist occupies the accommodation daily for the duration of the stay and thus the potential for satisfaction, or dissatisfaction, is that much higher. Most tourists can swallow hard and put up with a rough journey or an unpleasant incident at a visitor attraction; few will be as tolerant if their accommodation does not meet expectations. The discussion will be framed around three basic propositions which, it is suggested, generally apply to the choice of accommodation:

1 the tourist seeks *equivalent standards* (or superior standards) to those enjoyed at home.
2 The tourist seeks *flexibility* which is necessary to realise the particular objectives of the tourist stay.
3 The tourist expects *facilities* – both in terms of equipment and service – that make the stay easier and enjoyable.

There are obvious examples when one or more of these propositions do not apply. For example, the tourist on a trekking holiday in the Himalayas does not have a comfortable bed and a range of domiciliary facilities ready to hand. What he or she does have, however, is a degree of *flexibility* which is made possible by sacrificing equivalent standards and facilities. On this and other conceivable occasions, choice leads the tourist to alter or emphasise one feature or another and trade it off against a diminution in one or both of the other two.

A good example of the demand for *equivalent standards* has been two key trends which have affected, in particular, UK domestic seaside accommodation over the past 20 years. The first has been the demand by tourists to buy and consume liquor on the premises of their accommodation. For example, statistics show that in the UK, the consumption of wine, a drink more often taken with a meal than as a stand-alone drink, increased by 50 per cent between 1981 and 1991 (Central Statistical Office 1994a). Certainly, the need for active hotel and guest-house owners to acquire drinks licences was a live issue worthy of mention in the popular press in the early 1980s (Voase 1981). This is a good example of the way in which a social trend, that is, a shift from drinking in public houses to drinking at home, and acquiring a taste for a wider range of drink, imposes demands on the providers of tourist accommodation. The second trend has

been the demand by tourists for private *ensuite* bathroom and toilet facilities to accompany their rooms. The most likely explanation for this is the experience of improved standards at home, but especially of *ensuite* accommodation elsewhere, principally in the mass-market Mediterranean resorts, where purpose-built hotels dating from the 1960s and 1970s were furnished from the outset with private facilities and thus raised the general level of expectation. It was at the end of the 1970s that overseas packages began to bite deeply into the traditional markets for UK seaside resorts and so it is not surprising that the urgency to invest was recognised and addressed in the 1980s. Government support for such upgradings was available through the ETB in the form of grants issued under Section 4 of the Development of Tourism Act 1969, although the availability of this form of support was controversially withdrawn in England (but not in Wales) at the end of that decade. Nevertheless, with or without public financial support, upgradings took place and made a significant impact on the quality of the bedstock on offer in traditional resorts such as Margate (see Chapter 12).

The demand for *facilities* takes many different forms and is linked with the particular market sector which is being served. One of the selling points of Butlin's holiday camps was child care and children's activities which liberated time for parents to be by themselves. A conspicuous contemporary example is the effort made by major hotel chains to compete for business tourists by offering added value. Facsimile transmission and typing services, in-house pagers, plus room specifications which include trouser presses, drinks cabinets and satellite television have now become regarded as standard. An interesting development which began in the 1980s was the installation of health and leisure suites in major business hotels. Although very often the actual use made of these facilities by business visitors did not justify their installation, yet it was believed that the presence or absence of them was a significant feature in the decision to book. In other words, the businessperson was unlikely to use the facilities, but wanted the option: their presence was required arguably more for their symbolic than for their utilitarian value. The response of hotels was to seek custom for such suites by creating their own health clubs, thereby generating usage by local residents.

More general trends over the last 25 years have included the development of self-catering accommodation. Sacrificing the option of taking meals in-house is attractive to a number of groups, particularly families, but brings burdens in addition to the flexibility offered. For one thing, there is the need to prepare meals, plus the need to undertake shopping for groceries. The proliferation of the motor car has facilitated taking groceries on holiday in a way that was not possible when most holiday-makers were dependent on public transport, and the appearance of the supermarket, at home and abroad, has brought added ease to the buying-in of provisions. Also, as western wage inflation has generally risen faster than prices and made serviced accommodation relatively more expensive, self-catering has become an increasingly attractive financial option. In established destinations, a trend toward conversion from serviced to self-catering has been observed. In terms of the two resorts featured in Chapter 12 this was certainly true of Bridlington, but at Margate, perhaps influenced by the resort's proximity to London, other non-tourist uses made a rapid advance into the serviced accommodation stock which became available for re-use as tourist demand contracted.

The psychology of the home-from-home

Given therefore that the tourist has a number of expectations that need to be satisfied, and that these expectations may differ widely in accordance with the kind of tourist involved, are there such things as generic requirements, expectations of accommodation which are common to all tourists, irrespective of what kind of tourist they are? At one level that question has been answered in the three propositions regarding standards, flexibility and facilities, but is there a deeper issue, one of basic need, which is common to human beings when they are away from home? The following paragraphs examine people's relationship with their home environment, and assess the extent to which people need aspects of that environment to accompany them when they are tourists.

The science of environmental psychology begins its study of the relationship between human beings and their physical settings through a bifurcation of the surroundings into natural and built environments. The starting point is thus not dissimilar from that chosen as a basis for identifying what makes a tourist destination attractive (see also Chapter 4). Cooper, writing in Proshansky *et al.* (eds.) (1976, pp. 435–47), under the heading, *The House as Symbol of Self*, draws on the ideas of Jung and makes this observation on the role of the house in relationship to its occupant:

it [the house] has two very important and different components; its interior, and its facade. The house therefore nicely reflects how man sees himself, with both an intimate interior, or self viewed from within and revealed only to those intimates who are invited inside, and a public exterior (the persona or mask in Jungian terms) or the self that we choose to display to others. (in Proshansky et al. (eds.) 1976, p. 436)

Within this concept therefore are two notions: that the interior is self-furnished and, like the personality of its occupant, known only to intimates and to others who for specific reasons are admitted; the appearance of the exterior is also self-fashioned but moderated in accordance with the impression – signs – that the occupant wishes to offer the outside world. The house is therefore, in Cooper's words, a *symbol of self* and its interior arrangements are 'messages about ourselves that we want to convey back to *ourselves* [author's italics] and to the few intimates that we invite into this, our house'. '*Ourselves*' is significant because here, possibly, is an indication of that part of the home which the tourist may need when staying away. It is not uncommon for holiday-makers to regard the 'need to unpack' as a matter of some mild urgency when arriving at their accommodation; this may not be solely a function of the need to freshen up after a journey, but the need to use those objects and belongings which have been brought along on the trips as a means of creating identity and order within the temporary 'home' which has been assigned. Such a tentative hypothesis would seem to be endorsed by another of Cooper's observations: 'It seems as though the personal space-bubble which we carry with us and which is an almost tangible extension of our self expands to embrace the house we have designated as ours' (in Proshansky et al. (eds.) 1976, p. 436). The use of the term *personal space-bubble* is interesting inasmuch as there is an identity of terminology with the term used by the Henley Centre for Forecasting (1992) to describe tourists who seek to enjoy an overseas holiday inside an environmental bubble, by means of which indigenous customs, food, language and culture are kept at bay and within which the familiarities of the country of origin are carefully maintained and controlled. The need to recreate 'home' is likely to involve the extending of the personal space-bubble to embrace the hotel room; in some cases, compatriots from one particular country or region form a collective space-bubble to embrace the whole hotel, or even the resort.

The area of common need, if it exists, is affected by all kinds of other variables relating to personality and culture. For example, some people can live out of a suitcase with apparent ease, and will choose vacation accommodation which limits their ability to define their own space, for example camping. Yet those same people may be 'bubble-travellers', demanding an environment populated by the people and culture of their own country, perhaps even of their own region of their own country. One of the ways in which people's attachment to environments can differ, where preference for a particular environment exists, is between *generic place dependence* and *geographic place dependence* (McAndrew 1993, ch. 10). A person who is generically place dependent is said to be happy provided he or she is in a preferred type of environment, whatever that may be: say, for example, mountains. The person who is geographically place dependent may, when on holiday, form an attachment to a particular destination and may return to it year after year. The attachment can be formed to a particular hotel which is visited each year at the same time, and major disappointments arise when ownership changes and the hotel ceases to bear all the characteristics which have been instrumental to the attachment being formed. It is above all this kind of person who seeks a 'home-from-home' on holiday.

Other people can be just the opposite, regarding the tourist trip as an 'escape' mechanism which permits them the luxury of a different place every year. While both kinds of tourist regard the going away as a break and a change from home, the second of the two logically extends this to defining the holiday as an occasion when geographical place attachments may not be formed. Such are the widely differing reactions possible, arising out of similar sets of circumstances. McAndrew observes that place dependency of both kinds is more likely to be seen in children and the elderly, and in the case of the latter, place dependency does seem to become stronger with the passing of time (1993, p. 207). This has clear implications for the marketing of tourist products: domestic destinations, which appeal to young families and the elderly, can be expected to have a much more loyal clientele than, for example, a recently constructed Mediterranean resort. Conversely, the place dependency of such markets on a domestic resort can contribute to a place image which serves to exclude other less place-dependent visitors, causing an imbalance in the visitor profile and consequent long-term problems.

The other dimension to the concept of home, and which merits mention, is that of *territoriality*. This feature of life is widely observable in the animal kingdom and is shared by human beings, as anyone who has been in dispute with neighbours will confirm. Altman and Chemers included the following in their definition of human territoriality:

There is control and ownership of a place or object on a temporary or permanent basis . . . Ownership may be by a person or group . . . [it] can serve several functions, including social functions . . . territories are often personalised or marked . . . defence may occur when territorial boundaries are violated (1980, pp. 121–2)

This being the case, we could postulate that the tourists would seek to control and establish proprietorial rights over their accommodation even though its occupation is temporary; they may do this by themselves, or in the company of others, normally compatriots; and may seek to establish social control by, for example, the singing of popular anthems (such as football songs) at evening entertainment events, or establishing user rights around the swimming pool by marking out territory with towels. This kind of scenario will be familiar to anyone with experience of mass-market Mediterranean destinations which are shared by several north European nationalities. It surely qualifies the notion, which is advanced in some circles, that tourism enhances international understanding; it can be strongly argued that tourism causes and sustains stereotyping.

Altman and Chemers identify different types of territory, in relation to which different levels of territoriality can expect to be observed. *Primary* territory would include such places as a family home or personal bedroom, intrusion into which would, in the words of the authors, engender 'strong defensive actions'. *Secondary* territory would include the neighbourhood public house, or the neighbourhood street: public areas for which local people feel some proprietorial attachment. *Public* territory would embrace those places to which all comers are entitled to usage, subject to the observation of common rules (1980, pp. 129–35). Thus, humankind can mix happily on a Sunday afternoon in a public park, but a person allowing a dog to foul where children are playing may find him- or herself receiving unofficial, if not official, admonishment. Perhaps some of the territorial horror stories which seem to accompany visits to hotels where nationalities mix are the result of hotel facilities falling into the grey area between secondary and public territory: the customers are paying for the facilities, so they are not public in the full sense of the word; and yet the demands placed on such facilities by customers make them some of the most authentically public places in the world, with wide scope for cultural collision. One sad story, which made front page news in an English provincial newspaper, was of British holiday-makers on holiday in Turkey who became aggrieved when they discovered that their hotel restaurant had been used by well-to-do locals for a circumcision ceremony (Mellor 1993). The event had taken the form of a private hiring, and thus any offence existed entirely in the mind of those aggrieved. The episode was given added poignancy in that the Turkish hosts had invited all the overseas hotel guests to the reception afterwards (as opposed to the ceremony itself) in a gesture of generosity for which northern European society is not noted. Unhappy stories like this are almost inevitable because, at risk of being patronising, it is frankly unrealistic to expect high standards of cultural mobility amongst the massed ranks of north European holiday-makers. Continual, instinctive attention is needed either to anticipate or to minimise the immediate effects and aftermath of incidents such as this one.

Is there, then, such a thing as a generic requirement for a home-from-home; that is, common expectations which are shared by all tourists? A useful thesis may be that tourists seek to have their basic needs for food and security provided for, plus some (though not all) of the elements of *belongingness* which are associated with that place called home. This can be better understood if considered in terms of the work of the psychologist Abraham Maslow whose theoretical 'hierarchy of needs' is used and applied in Chapter 6 as a model for explaining tourist motivation and is also referred to in Chapter 2 in the context of motivation in the workplace. Essentially, Maslow said that an aspect of human behaviour could be analysed in terms of the drive to seek the satisfaction of needs for food and shelter as an antecedent to the satisfaction of 'higher' needs such as love and a sense of belonging. The thesis could be explained in this way: the tourist trip is by definition temporary, therefore the accommodation arrangements are temporary. The tourist seeks more than basic food and shelter, but does not insist on all the other attributes of 'home' that create a sense of belonging. The tourist may even actively avoid certain of these attributes, as may be theorised from the following hypothetical examples:

1 A *business traveller* is content to stay in a large business hotel where the sense of identity enjoyed at home is absent, replaced by a degree of anonymity; but where convenience in terms of service and gadgetry compensate in part for the absence from home. The business traveller is deprived of spouse and family, and access to personal home-based pursuits, but enjoys creature comforts as

compensation. As a temporary arrangement, it is suitable.

2 A *mass-market package holiday-maker*, intent on intensive recreation, may be accommodated in an impersonal hotel which is in some ways similar to the business hotel, though with a more limited range of facilities. This tourist is not bothered about anonymity because he or she either is accompanied by compatriots whom he or she knows or intends to get to know during the holiday, or views its anonymity as a positive advantage inasmuch as the intended process of intensive recreation is not fully compatible with behavioural mores in his or her home environment.

3 A *bed-and-breakfaster on a rural short break* has little in common with the example above, although he or she could conceivably be one and the same person doing different things at different times. It is here that the 'home' is sought out and re-created in its fullest form: elements are the presence of the farmer's wife or landlady whose home cooking is a feature of the accommodation; it may be a historic property, furnished with the proprietor's own belongings; and the holiday-maker may have the responsibility of locking up if arriving in late after a night out. Joining the rural 'family' for two or three days is a prime attribute of the product and, possibly, the whole point of it.

4 A *participant on a self-catering group holiday* may be accommodated in a chalet or tent and therefore does not benefit from the basic facilities offered in the other examples. However, if an objective of the holiday is to achieve, quickly, a depth of relationship with other group members, then the exigencies of the form of accommodation throw people together in a way that is not offered in serviced accommodation. The camper forgoes some of the creature comforts of home but seeks instead a depth of rapport with established family and friends and new acquaintances.

Choice in accommodation can thus be regarded as an outcome of the interactions of motivations determined by practicality, level of aspiration and the selective screening out, or alternatively the retention, of the covert comforts of the home environment. With the obvious exception of those types of accommodation such as country cottages and art deco hotels whose appearance and character can have signifying properties for the tourist, the scope for 'symbolic consumption' through accommodation, though possible, is limited. It is in this respect that transport differs from accommodation. An insight into the symbolic and signifying properties of various types of travel chosen has to be framed to some extent in a context of history, because, as will be argued, the range of transport opportunities available to the contemporary tourist represents an accretion of different forms which have evolved through time. This evolution in its turn is in part the consequence of technological innovation and the particular economics of the transport industry. Before considering travel choice in a semiological context, it is proposed to introduce transport in the context of its historical evolution.

Transport in a historical context

It is tempting to view travel for tourism as a simplistic progression from feet to wide-bodied jet as the technology of travel advances, with forms of transport such as passenger ships and railways becoming unfashionable along the way and being consigned to the dustbin of history. This is a fallacy, akin to suggesting that tourists have deserted coastal resorts for historic cities, have spurned Spain in preference for the eastern Mediterranean, have rejected the domestic long holiday in favour of the short break. Advances in the technology of transport have added to the repertoire of forms of transport available to the tourist, without eliminating any of the forms which in some ways have been 'superseded'. In fact, for example, not only are journeys by rail on the increase, but there is evidence of a resurgence in archaic forms of travel as an integral element of a specialised holiday experience. An example may be the attraction of trekking on horseback in the interior of Spain, one of a number of images used by the Spanish National Tourist Office in an advertising campaign designed to broaden the UK public's perception of the potential of Spain as a destination for something more than a beach holiday. However, travel in the mass-tourism market tends to be a means to an end, and thus favours speed and cheapness. This in turn tends to lead to the adoption of each more technologically advanced mode of travel as it arises. It is quite simply that short journey time, a capacity to transport large numbers, and at low cost, are critical attributes for the mass market.

Transport in an economic context

Requirements within markets may vary. For the business tourist, for example, a short journey time is likely to be set at a greater premium than low cost. Mass-market tourists seek low cost, but are also drawn to short journey times because they may wish to spend as much of their vacation time at the destination as possible. So, for example, as discretionary income rises and costs of air travel come down, and developments in airliner technology facilitate the transport of greater numbers and hence further economies in operating costs, increasing numbers of people travel by air. This was not just a transfer of business from ships; cheap air travel opened up new markets of its own: for example, the long-haul holiday. In the incipient days of transatlantic sea travel and, a century later, transatlantic air travel, costs limited the customer base: when technology and economies of scale improve, the customer base becomes larger and thus more accessible to the mass market. This is not an inexorable progression, as the example of Concorde demonstrates: having been developed in the 1960s, it began as a niche opportunity for business tourists for whom travel from Europe to New York in 2.5 hours had a value, and which made the cost of the ticket worth while. This is still the niche in which Concorde operates; guest appearances at airshows and special try-it-out trips to nowhere and back, are the limits of the mass market's access; plus vicarious participation in its prowess as when in 1985, for example, the rock star Phil Collins managed to appear at both the New York and London Live Aid concerts, by hopping on Concorde from one to the other, taking television cameras with him so that the

public could share the experience. Mass-market use of supersonic air travel now seems as unlikely as routine space travel, but the real emancipator of the world of passenger aviation was the Boeing 747, the so-called Jumbo Jet, which entered service shortly after Concorde, in 1970. Equipped with a capability to carry 400 passengers, it offered three times the capacity of the largest airliner to date and played a crucial role in making long-haul travel affordable to the leisure traveller.

Semiology and transport

Insights into the nature of choice in travel behaviour can be gained by considering such choices in terms of their signifying properties. When Christ entered Jerusalem in triumph on what is now celebrated by the Christian Church as Palm Sunday, he did so riding on a donkey, a pack animal of low status. As a cultural statement that denoted at the time, as now, humility; but centuries earlier, Solomon, the legitimate heir of King David, rode to his enthronement on such a beast (I Kings 1). This would have been well known to the crowd which welcomed Christ. The 'statement' was one of kingly authority combined with humility, and Christ would have been in no doubt as to its dual significance to the crowd. Choice of travel can have stylistic, signifying or symbolic importance. Sometimes, travel is simply a means of reaching the destination and is an inconvenience to be cleared out of the way as quickly as possible: for example, driving overnight to the West Country. On other occasions it is an integral part of the trip and may embody and manifest a range of signifying meanings for the traveller.

Semiotics, the study of symbols and their meanings, has received considerable attention in French intellectual thought over the last few decades. Barthes (1972, pp. 112–13) suggests that 'any semiology postulates a relation between two terms, a *signifier* and a *signified* [author's italics]'. By way of explanation, he cites the example of a man offering red roses to a woman: the roses are a *signifier* of something else, namely his love for the woman; his love is therefore that which is *signified*. The act of giving the roses, imbued with two qualities of being literally roses and at the same time representations of his love, becomes a *sign*. A further understanding of this process can be gained from an early (1923) English source in the writings of Ogden and Richards, referred to in Broadbent (1980, p. 20). These writers introduced the term *referent* to describe the thing to which the 'sign' refers. Thus, in Barthes's example, the *referent* could be identified as the generic love and passion which is known to arise, on occasions, between men and women.

Broadbent (1980, p. 21) cites the writings of Peirce (1960) in defining a *symbol* as a sign, but for which 'the relationships between the signifier, the signified and the referent *have to be learned* [author's italics]'. As an example he suggests that religious buildings such as cathedrals or mosques, with a distinctive signifying form, are symbols: when we spot specific architectural features such as spires or domes, we conclude that we are looking at a place of worship of some sort. Interestingly, Broadbent notes that because the meaning of symbols is learned, *their meanings cannot stay constant* (Broadbent 1980, p. 22). Brown points out the role of the travel and tourism industry and its agents in influencing choice and refers, albeit indirectly, to the need to examine consumption patterns on a 'longitudinal' basis because the constancy of symbolic meanings cannot be taken for granted:

Included among those playing 'tangential roles' in the assignment of symbolic meaning to the destination would be the mass media, advertising agencies and various sectors of the tourism industry . . . symbolic consumption . . . is frequently a longitudinal process. Thus, it is necessary to examine the consumers' perceptions of the symbol not only before and during purchase, but especially after the purchase has been made and during the life of the symbol as it is being consumed. (in Johnson and Thomas (eds.) 1992, p. 59)

As an example of the principle of symbolic consumption, Brown cites research undertaken by Wynne (1979) which compared the lifestyles of two middle-class populations on a particular housing estate. The two groups differentiated themselves in terms of level of education and job, plus holidays: one group saw an *à la carte* holiday

as the route to self-definition, whereas for the other group the aspiration was to 'holiday abroad in a hotel rather than in a tent' (Johnson and Thomas (eds.) 1992, p. 59).

Wernick, writing about the imaging of motor cars, defined the 'constructed symbolism' of car design as following three divisions in their markets which he defined as 'imagistic' (sports cars, roadsters); 'abstract Tradition' (luxury vehicles whose interiors and exteriors owe much to archaic traditions) and the 'symbolic mid-point' of the family sedan, whose mixed imagery can hint at sportiness, modernity or taste (1991, pp. 71–2). These latter products, though substantially similar in appearance, are segmented by engine size and badging exercises in order to appeal to the sportier end of the range (e.g. 'GTi', 'MG' etc.), and the re-creation of interiors redolent of the archaic traditions of the luxury limousine for the more sedate end of the family sedan market (as in the Van den Plas versions of various Rover mid-range saloons).

Where motor vehicles are used in tourism advertising, the choice of vehicle will invariably match the presumed lifestyle characteristics of the targeted market. For example, imagery calculated to invite an English target market to enjoy a bohemian life in rural France for the duration of a main holiday may feature a Citroën 2CV, or even more probably, a bicycle. For example, a brochure for a magazine launched in the UK in 1994 and entitled *France*, aimed at the 'increasing numbers who flock across the Channel to delight in *la différence*', featured as a front-cover illustration a French peasant wearing blue overalls and crowned with a beret, riding a well-used bicycle down a country lane. The image was completed by the presence of a *baguette* strapped to the rear of the machine, and by the humanizing presence of a little boy, presumably the peasant's son, riding behind his father on the luggage rack.

It has been suggested that the majority of tourists favour a form of transport for its speed, or at least the shortness of the journey (not necessarily the same thing), and for its economy. Yet choice and mode of transport is determined also by a range of cultural factors. Even at the most basic level, the use of feet, manner and appearance can combine to give a clear sign. In a newspaper feature article about the use of the countryside by ramblers, the complaints of a particular landowner included a litany of alleged problems supported by a portfolio of case examples, and a remark that it was those with the 'red socks' who were allegedly the most insensitive in exercising rights of access to other people's land. Whether the choice of the colour of rebellion on the part of the walkers was deliberate is unknown, but the landowner certainly saw it as a signifier. As a second example, a meeting of a local authority resort leisure committee was debating the growing use of jetskis by the general public. The use of these machines was creating cause for concern: jetskis are great fun, but generate a certain amount of noise nuisance and can be a hazard to bathers. An officer painted a verbal picture of a typical beach scene on a fine Sunday afternoon, describing how jetski disruption is heralded as 'the XR3s roll up, towing the machines behind them'.

The choice of travel says something about the traveller. It conveys a message, a statement about who you are, where you are going, who you intend to be. Perhaps choice of travel does not quite equal choice of clothes in terms of personal statement, but for many people, how they travel, what car they drive, what walking boots they own, maybe what colour walking socks they wear, is an opportunity to signify to like-minded people and the world in general an identity with a certain subculture, having achieved a certain level of material success, or having rejected material success, and so on. In Chaucer's *Canterbury Tales*, the Wife of Bath, a formidable woman who had outlived four husbands and was now on her fifth, acquired considerable wealth through inheritance, and rode her horse side-saddle. It was the practice of well-born ladies not to sit astride a horse in a less-than-ladylike position, but to sit sideways, thereby keeping the legs together. Chaucer imparts this information about the Wife with a hint that the signification of riding side-saddle was incompatible with her social standing and character. She was neither well born, nor a lady, as a reading of her Prologue and Tale will reveal. This equestrian style of well-born ladies is not quite ancient history: any tourist watching the Trooping of the Colour on the Queen's official birthday will see Her Majesty riding side-saddle. The practice lives on, the message clear.

The role of signification at the feet-and-animals level can be instructive in understanding the statement and style involved in more sophisticated forms of travel used by tourists. Two contrasting heroes and their steeds can be considered: first, one drawn from fiction. Clint Eastwood, playing the protagonist in the spaghetti western *A Fistful of Dollars*, rides into a town which is dominated by two competing families: the Baxters and the Rojos. Eastwood's character, the 'hero', manipulates the situation to his own ends by causing the rivalry between the two clans to escalate. His initial move is to seize an opportunity to kill some of the Baxters' hirelings in response to their mockery of his choice of steed, a *mule*. Their firing of guns into the air makes the animal take fright. The 'hero' demands that the hirelings apologise, not to him, but to the mule; thereby guaranteeing that an apology will not be offered and giving him the opportunity to gun down the three men when they draw their weapons. This 'hero' is totally secure and self-contained, is a bounty hunter, and thus does not seek to advertise himself: indeed, he is known only as *The Man With No Name*. The use of the mule appears to signify a rather dubious symbolic analogy with Christ's entry into Jerusalem and subsequent turning upside-down of the town. The second example is a military leader in the business of self-advertisement on a grand scale, and arguably lacking the personal self-assurance of *The Man With No Name*. Napoleon Bonaparte, sometime Emperor of France, applied an individual style to the management of his self-image: this included seizing the crown from the hands of the Pope at his own coronation, and crowning himself. Another was a penchant for white horses. One of a number of portraits of him accompanied by his mount was painted by Baron Antoine Jean Gros in 1808, entitled *The Field of Eylace*. It portrays the Emperor on a white steed, surrounded by his troops and followers. The message is unmistakable, a low profile unthinkable.

Travelling by foot, unaided by technology or an animal, can also be imbued with signifying properties. Quite apart from its role as a part of human body language, perambulating for its own sake on the promenades of Victorian seaside resorts accompanied by the restrained courtship practice of dropping and retrieving handkerchiefs is perhaps an example. A related example can be located during France's second Napoleonic era (1851–70) when the nephew of the original Bonaparte became Napoleon III. During this Second Empire, major alterations were made to the face of Paris, including the construction of the wide tree-lined avenues known as *boulevards*. A by-product of this remodelling was the lining of the boulevards with shops and cafés giving rise to a leisured atmosphere, which gave birth to the term *café society*, to be celebrated by writers and artists during the subsequent decades. A particular kind of leisured stroller, a *flâneur*, became a feature of this society. The aim was to see and be seen, to combine style, nonchalance and chic in that unique way which is associated the world over with *la vie parisienne*. (See Urry 1990, ch. 7 for a further discussion.) Contrast this with pilgrims visiting the shrine of Lourdes. Some visitors have been known to walk the final distance on their knees, signifying contrition.

In more recent times an increased diversification of available tourist experiences has been matched by an increased diversity of travel choice, in which nostalgia is frequently incorporated either into the product itself, or into the way it is promoted through the medium of advertising. Nostalgia for the 1930s has been used creatively in advertising for cross-channel ferries: one 1994 advertisement for P&O portrayed a couple in an open-top 1930s sports car, driving away from a ferry which, depicted in the style of 1930s poster art, looked more like a cruise liner. Similarly, an advertisement for Brittany Ferries also makes use of the style of 1930s poster art and depicts alfresco eating on the deck of the boat, the passengers being waited on at table and receiving a yesteryear standard of service. *The Royal Scot* and the *Orient Express* are examples of holiday products based on railway nostalgia: not on this occasion for anorak-clad collectors of locomotive numbers, but for people with the desire and resources to buy themselves into the leisurely world of the inter-war years. In the case of the Orient Express, authenticity is added through the use of original rolling stock, collected from throughout Europe and reconditioned for the purpose. Of more recent yet no less potent nostalgia value is the re-created Ferry Across the Mersey, operating out of Liverpool and associated internationally with a style of popular music whose origins are located in that city.

The perspective of the consumer may very often be to regard accommodation and travel as part and parcel of a seamless whole. This is most likely to be the case when the tourist has bought a specific product such as a package, which includes transport, accommodation and services at the destination. The independent traveller by contrast has the discretion and, very possibly, greater interest in itemising the choice of travel and accommodation and making that choice on the basis of separate motivations. Travel statistics show that between 1987 and 1989 in the UK outbound tourism sector, the flight package market declined from 11.8 million to 11.1 million trips, whereas the total number of holiday trips by air rose from 14.2 million to 15.5 million (Economist Intelligence Unit: 1992b, p. 3). The continuation of such a trend would increasingly create circumstances in which tourists can choose travel and accommodation on the basis of symbolic consumption. This trend would be further fuelled by the increasing maturity of tourists as travellers: the Henley Centre for Forecasting has addressed this issue in its model for international holiday-taking which is discussed in Chapter 14. For the present, an understanding of the tourist's response to visitor attractions and to destinations is the next subject to be addressed. The success of individual visitor attractions rests on their ability to satisfy the needs of the market which they aim to serve, and their success – combined with the quality of environment and accommodation – can make or break destinations. The survey which follows takes a perspective based in that concept of ubiquitous presence and elusive meaning, 'taste'.

Chapter 4

Attractions and destinations

The purpose of this chapter is to consider what it is that makes visitor attractions and tourist destinations attractive, using as a basis the elusive concept of 'taste'. It seeks to identify an interaction between taste, tourism and time. Consideration is given, first, to whether there are such things as generic tastes, and secondly to how and whether visitor attractions and destinations address these generic tastes. The third theme which adds to the complexity of this discussion is the passage of time. Whatever 'taste' is, it is an evolving concept which changes through time, causing consequent changes in its progeny, fashion, and has particular implications for attitudes toward 'heritage'. It must be stated at the outset that just as 'taste' is a fluid concept, the context in which the discussion takes place is also fluid: the complication arises out of two separate actualities, the *visitor attraction* and the *tourist destination*. A visitor attraction may be a stand-alone entity such as a theme park which is located away from other attractions and destinations, or it may be an integral part of a tourist destination such as a museum in a city or an amusement park in a seaside resort. It may also be a stand-alone special event such as Glyndebourne Festival Opera, or an event which takes place within a destination such as the Glasgow Mayfest. Where a visitor attraction or a special event is located within a destination, their destinies are tied together and issues of taste, applicable to both, are arguably inseparable.

In summary, therefore, the approach is to examine and explain the extent to which generic tastes can be identified in consumption patterns; to consider in turn the position of visitor attractions, tourist destinations and special events as physical elements in the make-up of 'attractiveness to tourists'; to introduce the variable of time in consideration of the evolution of tourist destinations, the effect of the passage of time on generic taste, and finally to give special consideration to what has been termed the 'heritage dilemma'.

Accounting for taste

This word (taste), which formerly signified no more than 'discrimination', was hijacked and its meaning inflated by an influential élite who use the expression 'good taste' simply to validate their personal aesthetic preferences while demonstrating their vulgar presumption of social and cultural superiority. (Bayley 1991, p. 3)

Tastes are props to the personality, and provide the individual with the impetus to enjoy preferred interests and activities. To indulge tastes may involve being surrounded by like-minded people in a place where such people congregate, so that the tastes and their indulgence can be jealously guarded. For this particular reason tourism, perhaps more so than other forms of consumption, is an activity in which the exercise of taste is fundamental. The reality of the present-day tourism environment is that the industry has produced a whole range of holiday opportunities to cater for increasingly diverse demand. It is very tempting to think that people themselves are becoming increasingly different in their tastes. It is certainly true that people *express* their tastes in a more diverse way than was the case 20 years ago, and part of the reason for that is that expressions of taste *have* become more diverse, encouraged by a proliferation of the means of self-expression through consumption. But in this chapter, the purpose is to get to the heart of intrinsic taste and argue that there remains a degree of commonality in the nature of taste and means of expression.

The fascination of the abnormal

Self-evidently, a holiday or even an annual business conference is 'abnormal', in the sense that it is infrequent, a break from routine, and arouses expectations of pleasure and interest which the daily round does not offer. The vacation tourist in particular has a choice as to where the vacation is spent, thus enabling the tourist to identify the destination or type of holiday which is most likely to deliver the required degree of 'abnormality'. The term is used deliberately, because some forms of vacation activity do not make logical sense: what, for example, is the purpose behind paying good money to be frightened to death on a roller-coaster for three minutes? The answer is that white-knuckle rides offer a threat and a thrill which is stimulatingly different from the daily round and not only that, the sheer purposelessness of it adds to the attraction: it is self-indulgence, a reward for many hours, days and weeks of enforced normality. This search for the abnormal reaches extremes in some forms of visitor attraction. Ghost trains, waxworks and freak shows are ever present in the glitzier seaside resorts of the UK, and yet tourism professionals would describe these, alongside moated manor houses and Elizabethan herb gardens, as 'visitor attractions'. They are as different as chalk and cheese, and yet visited by the same species, known as a 'tourist'. Are there two different types of visitor attraction for two different species of tourist?

The answer to that question may be illustrated by examining that part of television output which is designed for broad mass-market consumption, that is the TV soap opera. It could be argued that such programmes may offer a clue as to whether there is such a thing as a commonality of taste. *Emmerdale* is a twice-weekly soap opera whose appeal, like others of its genre, relies on the juxtaposition of normality with abnormality. In this case, the normality is a village setting with everyone going about their daily business but with a leaven of abnormal events occurring with such regularity as were they to occur in a real village, would beggar belief. The producer of the programme offered a rationale for his policy on story-lines:

We're on Britain's primary entertainment channel and people want a bit of entertainment before they settle down for the evening. At seven o'clock they'll be there with their chicken and they'll stop eating to watch the Post Office blow up. We have to find something that will make them pause between bites! (Garner 1994).

Emmerdale residents, in addition to a raid on their Post Office, also endured a passenger aircraft crashing on the village with consequent loss of life and injury, an armed siege which ended with two deaths, all during the first six fictional months of 1994. *Emmerdale* is a programme which attracts over eight million viewers and whose fascination, in common with other soaps, is maintained by the interplay of the stressfully eventful with the routinely normal. Arguably the soap opera plays on the viewer's innate fascination with the abnormal if not the stressfully eventful, just as visitor attractions and many tourist destinations seek to offer an experience which is distinct from the routinely normal, or even the routinely sensible.

Some visitor attractions such as seaside freak shows and chambers of horrors play quite blatantly on tourists' fascination with the 'abnormal'. However, serious visitor attractions may also choose, as their subject matter, human trauma. The Museum of the Irish Famine which opened during 1994 in Strokestown, Co. Roscommon, was opened to commemorate the 150th anniversary of the event which claimed one million lives and led to the emigration of one-quarter of the Irish population. The positive intention of the visitor attraction, as expressed by the Irish President who opened it, was to 'strengthen and deepen our identity with those who are still suffering' (Sharrock 1994). A similar rationale applies to the new Museum of Tolerance in Los Angeles, which uses interactive displays to re-create the Holocaust and confront visitors with issues of prejudice. It was said to have been founded on the maxim of the Nazi-hunter Simon

Wiesenthal of 'reviving horrors of the past to prevent hatred in the future' (Norris 1994). While the intentions of the seaside freak show are salacious in contrast with the noble rationales advanced for the latter two examples, they are, all three, visitor attractions. And like all visitor attractions, their attractiveness has to evoke something more than a sense of public duty if they are to attract visitors. And yet other kinds of visitor attraction could not be less eventful. What commonality exists between the attractions of the Museum of Tolerance, and those of an Elizabethan herb garden? How come some tourists' stated objectives for a holiday are to achieve inebriation and sexual conquest, others to enjoy the natural beauty of heritage coastline? Can common motivations be detected amongst the diversity of abnormality? An answer may be found in a dichotomy in human nature with Pick referred to as the *twin natures of man* (1988, p. 10).

The 'twin natures of man'

Conventional discussion of taste gives rise to terms which emphasise a dichotomy of what shall be called, somewhat clumsily, *taste drives*. One person may analyse another's behaviour in terms of *nobler and baser instincts*. An administrator of a municipal theatre, keen to make the building available to the widest possible audience, will seek to achieve a balance between *high art* and *popular culture* in the theatre's programme. A person making an important decision in life may be torn between *idealism* and *pragmatism*. What seems to emerge is a picture of humanity in which two taste drives are apparent: one of them aspirational and idealistic, seeking to satisfy the mind and the intellect; the other to satisfy the sensual appetites. Arguably, to be fully human is to acknowledge and provide for the needs of both these drives. 'All work and no play makes Jack a dull boy' is counsel which has been liberally offered to the over-studious, while by contrast the character playing the title role in Willy Russell's comedy drama *Educating Rita* is convinced of her need to feed and develop her intellect, and sets about acquiring an education in a determined fashion. Most individuals, whether or not they formally recognise the existence within

themselves of these two drives, will experience conflict between the two and it is the function of society's ethical code to offer a broadly agreed set of guidelines by which such dilemmas are resolved.

The civilisation of classical Greece had acute insights into the dichotomy of human nature. Two schools of philosophy flourished, the Stoics who practised restraint and self-denial in pursuit of wisdom and insight, and the Epicureans who considered that the pursuit of pleasure was the highest good. The dichotomy was also acknowledged in the arts:

Great art both inspired and questioned the ideals of the Athenians. At the great festivals, obeisance was made both to Apollo, the god of pure idealism, and to Dionysus, the god of revelry, lust and revolution. In the arts therefore the twin natures of man *were held to be reconciled (Pick 1988, p. 10, author's emphasis).*

The vital point to understand about the twin natures of man is that they co-exist within every human being. Inevitably, in any given person, one may be more apparent than the other.

These 'twin natures' can sometimes be recognised in works of drama, in terms of both the contrasting personalities of protagonists and the efforts of the dramatist to provide for the audience a balance of seriousness and levity. For example, Shakespeare's angle on the conflict between Mark Antony and Octavius Caesar in *Antony and Cleopatra* is to portray Antony as a man of Dionysian disposition, somewhat over-prone to enjoying himself, in contrast with Octavius who comes across as a rather cold fish. In one scene, at a feast on Pompey's galley, Octavius is having difficulty entering into the spirit of the occasion and Antony's advice to him is, 'Be a child o' the time'. Octavius' reply is unequivocal: 'Possess it, I'll make answer: but I had rather fast from all four days than drink so much in one.' (Act II, Scene vii). As an example of providing a balance of intake for the audience, the 'porter' scene from Macbeth involves the humorous spectacle of the rousing from slumbers of a hung-over doorkeeper immediately following the trauma of the murder of King Duncan. Some people have marvelled at Shakespeare's insertion of this scene at such a serious moment, but at times of stress humour is a good outlet. The placing of the scene is quite deliberate: like the light-hearted '*and finally*' item at the end of ITN's *News at Ten*, it is there for a purpose. There are limits to the amount of serious matter which people can handle. They need something light to draw them back into balance.

A further insight into the twin natures of man can be acquired by examining the readership profiles of Sunday newspapers. At first sight, the profiles show that the heavyweight quality papers giving in-depth treatment of the big issues of the day, such as the *Sunday Times*, attract a readership of which nearly 80 per cent are from the professional and managerial classes. Only 25 per cent of the readership of the *News of the World*, by contrast, is made up of such people (Waterson (ed.) 1992, p. 107). But before drawing conclusions about the educated classes reading about serious issues and the rest being satisfied with salaciousness and gossip, a glance at the readership figures provides a contrasting picture: the *Sunday Times* enjoys a readership of 3.5 million, the *News of the World* 12.7 million (Waterson (ed.) 1992, p. 107). Seventy-nine per cent of 3.5 million is less than 25 per cent of 12.7 million. The *News of the World* reaches a little deeper into the professional and managerial classes than does the *Sunday Times*. What presents itself is a picture of a household which perhaps takes both, providing a diet of Apollonian and Dionysian reading for a lazy day: the 'twin natures of man' in action.

Taste is the predisposition of the tourist to find certain things attractive or unattractive as the case may be. Taste is very much in the mind; to do with perceptions, preferences and prejudices. But taste does not exist in a vacuum. Its very existence is dependent on its being practised, on the person's exercising judgement on what is or is not to their liking. *Taste drives* are predispositions; the exercise of taste depends on physical stimuli from outside provoking what we may call *taste reactions*. These reactions may be triggered by the physical appearance of a destination, the way it is laid out, indeed the clientele which visits it. To some, the garish appearance of amusement arcades on a seafront is an offence to the eyes; to others, heritage trails are an exercise in publicly

funded tedium. Because Apollonians are more apt to air their views publicly than Dionysians (the chatter of the so-called chattering classes has a habit of appearing in newspaper letter columns), amusement arcades receive a heavier knocking than heritage trails, but in terms of volumes of usage are probably way in front.

Visitor attractions

What are the implications of this for tourism? First, let us consider the 'visitor attraction'. This may or may not be located within a resort; many, such as country houses and theme parks, are located by themselves away from centres of population and customers must make a specific decision to visit: they are often referred to as 'day-out destinations'. The implications for the visitor attraction are not necessarily that they should try to cater for both of the twin natures of man; in fact, such a policy may not only be difficult to implement on one site, but would not make commercial sense. People's expectation of a comparatively short visit to a day-out destination, lasting maybe a maximum of one day, is that it should provide an identifiable experience to meet a certain need. For the visitor attraction, this will usually mean determining the character of the experience, opting for either Apollonian or Dionysian, and making the best possible job of presenting that experience.

The National Trust, for example, protects the country houses in its stewardship and conserves them in a fashion which is close to their original form and purpose. The tone of presentation is unashamedly reflective of the Apollonian tastes of the county (as opposed to the *nouveau-riche*) middle class, venerating heritage and resolutely rejecting compromises with commercialism: amusement machines will not be found in the corner of cafeterias, neon signs are absent. Without doubt this approach has been successful, to the extent that membership of the Trust increased from about 280,000 in 1971 to 1.4 million in 1987 (Thrift in Hamnett *et al.* (eds.) 1989, p. 27). And yet such an approach, though successful, has limitations: children, in particular, have a low threshold of Apollonian intake and, no doubt with some exceptions, ultimately prefer playgrounds and hamburgers to herb gardens and carrot cake. But the approach is successful because it presents, in a fashion *par excellence*, an experience of Apollonian grandeur from the past. Of course, the novels of Jane Austen document the reality of life in such houses as more redolent of an American soap opera than the art-venerating trusteeship of the present day, but that is another discussion.

A contrasting type of visitor attraction is the theme park. If the National Trust's stately homes are the apogee of Apollonian interpretation, theme parks are surely the equivalent in Dionysian experience. Brash and noisy, the experience on offer is consumable excitement, thrills, escapism with an element of fantasy; catering normally will be conventional fast-food. In some ways there are more similarities between these two examples than meet the eye: both are offering a form of escapism, the one into an Apollonian past, the other into a determinedly Dionysian version of the present; both seek to push the character of the experience to extremes, and thrive on so doing; and the value of both experiences to the customer is not just their character, but that they are ephemeral: in short, their *abnormality*.

Tourist destinations

Tourist destinations, by contrast, have a more complicated task on their hands. For one thing, the staying visitor will be present in the destination from one night to up to one, two, maybe even three weeks. This experience is not ephemeral and therefore consideration has to be given to if and how the whole range of dichotomous human taste is to be catered for. Specialisation is seen to work: tourist resorts such as Blackpool which resolutely specialise in Dionysian dissipation tend to have proved more durable than those which maintain a limp attempt at 'something for everyone'. Similarly those inland towns which can be termed 'tourist-historic' cities, such as York and Chester, offer an assemblage of attractions such as cathedrals, historic architecture and museums which quite clearly appeal to the nobler rather than baser instincts, and similarly enjoy durable success. The significant success story of the last 15 years,

which is discussed in detail in Chapter 7, is the emergence of what could be termed 'post-industrial cities', such as Bradford and Glasgow, as tourist destinations. These, unlike coastal resorts which have mostly grown up around tourism as a central industry, and unlike the tourist-historic cities which tend to be town-size in scale, offer cultural facilities which are of the first order alongside a wide range of purely-for-pleasure facilities, for example their shops, public houses, restaurants and clubs, which have built up to service the requirements of a large resident population. These cities are thus equipped to share their 'experience-opportunities' with visitors who, like the city's residents, can sample a variety of experiences under the umbrella of the anonymity which the city, uniquely, offers:

For better or worse, it [the city] invites you to remake it, to consolidate it into a shape you can live in. You, too. Decide who you are, and the city will again assume a fixed form around you. Decide what it is, and your own identity will be revealed, like a position on a map fixed by triangulation. (Raban 1974, pp. 1–2)

Perhaps the secret of the attractiveness of the city as a tourist destination is precisely that the experience is not prescribed. Resorts, whether coastal or tourist-historic cities, wear their hearts on their sleeves and offer a repertoire of off-the-peg tourist experiences for consumption, but demand in return a degree of conformity on the part of the visitor. Mannered discourse in a night-club in Ibiza would be as intrusive as bacchanalian revels in the Pump Room in Bath. The post-industrial city makes no such demands. A visitor can opt in and opt out of the diversity of lifestyle experiences which the city provides, revelling in the process of discovery, the immensity and diversity of the place, making it possible to go unnoticed. In a resort, a tourist is just another tourist; in the post-industrial city, just another person.

Terminology needs to be used with a little care: when talking about the 'attractions' of a destination, we may be discussing a range of physical factors which make the destination attractive. These may include undertakings which we would formally call 'visitor attractions', such as a museum, amusement park or theatre, and other factors such as the natural scenery, historic town centre, good shopping opportunities and so on. In the broadest terms, those factors that make a destination attractive fall into two categories: the natural environment, which may include such things as beaches, coastlines, rivers and rural landscapes, and the built environment which will include, for example, buildings, harbours, waterfronts and historic town centres. Both categories can include factors which can be formally regarded as 'visitor attractions': a cathedral may not charge for admission, but its operation is to some extent geared toward receiving tourist visitors. Similarly, a beach is cleaned and managed and there may be a water-safety service available, even if no charge is made for its use; similarly, a nature trail which introduces and interprets the natural environment to tourists is also maintained and managed and may be regarded as a visitor attraction. Specific events, such as festivals, may also be major visitor attractions for particular destinations and while technically not part of the physical environment, are nevertheless man-made and thus manu-factured to enhance the attractiveness of the destination.

Burtenshaw *et al.* (1991, ch. 9) categorised attractions in terms of their importance in attracting tourists. The major features of the destination, such as cathedral, castle, beach, museum, amusement park, they described as *primary resources*. These were seen to be the factors which, together or in the case of a major attraction, perhaps singly, made the destination credible for a tourist visit. They are the attractions which feature prominently in resort literature, the ones which visitors can generally name before they arrive, and should be present in sufficient quantity to make the destination able to support the length of visitor-stay to which it aspires. It could be said that the attractions need to achieve a certain 'critical mass' to become credible. Recently emerged destinations, such as some of the post-industrial cities, have specifically planned the acquisition of this critical mass. Since 1980, the City of Portsmouth has complemented the presence of Nelson's flagship, HMS *Victory*, with a range of additional maritime attractions including a Royal Naval museum, HMS *Warrior*, and the celebrated tudor warship *Mary Rose*

which, having been raised from the sea just off Spithead under the eyes of the world's media, is now open to public view. The City of Bradford, similarly, made premises available for the relocation of a branch of the Science Museum, the National Museum of Photography, Film and Television. This rapidly became one of the most visited attractions in Yorkshire and was followed by the refurbishment, with assistance from the European Regional Development Fund, of the nearby Alhambra Theatre. The village of Haworth, home of the Brontë family, is also located within Bradford's municipal border and the packaging and presentation of these and other attractions created an effective short-break holiday product.

The *secondary resources* identified by Burtenshaw *et al.* can be defined as those facilities which do not necessarily feature as reasons for visiting, but are required to make the trip possible or are needed during the visit. Examples would be cafés and restaurants, car parks, public houses, public transport services, tourist information services, and self-evidently, hotel accommodation. Arguably there is a third class of facility which could be termed *tertiary resources* which are required as a consequence of the usage of the secondary resources. Examples may be public toilets, cash-dispenser machines, effective street signing for pedestrian use (possibly in more than one language) and so on. Local authorities which cater for tourists as well as residents will inevitably encounter occasions when the needs of visitors and the needs of residents are in conflict. For example, residents in a resort area may argue for charging for the use of public toilets in order to recoup from the visitor a proportion of the cost of providing the service. However, to do so would not necessarily be in the overall interest of the community if visitors find that they are required to produce a sum of money in the right coinage at a time when they have just come off the beach, and are least likely to be equipped to meet the requirement. In a city which is emerging as a tourist destination, museums may traditionally close for part of the weekend, but this would conflict with the needs of tourists who are being invited to the town as short-break holiday-makers specifically to enjoy its cultural attractions. Burtenshaw *et al.* observe that planning for tourist as well as residential and business use demands the formulation of reconciliation policies by means of which the needs of the tourist city are integrated with those of the residents' city and the business city.

Special events

By 'special events' we mean major events, the larger ones of which have been described by Hall (1992) as 'hallmark tourist events' in his book of the same name. Many post-industrial cities, using their considerable cultural and financial resources, have used special events to develop an image. An example of apparent success was Glasgow's City of Culture celebrations in 1990. Some smaller destinations have also successfully selected specific kinds of event to generate profile and visitor nights, and one popular way of achieving this over recent years has been through literature festivals (*Economist* 1994f). Such events were said to have proliferated because of their capacity to generate high levels of attention, coupled with relatively low cost. Examples are the 1994 Hull Literature Festival which focused on Andrew Marvell and Philip Larkin, both of whom had been locally based, and plans by the City of Bath to inaugurate a similar venture in 1995 focusing on famous writers associated with that city including, amongst others, Jane Austen and Richard Brinsley Sheridan.

The point about the big-city successes is that they are frequently, as in the case of Glasgow, made credible by significant capital investment in cultural and leisure facilities which very frequently have been supported by the Government's Urban Programme and European Union (EU) funds, and are built on an existing critical mass of attractions which have hitherto been provided and supported for residents' use and are now being adapted to the purposes of tourism.

Special events can be a major contributor to the success of a destination, of that there is no doubt, but the *concept* of the event must be appropriate to the *context* in which it takes place, as with the cases of Hull and Bath and their literature festivals. Simply transplanting a concept from one context to another will look odd, and the public reaction may be one of avoidance rather than interest. For example, an attempt to hold 'the world's largest meeting since the Rio Earth Summit' in Manchester in 1994 was in trouble only five months in advance of its scheduled happening. 'Global Forum '94' aimed to attract 15,000 delegates and 200,000 visitors and was backed with a budget of £2.6m from public sources, but it was said that only 13 hotel rooms had been booked and that the second chief executive in six months had resigned (Vidal 1994). There is also the problem of overplaying particular ideas. This is perhaps evident in the proliferation of commemorative events which the *Economist* referred to as a 'glut of anniversaries', prompted by the competing attentions of anniversary events for the Woodstock Pop Festival, the first moon landing, the D-Day commemoration and others. It was suggested that proliferating commemorations may in the end be 'subject to the law of diminishing returns' (1994g).

A number of risk factors concerning special events should be taken into account when their use is under consideration:

1 Special events only generate visitor nights for the duration of the event itself. Longer-term benefits come from the image-building success as a consequence of favourable media exposure, but such benefits depend on the concept and context being right, and a long-term commitment by the promoters to keep it going year-on-year until the long-term benefits are realised.
2 Special events are costly to organise, being particularly labour-intensive. These costs include not only the organising, publicising and stewarding of the event, but other less conspicuous costs such as additional policing and the creation of temporary additional car parking areas. These events also demand substantial marketing budgets.
3 The success of special events can be deceptive. Local people may turn out in force and, with the presence of day-visitors, the destination may appear to be heaving, conveying the notion that the event has been successful. The real barometer of success is the volume of staying visitors achieved, and any special event should be accompanied by research to assess its real value in terms of the economic contribution made to the local economy.

4 Special events, even if successful, can cause long-term damage to the destination if the expectations of new visitors are not matched by the quality of the environment and the standards of service on offer. In this respect it is important to ensure that the event attracts a profile of visitor whose demands can be met. When, for example, visitors find that their preferred kind of accommodation is not in sufficient supply in a resort, they are compelled to 'trade down' and complaints can be expected to spill over into the media.

5 Special events, if they run into trouble, expose the destination to mockery on a grand scale and the wounds in terms of negative image can take a long time to heal. The Sheffield World Student Games of 1992 was just such an example. The Games happened and were effectively a success; but this success was eclipsed by financial embarrassment. At the planning stage, the capacity of this particular event to attract television coverage and hence commercial sponsorship had been over-estimated, resulting in an annual burden of debt charges of £10m.

The tourist destination and its life cycle

It is demonstrably true that many tourist destinations have passed through what can be described as a life cycle, from beginnings to growth, maturity and eventual decline. Two such examples are discussed in detail in Chapter 12. The nature of the progress could be viewed in any one case as being determined by a combination of factors which may include social, economic, technological and political change. The concept of a life cycle has been applied generically to products by marketeers such as Kotler and Armstrong (1991, p. 299) to illustrate the way in which, for example, a particular model of motor car passes through different phases before entering obsolescence and finally being withdrawn, by its manufacturer, from the market. The initial stages, of development and introduction, involve significant investment in developing and launching the product. Only when sales take off does the model become profitable for its manufacturer. As time erodes its attractiveness to the consumer, sales fall and its profitability declines.

Butler (1980) applied the life-cycle concept to resorts. His terminology involved characterising the product development stage as *exploration* followed by *involvement*. As the nascent resort increases in popularity and visitor numbers grow, the resort passes through the *development* stage until it reaches an optimum size and must reinvest in itself in order to sustain its level of business. This was termed the *consolidation* stage. As market tastes evolve through time, the resort finds itself appealing to discrete and limited visitor markets and entering a *stagnation* stage. This will be followed by a *decline* stage. Butler's argument was that not only was significant investment required in the initial stages of the evolution of a resort, in common with manufactured 'products', but that progress into obsolescence was inexorable and that crucial decisions were required during the phase which Kotler and Armstrong describe as 'maturity' and Butler terms 'stagnation'. Such decisions can usefully be described as *turning-point decisions* and can seek to secure either rejuvenation and further development, or a modicum of renewal resulting in the retention of present position. These together can be termed *extension strategies*. To do nothing is equally a turning-point decision by default, and will usually result in continued decline. Some turning-point decisions may entail the deliberate neglect of the tourism industry either through conviction that renewal is not possible, or to favour other purposes, in which case the consequence will be accelerated decline.

The British seaside resort, as a mature holiday product, is a good vehicle for demonstrating the destination life cycle in action. The *exploration* phase occurred during the first half of the nineteenth century and before, when most incipient resorts were only accessible by stage-coach. Urry (1990, pp. 20–1) points out that the exploration phase was marked by the well-to-do visiting the seaside, attracted and influenced by the Romantic movement which was sweeping through art, literature and music, and which extolled the value of natural beauty. *Development* occurred very rapidly in the decades following the railway-building boom of the 1840s, which brought the seaside within reach of the industrial masses. The late Victorian and Edwardian eras saw copious public and private investment in hotels, piers, promenades and theatres. Following the First World War and the recession of the 1920s, the resorts entered a *consolidation* phase in the 1930s which saw further investment in resort facilities. This was brought to an abrupt end by the Second World War, after which, in a period of austerity which lasted until about 1960, the resorts enjoyed an Indian summer but did little to invest in the product. This can be identified as Butler's *stagnation* phase, which lasted until *circa* 1975 when visitor numbers started to decline. At the end of the 1970s the effect of competition from cheap overseas package holidays began to bite deeply into the British resorts' traditional markets and heralded the *decline* phase: the British Transport Commission's *Annual Abstract of Statistics* shows the number of holiday trips abroad increasing from about 8 million in 1975 to 20 million in 1987; the total number of holiday nights spent in British seaside resorts declined from 180 million to 116 million between 1980 and 1988: a fall of 36 per cent (Middleton 1989).

When we evaluate the progress of the British seaside resort over the whole of its life cycle, two factors in particular stand out: the role of private capital in providing access in the form of railway connections, and the role of local governments which either directly created the key man-made features of the destinations, or facilitated their creation by third parties. The effect of two world wars can be regarded as having lengthened the life cycle of coastal resorts by creating conditions which, for much of the twentieth century, inhibited the development of overseas holiday-taking. The failure to invest in new facilities during the resorts' Indian summer of the 1950s can hardly be regarded as culpable in a climate of post-war austerity, and the continued failure to invest during the boom years of the 1960s does not mark out the domestic tourism industry from other sectors of the UK economy: the general failure to invest in new plant and machinery, relying instead on labour to provide the requirements of expanding demand, may have created near-full employment but sowed the seeds of the economic crises of the 1970s when the consequences of earlier failure to invest became

apparent. Likewise, domestic resorts found themselves during the 1970s in competition not only with the Mediterranean sun, but with a quality of accommodation, in newly built hotels with *ensuite* facilities as standard, which raised and changed customers' perceptions of the standards required. The seaside landlady, always renowned in music hall jokes as a figure of endearing fun, became an anachronism symbolic of an old order which, in the space of a few years, was overtaken by overseas alternatives which, if less personal, were more professional.

Even then, businesslike domestic resorts were making *turning-point decisions*. For some, this meant a reappraisal of what sector of the tourism market they intended to serve. A seemingly inexorable fall in the demand for domestic main holidays led some resorts to concentrate on growth sectors, such as the demand for conferences. Resorts such as Brighton, Torquay and Bournemouth, which were well equipped with a stock of good-quality beds, invested in new conference facilities. Smaller resorts such as Rhyl and Bridlington, which saw their futures in retaining a slice of the contracting domestic family holiday market, invested in leisure centres which offered an indoor tropical environment as an option for those days on which the climate failed to deliver.

In the 1990s, the power of local governments to fund capital projects such as these became severely limited by central government; there are even limitations on the purposes to which a local authority may use its capital receipts, that is money which it accrues through (for example) selling council houses or surplus land. One of the last resort attractions built before the most stringent of the government's constraints were applied was the White Cliffs Experience in Dover, a £15m. visitor attraction opened in 1991 and which was substantially funded with receipts from sold assets. This attraction plus investments in Dover's Town Gaol Museum and other facilities, plus a substantial and consistent programme to market Dover as a visitor destination, was intended to create a new economy and image for Dover in preparation for the opening of the Channel Tunnel after which, it was feared, Dover would lose several thousand port-related jobs plus its perceived *raison d'être* in the eyes of the nation as the principal link with the Continent.

It is worth noting that the established mass-market resorts of the western Mediterranean started to encounter the problems of maturity and incipient decline at the end of the 1980s after an accelerated life cycle of little more than 20 to 25 years. Bierce (1991/92) observed that the decline of beach tourism visits and revenues to Spain (see Bunting 1990) had been partially masked by an increase in urban tourism in that country, which she attributed to a growth in business tourism such as conferences and seminars. The decline in Spanish beach tourism she attributed to a loss of competitive edge in the British and German markets, where Spanish holidays were sold on sun, beach and price, and the fact that developments in air travel were now such that a flight to the Caribbean cost the same as a flight to the Canaries. Her prescription for recovery included attention to increased quality in service delivery, creating 'une culture dominée par le client', by which she might well have been speaking of the need for the practice of the hospitality instinct.

So, tourist destinations can be shown to evolve through time. At this point we retain the theme of time and reintroduce the earlier theme of taste, in order to examine the way in which the two interact and their consequent implications, in particular toward the attitude to 'heritage'.

Taste and the passage of time

The best illustration of the link between taste and time occurs in that area of life which is the progeny of the two, namely fashion:

Indecent	10 years before its time
Shameless	5 years before its time
Outré	1 year before its time
Smart	–
Dowdy	1 year after its time
Hideous	10 years after its time
Ridiculous	20 years after its time
Amusing	30 years after its time
Quaint	50 years after its time
Charming	70 years after its time
Romantic	100 years after its time
Beautiful	150 years after its time

('The cycle of fashion' from James Laver's *Taste and Fashion* (1945), reproduced in Bayley 1991, p. xiv)

Time is also, it is said, a great healer. Like most sayings, this is partly truth and partly wishful thinking: there is a sense in which the passage of time heightens the sense of enjoyment of good times remembered, and erodes the trauma of unpleasantness. Yet there is also the fact that, for example, to lose loved ones as the victims of crime is an ever-present grief for close family, even if such incidents become memories and statistics for the rest of the world. There is also the fact that, in the eyes of the law, wrongdoing must be atoned for irrespective of the passage of time. There is therefore something of another dichotomy of perception: for the mass of the people, notorious acts take their place alongside other events of history. For loved ones of victims, and in the eyes of the law, notorious acts remain fresh in their notoriety. But notoriety also attracts the interest of the public: and hence a dilemma of taste arises. For example, in 1981 – on Trafalgar Day, 21 October – the English Tourist Board launched a major promotion entitled 'Maritime England'. Heralded by the ignition of a beacon by the present-day descendant of Admiral Lord Nelson, the promotion was cleverly conceived because, with few exceptions, most neighbourhoods in the country could lay claim to maritime connections. The promotion was to run for the duration of 1982, and indeed did so, except that something entirely unexpected happened in the south Atlantic: the invasion of the Falkland Islands by Argentinian forces. The sending of a maritime task force and subsequent recapture of the islands has now taken its own place in history, but at the time there were certain implications for the handling of the Maritime England promotion: talking at a distance of naval glories past is the stuff that tourism promotion is made of, but doing it while present-day ships are being sunk and lives are being lost is a different matter.

Another example of taste's relationship with time is a museum which was established in the late 1980s in the warehouse in Dallas, Texas, from which Lee Harvey Oswald is thought to have assassinated President John F Kennedy. The actual floor from which the crime is said to have been committed is now laid out as it was on that day in 1963 when the assassination took place. It is unlikely that taste would have permitted the establishment of such a museum any earlier than the late 1980s. A tawdrier example arose in 1981, shortly after the sentencing of the serial killer Peter Sutcliffe, known as the 'Yorkshire Ripper'. The operator of a seafront waxworks in Bridlington displayed a model of the criminal accompanied by the tools of his trade and a recording of his Old Bailey sentence (McClarence 1981). This, when discovered by the tabloid press and communicated to relatives of Sutcliffe's victims, caused distress and calls for the resort to be boycotted. The mayor of the resort prevailed upon the waxworks operator to remove the exhibit, but the incident serves to illustrate, once again, the link between taste and time. It was seen as indecent and a violation of taste to contemplate documenting the notoriety of Sutcliffe at that time and in that way.

In summary, it seems that where public fascination and personal grief concide, a dilemma of taste may arise. Empathy for the victims of trauma may determine that their experiences should not become an object of public curiosity. On the other hand there is a worthy belief that episodes such as the Holocaust will not recur if former concentration camps are conserved and opened to the visiting public. It seems that when trauma is so distant in the past as to be depersonalised, the depiction of, in Burns's words, 'man's inhumanity to man', attracts less controversy. For example, scenes of mediaeval torture as may be found in certain kinds of visitor attraction may not acquire general approval as being 'tasteful', but are insulated against controversy because the acts themselves took place so long ago, the victims lost in obscurity or, in some cases, elevated to martyrdom.

The heritage dilemma

Also arising out of the linkage between taste and time is a dilemma over the depiction in the present of the past. The origins of the explosion of interest in 'heritage' are to be discussed in Chapter 7, but the outcome in terms of tourist activity has been a proliferation of museums and the emergence of

new kinds of visitor attraction which seek to combine, very roughly, the presentational attractions of a theme park with some of the authenticity and credibility ascribed to traditional museums.

The first and perhaps best-known example in the UK is the Jorvik Viking Centre which opened early in the 1980s. Its unique success as a visitor attraction, for it is still drawing about 800,000 visitors per annum, put a new kind of visitor attraction centre-stage. The purpose of these visitor attractions was easy to describe: they took a historical theme and, using displays, new audio-visual technology and design skills, created a *visitor experience* in which the customer was carried, in the case of Jorvik quite literally, through a depiction of life during the time of the Viking kingdom of York. The 'experience' included not just sights and sounds, but smells, albeit suitably sanitised. While everyone knows what this new breed of visitor attraction does and how it does it, a satisfactory name is still elusive. 'Museum' springs to mind, but museums they are not: a museum, according to the Museums Association, 'collects, documents, presents, exhibits and interprets material evidence and associated information for the public benefit'. Such visitor attractions may do all of these things; Jorvik in fact includes a small display of real objects, but it is only a small part of the overall operation. 'Exhibition' is not appropriate because it implies something static and impermanent. 'Heritage Centre' is not quite right either, because both 'heritage' and 'centre' are overworked words which mean everything and nothing. In the case of Jorvik, the City of York could arguably be regarded as the 'centre' of the Viking kingdom and hence appropriate. Similarly the National Fishing Heritage Centre (Grimsby) could reasonably claim to be in *a* centre of the fishing industry. Some attractions have sidestepped the problem by choosing names which avoid a label, such as 'Canterbury Tales' (Canterbury) and 'A Day at the Wells' (Tunbridge Wells), or have opted for the suffix 'Experience' as in 'White Cliffs Experience' (Dover).

The importance or otherwise of this breed of visitor attraction has attracted much debate and ruffled feathers in the world of traditional museums (see Davies 1989). Traditional museums see the use of an excess of design and audio-visual technology as a usurpation of the role of authentic objects from the past which, it is argued, suitably presented and interpreted in a museum, can act as a better stimulus to the imagination than the prepackaged completeness of the heritage centre. In the end, the issue is to consider what the attraction is aiming to achieve. There is no doubt that heritage centres have provided brightly packaged competition for traditional museums. Even though the objectives of heritage centres are in many cases commercial and of museums in most cases public service, they are perceived by the public to be in the same business. The term 'edutainment' has now been commonly ascribed to heritage centres because, while the nature of attraction may be one of a creative display to entertain customers, their objectives are to convey authentic history and as such are educational.

Museums can find themselves in something of a dilemma: are they in the business of education, or entertainment? As 'heritage' rose to prominence in the period post-1970 not just as part of the UK tourist product but as something of a national obsession (see Chapter 7), the public looked to museums as custodians of the nation's heritage to equip themselves for the demands of a mass audience, a trend which was encouraged by the very success of the 'heritage centres'. What has tended to happen is a degree of convergence, with heritage centres seeking to maintain credibility as authentic portrayers of the past, and museums applying new interpretive techniques to present and exhibit their collections in a fresh and entertaining way. Participatory displays, the so-called 'hands-on experience', has been a major innovation in this respect.

A second area of dispute arises when different people have different perceptions of how 'heritage' should be conserved and presented. Admittedly that is what the previous area of dispute is about, in that museums and heritage centres are serving the same publics and may disagree on method and emphasis. But that is essentially a dispute between producers, professionals disagreeing on how it should be done. The visiting public are more interested in having a satisfying experience than in professional rivalries. In other circumstances,

however, sections of the public can be very vociferous about what they want to see done, particularly when cherished tracts of land, or cherished buildings, are at stake. Professionals such as statutory conservation bodies or local authority planners can become involved in disputes between different groups which have different designs for the same piece of 'heritage'. Alternatively, different stakeholders, to use a currently popular term, may have differing views on how, for example, a cherished building should be conserved.

One such example was reported in the *Yorkshire Post* (Brown 1994) and illustrates rival perceptions so well that it is worth relating. A hereditary peer, Viscount Scarsdale, handed his eighteenth-century family seat, Kedleston Hall in Derbyshire, to the National Trust in 1987. The peer retains residence in one wing, and the Trust administers the rest of the house. The substance of the news report was of disagreements over levels of consultation between the peer and the Trust and which are not germane to the present discussion, but the philosophical issue at the heart of the dispute is one which has to be faced in the interpretation of any historic building: should it be interpreted as it stood at one particular time, for example shortly after it was built; or should it be interpreted as a continuum through time? It can be argued, for example, that the twentieth-century use of an eighteenth-century historic house is as relevant as its use two centuries earlier. The differing philosophy of the peer and the Trust is apparent in the comments quoted in the *Yorkshire Post* article:

Kedleston Hall has always been a pure reflection of the Georgian period . . . we have arranged furniture in a way that makes sense – removing some of it from the centre of rooms to the edges, which is how it would have been arranged for most of its time in the hall. (National Trust spokesperson, quoted in Brown 1994)

It is a family home and should reflect the changes throughout history . . . I'm not trying to say that the Trust is destroying the house but it is trying to change its character. (Viscount Scarsdale, quoted in Brown 1994)

Hewison reports that a chairman of the National Heritage Memorial Fund, when asked what the word 'heritage' meant, is said to have replied, 'Anything you want' (in Uzzell (ed.) 1989, p. 15). This comment in its untethered generality supports a relevant point: that a family like Viscount Scarsdale's which has apparently lived on the same land for 800 years is itself as much part of the heritage of the site as the house and the furniture. It can be argued that conserving the house as a two-dimensional snapshot from the eighteenth century risks creating what can at best be a vision of what twentieth-century knowledge and aspiration considers the past could or should have been like or, as Hewison (1987, p. 8) put it, a 'crash course in the bourgeois myths of history'.

The Kedleston example is interesting as a microcosm of disputes which occur more widely when the stakes are higher and there are more stakeholders. The acronym NIMBY (not in my backyard) was coined for individuals and groups who discovered the power of lobbying to resist development close to their domiciles. Blackhurst, writing in the *Observer*, claimed to have identified a new species. Under the banner heading 'Notes: The rural taste tyrants', Blackhurst claimed that:

Not content with telling people Not In My Backyard, the Nimby has gone a step further – at least in the national parks of England and Wales – and is saying Not Over There Either. Buoyed by civil servant allies in Whitehall – who prefer the acronym Bananas – Build Absolutely Nothing Anywhere Near Anything – Notes are making life hell for ordinary country folk. (Blackhurst 1994)

Blackhurst identifies NOTES as refugees from the city, owners of holiday homes and commuters whose fierce resistance to change is complemented by skills in lobbying, petitioning and writing to newspapers. Specific examples quoted include North Yorkshire Moors National Park planners banning reoccupation of a farmhouse because the presence of washing on a line would harm the view, and officials in the Lake District using a helicopter to check whether occupiers had reroofed using artificial slates which, it is claimed, are barely discernible from real Westmoreland slates. A Derbyshire councillor is quoted as saying that villages such as Birchover 'are being dragged towards museum status'.

Blackhurst credits Lord Shuttleworth, chairman of the Rural Development Commission, as having coined the term NOTES and who expressed some optimism that the government may act to ensure that policies for national parks guarantee a future for their indigenous inhabitants. An article in a magazine published by what was described as a Notist body, the Friends of the Lake District, was also quoted as evidence of self-criticism by NOTES and brings to mind Hewison's words about the 'bourgeois myths of history'.

The popular image of the Friends is as an organisation whose main purpose is to try to prevent change of any kind and to condemn the inhabitants of the Lake District to a way of life fossilised in some idyllic past age and deprived of the benefits of modern civilisation. (R Gambles, quoted in Blackhurst 1994)

Tastes as signs

We have considered the appeal of visitor attractions and tourist destinations in the context of a commonality and a diversity of taste, and explored the influence of the variable of time by which tastes change, and popularity is affected. It has been argued that destinations pass through an evolutionary process of incipient discovery, popularity and decline, giving rise to what has been described as a resort life cycle. The interaction of taste and time, with consequent implications for attitude to 'heritage', has also been discussed. In a sense, conclusions at this point are as elusive as taste itself. Tastes could be said to be but superficial signs of deeper intrinsic human traits, needs and values which are the product of education and cultural conditioning. The next three chapters aim to achieve some more insights by taking an anthropologist's view of the role of endeavour in the tourist experience, the existence or otherwise of a fundamental 'need' to tour, and cultural conditioning as a determinant in tourist behaviour.

Chapter **5**

An anthropology of tourist endeavour

This chapter aims to examine the nature of 'endeavour' in the context of tourist activity, and how the achievements of endeavour are documented and communicated through the acquisition, exchange and sharing of objects such as postcards, souvenirs and photographs. It will be suggested that these objects are important for their symbolic rather than their real value. The chosen perspective owes much to that of the social anthropologist, and it will be argued that there is a commonality of motive, behaviour and imaging which is as observable in major examples of human endeavour, such as the moon programme and military activity, as it is in the behaviour of the individual tourist. The intended outcome is to provide a basis of insight for the more detailed discussions relating to individual and societal motivations, which are the themes of Chapters 6 and 7.

'Otherness' and the tourist trip

One of the themes of the previous chapter was the attractiveness of 'abnormality', usually defined by anthropologists as 'otherness', in the tourist experience. The abnormality was held to have meaning both in the sense of the pursuit of the bizarre, such as a ride on a roller-coaster, and in terms of difference from routine. Shakespeare observed that 'If all the world were making holidays, to sport would be as tedious as to work' (Henry IV Part 1, Act X, Scene x) and it is true that in the case of holidays or business trips, or visits to relatives, the pleasurable aspects of such trips are in part dependent on their infrequency. The problems caused by frequency of exposure came to the mind of the author, one fine day in March

1993, sitting in a restaurant in Palma de Mallorca, capital of the Balearics. Observation of early-retired British expatriates at their leisure gave an impression that, somehow, retirement in Spain was not the permanent holiday that might be anticipated. An absence of mirth, absence of conversation, and purposelessness of facial expressions spoke powerfully of the dangers of leaving the community where work and social role offer a sense of identity, and entering another community where personal roots and recognition do not exist. Equally, there are many stories of expatriates whose experiences match their expectations, but on the other hand many tourists will admit that 'coming home' is in some way one of the pleasures of the trip. Perhaps therefore the 'otherness' of a tourist trip cannot be relied upon to provide sustained satisfaction if converted into residency, in much the same way as a diet of chocolates cannot provide sustained nutrition.

Other kinds of tourist may, like the retired expatriate, seek to prolong the satisfactions of the tourist trip but by adopting a very different approach. Explorer-tourists are people who may describe themselves as 'travellers', and as a group may be subject to varying degrees of addiction to travelling. The explorer does not look to residency to prolong the satisfactions of 'otherness': satisfaction, by contrast, is achieved through being constantly on the move, and in extreme cases the explorer finds it impossible to adapt to the rigours of residency and stability. In its mildest form, the traveller simply perceives a need to have more holidays, or travel more frequently, than the ordinary person. The more seriously afflicted find themselves locked into a state of endemic itinerancy. A recent example encountered by the author was a 30-year-old who had travelled the world for years undertaking a range of seasonal jobs, plagued by a perennial struggle to convince himself of the need to enter higher education as a prelude to a more settled pattern of work and lifestyle. A yet more extreme form of endeavour-addiction may be evident in explorer-tourists who combine prolonged travel with feats of endurance. Clouston, writing about round-the-world walker Ffyona Campbell, speculated on reasons to explain her 'phenomenal staying power in the face of stone-throwing Africans, Australian droughts and sundry marauding males'. A psychologist was quoted as advancing various explanations, included amongst which was the suggestion that her capacity for doing without the company of other people was 'enormous', but observing that a simple liking for 'seeing other places' was also a possibility (1994). In the absence of further information, it is only appropriate to speculate that a need for self-testing through endurance, a difficulty in adapting to residency, an enormous appetite for seeing other places, or a combination of these factors, may explain the feats of explorers whose thirst for endeavour is not quenched by frequency of exposure.

The thirst for endeavour

Major feats of endeavour as undertaken by Ffyona Campbell are significant not solely as individual achievements: they have the benefit of the vicarious support of large numbers of others who, although not fellow-travellers in the literal sense of the word, follow the progress of explorers through the media and share in their sense of accomplishment. Examination of major organised efforts of human endeavour shows that there is a commonality of motivation, behaviour and imaging which, it is argued, can be directly related to the behavioural features of the ordinary tourist trip. Two examples are chosen: first, the moon programme; and secondly, military activity.

THE MOON PROGRAMME

In 1969, the United States of America successfully landed astronauts on the moon. That was a seminal event in the memories of those who were alive at the time, and the words of Neil Armstrong who first set foot on the lunar soil have earned an entry in the annals of soundbites: 'That's one small step for a man, one giant leap for mankind.' Armstrong and his crew were away from home on the business of their employer and, technically, were business tourists. What is more, the salient behavioural patterns of the astronauts while on the moon coincided quite closely with known patterns of tourist behaviour. Photographs were taken of the destination, some of them featuring the astronauts in the foreground. The visual record was shared with members of the global family through the medium of television. Souvenirs were acquired in the form of pieces of rock (of the inedible kind) and brought back. Some of these souvenirs were presented to other nations for scientific use, and display in museums. This is not an attempt to trivialise endeavour but to point out that the moon landing was *de facto* an enormous tourist trip and the motives of discovery, self-betterment and adventure, shared by all of those who followed the progress of that mission through the medium of television, have a lot in common with personal, individual reasons for touring: tourism as *exploration*.

MILITARY ACTIVITY

Participants in military activity are undoubtedly participants in endeavour, though a 'thirst' for authentic military action is presumably confined to very few. The reality of soldiering in peacetime is of retaining a preparedness for action, and similarities with tourism are seen particularly in the imaging of soldiering which is used to attract recruits. Until comparatively recently, the advertising images used by the British armed services were very much based on 'seeing the world', the invitation being accompanied by images of leisure and sporting activities being undertaken by military personnel at their ease in overseas locations. The nature of formal advertising for professional recruits has become noticeably more reflective of late, yet still focuses on overseas experience and contact with other cultures: a contemporary (1994) cinema advertisement seeking officer recruits for the Army reports the role of an individual in successfully facilitating the development of a self-help project on a Pacific island, revealing at the end of the piece that the achievement was that of a full-time army officer. From time to time in provincial newspapers, small syndicated news items report the progress of some local young person serving abroad in the Services, usually detailing the attractive leisure pursuits which are enjoyed by him or her during free time. The anthropology of military activity may also be regarded as comparable with that of tourist activity in the acquisition of objects to document participation. These are of official and non-official origin: first, the receipt of medals from an official source; and secondly, the acquisition of items of ephemera such as badges, insignia and personal mementos, whose value to the participant is as unofficial but personal souvenir documentation of the endeavour. In common with the moon programme, armies on active service have their progress documented through an official visual record, for example cinema newsreels during the Second World War, which enables non-combatants at home to participate vicariously in the endeavour.

The suggestion is, therefore, that the tourist trip shares features in common with major efforts of human endeavour such as those outlined above. This commonality is internal inasmuch as the tourist trip is an adventure demanding of the tourist qualities of courage and the ability to organise and adapt to new circumstances, while being deprived of the full resources of the home environment. The commonality is external inasmuch as the tourist trip is documented through a visual record, the acquisition of objects and the sending of visual messages which are intended to communicate and share the experience with other people. We now turn to consider the documenting process in detail.

Documenting the trip

TAKING PHOTOGRAPHS

'Next Monday afternoon we're arranging for X to show his pictures of the Paris trip. Don't look so enthusiastic.' These words were uttered recently to the author by an academic colleague. Just why does the prospect of viewing other people's travel photographs evoke mixed feelings? First, the photographic record tends to be *personal*. It involves the placing of self, family and friends in the context of a famous, attractive or otherwise noteworthy place, or simply enjoying personal pleasure. What is of personal interest or amusement does not necessarily have the same significance for others. Interestingly, the visual record of one of the later Apollo moon landings showed an astronaut taking a swing with a golf club on the moon. After the initial fascination of seeing a man walk on the moon, and beholding the beauty of the earth as seen from the moon, there was frankly little more to see or do and the visual record degenerated into self-amusement.

Secondly, the photographic record is *predictable*. Where the photographs are of the 'sights' rather than the personal variety, there is every likelihood that prospective viewers will already know (for example) what the Eiffel Tower or the Taj Mahal looks like; not only has it been seen before, but its image is frequently exposed through a variety of media. It can be argued that tourist photography is one facet of the souvenir-collecting process inasmuch as it is a personal record, available to wider scrutiny, documenting the sometime presence of the tourist in a certain place with certain people. Having oneself photographed with Mickey Mouse at Disneyland Paris is an example *par excellence*.

Urry follows this argument by suggesting that 'to photograph is in some way to appropriate the object being photographed. It is a power relationship' (1990, pp. 138–40). In this way our *personal* relationship with the object accompanying us in the photograph is documented and available for wider scrutiny; or maybe our power to acquire a bite of consumer-correct lifestyle, reclining on some foreign beach whose overseas provenance is documented by examples of exotic plantlife in the background, such as a palm tree. The *predictable* nature of our photography is determined by the fact that, when photographing noteworthy sights, we have learned through previous exposure to these same or similar sights, to photograph them in a certain way. For example, visitors to the City of York who have walked the city walls will notice that when walking north-eastwards toward Lendal Bridge, the generic 'view' of York which regularly features in tourist brochures is readily recognised. Other tourist landmarks can be similarly recognised and photographed from agreed vantage points. At Niagara Falls, for example, such locations are physically marked to assist the tourist acquire the best photographs. Other material included in photographs serves to endorse the location: the palm trees on the exotic beach, the Frenchman in a striped jersey in the foreground of a Provençal landscape, the barbary ape on the Rock of Gibraltar. In this way tourist photographers choose material for its signifying value: the tourist is, in Urry's words, an 'amateur semiotician' (1990, p. 139).

An effective and widely disseminated example of amateur tourist semiotics was the photographing of the Princess of Wales in front of the Taj Mahal during a state visit to India. The view of the Taj Mahal was the predictable one; she located herself in the foreground, alone, providing a photo-opportunity for the world's media. This well-staged gesture was doubly significant: first, she was present at this world-famous site, and secondly she was alone at a place of which her husband was on record as having said that he wished to show her its beauty. The meaning of this demonstration was not lost on the world's media. More commonly it is the presence rather than the absence of loved ones which the tourist wishes to document. Tourist photographs are, in Urry's words, 'the outcome of an active signifying practice' (1990, p. 139).

BUYING SOUVENIRS

When the miniature replica of the Eiffel Tower is purchased, it can be simultaneously enjoyed as a piece of kitsch, an exercise in geometric formalism and as a socially revealing artefact. There is no need to make a fetish out of the correct interpretation since the post-tourist can enjoy playing at it being all three. (Urry 1990, p. 100)

Witless adaptation, diminution and relentless cheapening categorise kitsch. (Bayley, 1991, p. 65)

Post-tourism, post-modernity and *playfulness* are concepts which are further discussed in Chapter 7. For the present purpose, we assume that souvenirs are acquired and collected, as Urry suggests, for a multitude of purposes. First, they may be bought for the purchaser's own enjoyment, or as a gift to a friend or relative on returning home. Secondly, souvenirs are generally items which have no functional value within the range of regular consumption. They are not household essentials: a stick of rock has minimal nutritional value, a kiss-me-quick hat has limited application as an item of everyday clothing. Nor are they household luxuries. They may frequently be regarded by both purchaser and recipient as something of a nuisance. The nuisance value of souvenirs may extend to the time of immediate pre-purchase, where a final morning on the beach has to be sacrificed in favour of acquiring items of ephemera to please, or placate, immediate family and friends who have not participated in the trip and whose wrath may be incurred if their loved one returns without evidence of having thought about them during the envied break.

Much souvenir material of this kind may fall into Urry's kitsch category and acquire a new role as a dust-trap on some mantelpiece. Its actual function, and hence reason for purchase, can be regarded as *symbolic*, and like its companion, the holiday photograph, it is acquired for its *signifying* properties. Souvenirs are often flippant purchases made out of playful motives and under the duress of some familial obligation. The souvenir purchased for personal retention may have aroused some genuine affection in its purchaser; the purchase for a third party may have benefited from less forethought. In both cases the item will symbolise the place: the stick of rock symbolising the seaside, the Eiffel Tower symbolising Paris, documenting the fact that the visit took place. Sticks of rock invariably carry the name of the resort of purchase, and many other souvenirs of the kitsch category will have the name of the destination applied to them. It is as if the recipient of a souvenir offered as a gift acquires a connection by proxy with the place of origin, by way of 'I know someone who . . .'. In this way the souvenir is, in Urry's words, a 'socially revealing artefact' (1990, p. 100).

At peril of ignoring Urry's warning that there is little reward in making a 'fetish' out of the interpretation of souvenir-purchasing, it is none the less interesting to notice that the acquisition and giving of souvenirs as post-holiday gifts has much to do with social *ritual*, of which the need for *reciprocation* is a key feature. As with other forms of present-giving there is the expectation that the recipient will respond by offering a similar gift, preferably of comparable quality and value, when the opportunity arises. Even when the souvenirs exchanged fall quite definitely into the kitsch category, the failure to reciprocate can engender offence. Being equipped with suitable items of ephemera is a must, for example, for a town mayor, whose visitors from other municipalities from home and abroad will come equipped with official souvenirs of their area. Framed engravings and bone china plates depicting the municipal arms are favourites. The givers expect, and receive, something similar in return. Typically these trophies are collected together for viewing, if not for the general public, then for the discrete set of visitors who are admitted to the mayoral suite.

Ethnographic parallels can be observed in some chiefdom societies, such as the Kyaka people of New Guinea, where ritual gift exchange has been a crucial means of maintaining understanding between different chiefdoms, accompanied by a cycle of mutual entertaining at feasts and festivities (Renfew 1972, p. 140). Further, items such as a town mace whose presence during the full meeting of the municipal body serves, like tourist memorabilia, a symbolic function, are also invariably displayed alongside the rest of the civic regalia to town hall visitors; possibly, even, with the ritual gifts from other municipalities accompanying them in the display, in a supporting role. Without wishing to labour this point, it does seem that municipal souvenir-collecting and personal souvenir-collecting share some symbolic meanings: both document *connection, association* and hence a kind of power alliance with the places of origin, resulting in an enhancement of status of the collector. An anthropologist viewed it thus:

Among societies where status grading tends to be of a nonegalitarian type, the status symbols . . . would normally be dictated by ideological symbolism which rationalizes and emphasizes the particular internal ranking system . . . [and] possession of certain forms may become exclusively restricted to certain status positions. (Binford 1962)

Complex western societies tend to be a mixture of egalitarian and non-egalitarian features. For example, an ordinary citizen has realistic opportunities to become involved in local politics, seek to become town mayor and enjoy an association with the symbolism and trappings of that office, but carrying the orb and sceptre at a state coronation lies beyond the ambitions of all but the heir to the throne as determined by birth. But as increasing wealth causes travel opportunities to proliferate, westerners can engage in an egalitarian rush to document their associations with the places they visit, or the places that their friends and relatives visit, by including souvenirs in their assemblage of material possessions.

Vicarious association with exotic destinations has been applied quite unselfconsciously by tourism businesses and destinations in pursuit of status enhancement. The ability of the mild climate of south Devon to support palm trees, a plant not indigenous to England, has not only created a hint of southern climes for the visitor to Torquay, but provided the promotional symbol for the resort, supported by the term 'English Riviera'. Likewise, an enterprising owner of a small hotel in a Yorkshire coastal resort created a 'Spanish Bar Lounge', a photograph of which in his advertisement depicted all manner of Spanish resort memorabilia affixed to the walls, and a 'Manhattan Coffee Lounge' whose backdrop was a mural of the New York skyline (East Yorkshire Borough Council 1983, p. 39).

Krippendorf (1987) perceived that the rush to acquire and exchange tourist kitsch risks taking the pursuit of triviality to derisory levels, and as part of his prescription for what he terms the 'humanisation of travel' invites the tourist to reject conventional souvenir consumerism:

Find happiness in small things instead of wanting more and more. Not the superlative, the most expensive, the extreme. Have an eye for the small joys, for the found and discovered. Find your small holiday booty. Collect rocks, shells, starfish, cones, feathers. Take home your personal souvenir. (Krippendorf 1987, p. 131)

Such advice is enacted effortlessly by children, and offers the benefits of saving both time and money for their parents. But the reality of consumerism is that its power to conform is considerable, and the ritual of adult gift exchange demands evidence of both time and money expended. Auntie may be satisfied and even touched by a gift of a cone or a feather from a 7-

year-old niece, but may have higher expectations of the adult members of the party. On the other hand, similarly minded people may willingly co-operate with each other, on a reciprocal basis, in exchanging *personal* rather than *purchased* souvenirs. Consumer purchasing patterns are determined by a number of variables, of which taste, a theme of the previous chapter, is one of the most difficult to define. Where does *kitsch* stop, and *taste* begin?

There is a need here, perhaps, for a dose of healthy iconoclasm. The National Trust, in England, has developed a model of minimal commercialisation of its properties which are displayed to the public in a state of exemplary 'good taste', and yet the *objets d'art* with which many such properties were endowed by their former aristocratic owners could be viewed in their contemporary context as items of bought-in culture whose acquisition at the time was made possible by the availability of surplus wealth. Did these landowners understand, at the time, that they were exercising 'good taste', or were they simply doing what other aristocrats were doing and collecting exotica in a process of, to use Bayley's words, 'witless adaptation'?

Significantly, the actual cultural and financial value of antiquities often eludes all but the initiated. 'Taste' in relation to *objets d'art* is surely a relative concept, determined partly by knowledge of the object's significance, partly by the value placed on the object by society, and partly by level of interest. An object which is valued as a signifier becomes an embarrassment when that which it signifies becomes unfashionable. Oliver Cromwell, on dissolving the Rump Parliament in 1653, robustly dismissed the mace with the words, 'What shall we do with this bauble? There, take it away.' The journey from valued symbolic object to kitsch is a short one.

SENDING POSTCARDS

The sending of postcards as a holiday-related activity combines the features of photography and souvenir-purchasing, and can thus be regarded as a hybrid of the two. The postcard depicts, usually, a photographic illustration of the destination visited and as such documents the sender's association with that place. It is sent to a third party and in this way is akin to a souvenir. Many

will testify that choosing and writing postcards, finding a place which sells stamps and then sending them, rivals the obligations of souvenir-buying as an irritation. There is for most people a sense of social obligation about sending postcards, but equal frustration at the time it takes, particularly if the postcards are sent from an overseas destination and the sender arrives back home before the postcards. The creative solution of one acquaintance of the author is to send postcards from the airport either on departure or on return, thereby making productive use of 'dead' time and guaranteeing prompt arrival. Once received, the postcards receive similar treatment as souvenirs and are assembled in some conspicuous place in the household as trophies of destination associations enjoyed through third parties.

Thus, to summarise so far, the phenomenon of tourism enjoys a commonality of form with human endeavour. The urge to tour is equalled by the urge to document, and not just to document but to communicate and share with others. Features of tourist endeavour which are shared with examples such as the moon programme include the option for vicarious enjoyment of the trip by non-participants. The following paragraphs set out a context for vicarious travel and suggest that it is an under-researched area which arguably should be regarded as an integral part of the travel and tourism industry.

Vicarious travel

Earlier in the chapter, an extreme type of tourist behaviour which was termed explorer-tourism, motivated by endeavour-addiction, was considered. Logically it is useful to consider whether, like most extremes, endeavour-addiction has its opposite. Armchair tourism, what Hamilton-Smith termed 'travelling vicariously' (1987, p. 340), may be that opposite. Readership of travel books in 1986 amounted to 1 per cent of the total readership of fiction and non-fiction in the UK (Policy Studies Institute 1989, p. 15), comparable with the readership for books on gardening, DIY, leisure and religion, but far less than for the modern novel (13 per cent) and romance (28 per cent). But television programmes such as *Holiday* can rival soaps such as *Emmerdale*, attracting nearly 8 million viewers and placing it in the top 20 of weekly television listings, even during the month of April when many viewers have already booked holidays (*The Stage* 1993, p. 25).

Hamilton-Smith suggests that armchair travellers are more interested in living the experience of the traveller than in the nuts and bolts of what was achieved, and suggest this as a reason for Noyce's (1954) *South Col* having been better received than Hunt's (1953) *Ascent of Everest* (1987, p. 340). The television holiday programmes are something else, much more akin to a shop-window for holiday opportunities than conveying any sense of the personal enjoyment gained from travel, and it is perhaps more appropriate to regard travel documentaries and natural history documentaries as offering a more authentic experience for armchair travellers. It could be hypothesised that travel books and travel programmes may have a salient influence on the cultural agenda and in determining fashions and trends in trip-taking, and it is this in particular which may benefit from further research.

One of the advantages of experiencing travel through books and the media is that some of the less pleasant aspects of the real thing, such as airport delays, bowel disorders, and fall-outs with fellow travellers, are absent. The apogee of vicarious travel was surely represented in the 1990 science fiction film, *Total Recall*. Set in the future, the story-line begins with the attention of the protagonist, played by Arnold Schwarzenegger, being caught by an advertising poster which offers the experience of a holiday by implanting the sensations and memories of a trip into the mind of the customer. Despite advice from a workmate who counsels caution, Schwarzenegger visits the company which offers the experience. The sales pitch includes a litany of the inconveniences of travel: declaiming real holidays as 'a pain in the butt' and naming airport delays, misdirected luggage and expense as evidence, the invitation to Schwarzenegger is to 'take a trip from yourself'. The computer programme which delivers the model holiday offers a menu of options which relate not only to destinations and holiday activities, but to the physical appearance of a female travelling companion. What was intriguing about this episode was the suggestion that

Schwarzenegger's mental documentation of the experience, that is his own memory, should be tantamount to the equivalent of having experienced the holiday in reality. No offer of inauthentic external documentation for the trip was offered, such as a package of souvenirs, postcards sent to friends, and a set of photographs to peruse on a rainy Sunday afternoon: the 'holiday' was sold as seen, the remembered sensations being the prime attribute. This raises the issue of the intrinsic satisfactions of a holiday, to be discussed in the next chapter.

To conclude this chapter and form a further link with the theme of intrinsic satisfaction to be considered in the next, it may be useful to return to the moon programme. This venture was arguably, in its essence, a vehicle for vicarious travel of enormous proportions, being delivered visually and aurally into the homes of the world through the electronic media. The rationale advanced for the venture is not without its own significance. President John F Kennedy, when committing the United States to putting a human being onto the moon before the end of the 1960s, left the world in no doubt that prestige was the primary purpose (Sorensen 1965, pp. 523–9). Kennedy sought to justify his rationale by referring to the comment of the mountaineer George Leigh Mallory who, when asked why he wanted to climb Mount Everest, offered the oft-quoted response, 'Because it is there.' In science fiction as well as science fact, the urge to explore, for exploration's sake, has been advanced as an acceptable rationale. The mission of the starship Enterprise in the TV science fiction series *Star Trek*, now in its second generation of programmes, was to 'explore new worlds, to seek out new life and new civilisations'.

If the suggestion of this chapter, that there is a commonality of form and motivation in tourism and endeavour, is correct, then that may account in part for the extraordinary popularity of both tourism and *Star Trek*. Perhaps, as evidenced in Kennedy's rationale for the moon programme and Mallory's for climbing the mountain, the quest to boldly go where no one has gone before is both the means and the end. Tourism, being 'largely psychological in its attractions', is a drama of the mind, and requires no justification of material purpose. To this extent, the private adventure of the individual taking a pleasure vacation compares with the public adventure of Neil Armstrong and his crew. Of course, consumers advance a range of 'reasons' for taking a pleasure vacation, and for particular choices of vacation, and these are considered in Chapter 7. Similarly, the moon programme was supported by a range of ancillary 'reasons' such as technological progress and scientific research, but the primary rationale was the one advanced by the President himself at the inception of the project.

The twenty-fifth anniversary of the first lunar landing was commemorated in 1994, spawning a shoal of media features and documentaries in the search for a purpose beyond that first outlined by President Kennedy. It was noted that space exploration by human beings was now confined to the immediate vicinity of the earth's atmosphere, and that humankind's personal involvement with the moon appeared to have ceased with the conclusion of the Apollo programme. There was much speculation as to what outlets will be available in the future to satisfy humankind's urge to explore. The philosopher Edward de Bono, writing in *The Guardian*, suggested that greater benefits would have been realised by spending the moon programme's $25bn. budget on improving people's thinking habits (de Bono 1994). During a group discussion concerning the 25 years which had elapsed since the moon programme, broadcast on BBC Radio 4's *The World This Weekend* on 17 July 1994, contributors were lukewarm about the potential for further space exploration. One participant advanced an alternative: 'Man's inner space – the mind – that's the next great frontier.' The relationship between tourism and the human mind, framed in terms of its needs and wants, is the subject of Chapter 6.

Chapter 6

The 'need to get away'

T*he key to understanding tourist motivation is to see vacation travel as a satisfier of needs and wants . . . it is the difference between those travel agents who see themselves as sellers of airline seats and those who view themselves as dealers in dreams.*
(Mill and Morrison 1992, p. 17)

'I need a holiday'

The 'need to get away': is it real or imagined? Data from the Central Statistical Office shows that in the United Kingdom, four out of ten people in any one year do not take a holiday. This figure has remained fairly constant over the last two decades, in spite of the fact that 94 per cent of UK workers now enjoy four weeks' paid holiday compared with the early 1960s, when 94 per cent of workers had only two weeks' paid leave. Twenty years later, an identical percentage enjoyed double that amount. Even at the end of the 1970s, a holiday entitlement of more than four weeks was rare (1993, pp. 140–1). And during that same period, throughout the western world, disposable incomes grew to a considerable extent: in Germany, for example, the family leisure budget quadrupled between 1965 and 1982, of which one-third was spent on holidays (Krippendorf 1987, p. 91).

Who are these 40 per cent who live their lives without the annual holiday which, for many, is the pivotal event of the year? For some, lack of discretionary income precludes expenditure on holidays; one product of the 1980s has been a widening gap between the 'haves' and the 'have-nots'. Quoting recent research by the Institute for Fiscal Studies, the *Economist* stated that the wealthiest 20 per cent of Britons were, in 1991,

seven times better off than the poorest 20 per cent. They had been four times better off in 1977. A similar trend is discernible in other advanced countries (1994c, pp. 19–21).

It can be supposed that it is unlikely to be the same 40 per cent every year who do not take a holiday; but if significant numbers of the 40 per cent were *disposed* to take holidays, if not every year, then it would be expected that increasing affluence and lengthening holiday entitlements, not to mention the vigorous efforts of the travel and tourism industry in selling its wares, would have increased take-up during the course of the 1970s and 1980s. A consequence of increasing free time and discretionary income has indeed been an increase in travel and tourism, and yet the 40 per cent figure remains constant. The statistic refers to people who do not take a holiday of *four* nights or more, so some of the 40 per cent may be holiday 'snackers': takers of short holidays of one to three nights, a sector which is estimated by Beioley to have grown by between 15 and 20 per cent per annum during the 1980s. Research showed that in 1986, 28 per cent of adults had taken a short holiday in the UK, and 12 per cent had taken two, but data collected by the Wales Tourist Board in the same year showed that regular holiday snackers were also likely to have had a long holiday in the same year (1991b). The takers of long holidays and the short-breakers were largely the same people.

The point of this present discussion is not to delve deeper into the identity of these 40 per cent, but to establish the point that there are people, apparently many people, who make do without an annual 'main' holiday. If a holiday is truly a 'need', in terms of the refrain, 'I need a holiday', then in any one year four out of ten of the population could be expected to exhibit signs of vacational malnutrition, whatever those signs may be. Although we have all encountered people whose state of health and general appearance suggest that they 'need a break', to what extent is it a holiday that they need, or *something else* that a holiday provides, and which could potentially be acquired by other means? Certainly, a holiday does on particular occasions seem to be a prescribed means of achieving specific beneficial effects. The medical profession is known to recommend a holiday as part of a programme to recover from certain illnesses, and Health Authorities, trade unions and other organisations maintain convalescent homes, often located in established resort areas, to which their patients or members can remove in order to recover from illness and/or medical or surgical treatment.

One consequence of the working climate of the 1980s in advanced societies has been an increase in so-called prosperity diseases. In this regard it is interesting to discover that work-stress is not, as is sometimes believed, exclusively associated with particular kinds of work; Cooper refuted the notion that the 'need' for respite from work is greater amongst executive, managerial and professional employees, demonstrating that the stress symptoms of white-collar workers tend to be of the psychological kind, whereas stress tended to be manifested in blue-collar employees through physical symptoms. The origins of the stress were also different: in middle-managerial employees, it was frequently caused by the dual burden of responsibility and an uncertain operating environment; in blue-collar employees, by their impotence to change things for the better (in Kalimo *et al.* (eds.) 1987).

In anecdotal terms, it is not difficult to picture the jaded worker, whether employee, domestic spouse or whatever, and their perception of their own need for a change of scenery. What is sought is a break away from home, somewhere hot, perhaps, with something different to do, or alternatively the opportunity to do nothing. It would be an opportunity to spend time with the family, or escape from the family as the case may be. Above all, it would be an opportunity to feel fully in control of one's own activity: time to think, time to be active, time to relax, time for fun. The jaded employee's boss may share his or her enthusiasm: the company does not offer four

weeks' paid holiday for no reason, you are not expected to stay at home wallpapering, you are expected to take a proper break, at the moment you are making mistakes and getting crabby with everyone, if you can't take the heat, get out of the kitchen . . . at least, for a week or so.

Is, then, a holiday a *need*, or a *want*? There is much work yet to be done in understanding the psychology of tourism. Pearce and Stringer have described the field as 'undermanned' (1991, p. 143), and Gilbert has noted that the principal texts on tourism marketing tend not to cover consumer behaviour in any depth (in Cooper (ed.) 1991, p. 80). The purpose of this chapter is not to offer ready conclusions. However, an ambition to acquire and nurture the hospitality instinct demands that this subject be confronted, and a set of concepts acquired which illuminate understanding. That is what this chapter seeks to achieve. The discourse which follows uses a range of Schon's *displaced concepts* (see Chapter 1) and makes reference not only to psychological theory, but also to literature, and to the field of social policy, where the search for a definition of 'need' and 'want' is of vital importance, influencing the distribution of public resources. The concept of 'need' as expressed through select literature is the first subject of examination.

Reason not the need

Reason not the need; our basest beggars are in the poorest thing superfluous. Allow not nature more than nature needs, man's life is cheap as beast's. (Shakespeare, King Lear, Act II, Scene iv).

One of the achievements of Shakespeare's greatest work is its portrayal of and discourse on human need. It is worth examining this in some detail. Lear, King of Britain, wants to retire from the responsibilities of kingship, but does not want to hang up his crown. He divides his kingdom between two of his three daughters, but retains his title and 100 followers, and arranges to lodge for six months alternately with the two daughters. After the deal is struck, the daughters and sons-in-law decide they are less than happy with the lodging arrangements, in particular as regards the alleged rowdiness of Lear's followers. In a climactic scene where Lear confronts his daughters, they whittle away at the number of followers they say they are prepared to accommodate down to 50, 25, 10, 5 ... until the baseline is reached: 'What need one?' At which point, Lear responds with 'Reason not the need', quoted above. What he is saying, in essence, is this: whether I *need* my followers is not the issue: even beggars on the streets have some poor personal possession or other with which they could do without, which they do not actually *need*. If human beings are not to be allowed any more than is necessary to keep them this side of death, then the quality of life is as poor as that of a 'beast', a common animal.

Lear in effect admits that, as far as the 100 followers are concerned, he is talking about his 'wants' rather than his 'needs', while disposing of his daughters' appeal to 'need' as a reason for depriving him of his retinue. The prospect of losing his followers, the symbolic representation of his power base, causes him distress of a kind which strikes at the heart of his self-esteem. Lear is a king, and is accustomed to feeling secure in the trappings of being a king. Lear 'needs' the panoply of kingship, as the chairman of a major corporation 'needs' a limousine, and, quite possibly in this sense, the wealthier inhabitants of the world's leading economic powers perceive an entitlement, a 'need', for a holiday commensurate with their expectations. But there is another dimension to this episode in Lear's life, a *something else* of more importance than his 100 followers: his daughters' love. Lear is experiencing rejection by his daughters, and it is the apparent *withdrawal of their love*, measured in terms of the number of followers they will agree to accommodate, which cuts Lear to the quick. Lear makes this clear when he says to one of them, who at one point in the dialogue is offering the better deal: 'Thy fifty yet doth double five-and-twenty, and thou art twice her love.' Slighted by his daughters' rejection, Lear retires to nearby heathland, where night falls and a storm rages. Broken by his daughters' 'filial ingratitude', his 'wits begin to turn'. Lear takes leave of his senses. Only at the end of the play, when he is reunited with his third, loyal daughter and reassured of her continued, all-forgiving love for him, in spite of his earlier rejection of her, is his mind healed.

At one level, this episode is about an attack on the self-esteem of a self-important man who is not used to having his will challenged; at another level, about agreements, expectations and entitlements ('wants'); but at the deepest and most profound level, about Lear's innermost, basic needs for love and belongingness.[1] In the same way, at one level a holiday may be about an exotic experience in new and unfamiliar surroundings; at another level, as research conducted by Dann suggested, it may be about 'getting to know for the first time the person to whom they had been married for some years' (1977, p. 190). Research conducted by Crompton suggested that, in parallel with the 'Lear' episode, the apparent reasons given for taking a pleasure vacation were not the same as the real reasons, which in many cases related more to the recapture of what in effect was a sense of belonging in the form of 'enhancement of kinship relationships' and 'facilitation of social interaction' (1979, p. 418).

Mystery guests

The world is full of surprises. A door can open at any moment and someone will come in. We'd love to know who it is, we'd love to know exactly what he has on his mind and why he comes in, but how often do we know what someone has on his mind or who this somebody is, and what goes to make him and make him what he is, and what his relationship is to others? (Harold Pinter, playwright, quoted in Esslin 1970, p. 38)

Harold Pinter is a contemporary playwright, whose most celebrated output occurred during the 1960s. His contribution to modern drama was to reject an approach which required playwrights to 'motivate their characters totally and to disclose their motivation to audience' (Esslin 1970, p. 39). When the curtain rises on one of Pinter's plays, the audience has no prior knowledge of the characters revealed on the stage, demonstrating 'Pinter's rejection of the conventional exposition in drama, which, in a few bold and clever strokes, purports to introduce the principal characters to us with a handy do-it-

[1]*For a further discussion of 'need' in the tragedy of King Lear, see Ignatieff (1984, ch. 1).*

yourself kit to decipher their origin, background and motivations – all in the first ten to fifteen minutes of the action' (Esslin 1970, p. 39).

Arguably, people who work in the travel, tourism and hospitality industries are confronted, day in, day out, with scenes which might have been drawn from a Pinter play. The customer arrives in the travel agency, ostensibly to buy a holiday, but in practice seeking a *dealer in dreams*. There is no printed programme on sale in which the character's intentions are explained; there is no narrator to introduce the character; only rarely will the character conduct a conversation with those accompanying him or her to reveal key characteristics, intentions and motivations. That which surrounds the character is mystery, with perhaps a hint of aggression, uncertainty, melancholy . . . possibly, on occasions, of menace. And so it is in the travel agency, in the hotel, in the airliner, or wherever the mystery guests are encountered.

When people are encountered for the first time, nothing is known about them. It is only through dealings with them that knowledge of their hopes, fears, wants and needs are revealed. When Pinter applied this principle to drama, the clear artificiality of much of what had gone before was exposed. Referring back to Crompton's (1979) work mentioned earlier, his results elicited some surprise because of the covert nature of the pleasure-vacation satisfactions which had been uncovered. Crompton concluded that for the subjects, the research interviews had been 'an exercise in self-discovery' (1979, p. 421) and suggested the following:

The role of the travel agent may usefully be expanded to that of travel counsellor, offering similar services to those of the emerging leisure counsellors. Once the real motives for travel were elicited from interviews, then the counsellor would be in a much better position to recommend the most appropriate type of pleasure vacation and destination (1979, pp. 421–2).

The concept of need in social policy

In social policy, the concept of defining 'need' is of paramount importance, and is the subject of endemic debate. In the United Kingdom, the government's largest budgets are reserved for social security and the National Health Service. In offering support to families where income from paid employment cannot cover the family's outgoings, where do 'needs' stop and 'wants' begin? Do contraceptive pills fall within the concept of 'basic' health care? Should medical prescriptions be charged for, and if so, at what level? If a 'basic' charge is made for prescriptions, what level of charge can be identified as 'basic'? In 1988, the UK Government issued a Green Paper in which it outlined a continued commitment to 'the provision of the free basic library service at the public expense'; but also suggested 'charging for all charged services at economic rates'. By implication, using a publication which is in the stock of the local library service will be free; but if it is not in stock, borrowing from another library service via inter-library loan would be charged at full cost (Office of Arts and Libraries 1988). What constitutes a 'free basic library service': free access to those materials held by the local library, or free or subsidised access to the library stock of the whole country?

The pursuit of identifying *absolute*, or 'basic' needs is a difficult one and risks becoming fatuous, as King Lear would no doubt point out with elegant invective. There have been occasions when some person in public life attempts to demonstrate the adequacy of the benefits system by living on income support for a week, after which, sliding back into a life of comparative wealth, he or she announces that he or she was able to purchase 'necessities' for the week. Such persons can be grateful that King Lear is not available for comment. Basic necessities are virtually inseparable from the *relative needs* which arise as a consequence of living in a complex consumer society. Ware and Goodin observe that, paradoxically, one way of satisfying unmet needs may involve diminishing the means by which those needs can be satisfied (eds.) (1990, p. 12). A good example of this occurred in the late 1960s when, faced with a balance of payments deficit, the UK Government introduced a £50 travel allowance: no one going abroad could take more than this sum out of the country. Although the motive behind this move was economic, for the period of its enforcement it removed the 'need' for people to compete in extravagance in holiday spending in what was, at the time, a rapidly growing overseas package holiday market. Other governments, notably those located behind what used to be termed the 'Iron Curtain', simply forbade or strictly rationed overseas travel opportunities for their citizens. Under such circumstances, the 'need' for an overseas holiday was unlikely to arise.

Relative need has been summed up by Ware and Goodin as follows:

what you need depends on the society (its objective circumstances and its extant values) in which you find yourself . . . your needs depend not only on what local convention requires of you but also on how well everyone else in your society satisfies those requirements. Your needs-fulfilment is dependent on, and relative to, theirs. What you truly need depends on what they already have. The more needed resources they have, the more of them you need. (1990, p. 14).

As an example, Ware and Goodin cite the need for a television set as dependent on the proportion of the surrounding population which has access to a set, and the extent to which social conversation is dominated by the previous evening's programmes.

One writer on social policy, Jonathan Bradshaw, published a paper (1972) in which he outlined four definitions of need, as follows:

1 *Normative need*   This is the kind of need which is defined by 'experts', to what they consider to be a 'desirable standard': for example nutritional standards adopted by the British Medical Association as the basis for an adequate diet. A current example within the UK may be the initiative by the present Prime Minister (John Major) to apply normative standards to performance of public services, known as the Citizen's Charter. It should be noted that the establishment of normative needs can be paternalistic – 'we know what's good for you' – and the definition of needs can be limited by the perceptions of the experts.

2 *Felt need*   This Bradshaw equates with 'wants'. I, you, he or she wants a holiday, Lear wants his 100 followers. *Felt need* is said to be a crucial motivator within a free-market democracy. Companies are at liberty to provide for our felt needs for overseas holidays, politicians must respond to the electorate's felt needs, once every four or five years at the very least, if they wish to secure votes at election time. As with Lear, felt needs may not be the deepest needs; and they may be limited by the perception of the individual. For example, an individual with a felt need for an inactive holiday in the sun as escape from a routine job may simply discover a new form of boredom; his or her deeper needs may demand a more challenging sort of holiday if they are to be satisfied.

3 *Expressed need*   This is defined by Bradshaw as felt need turned into action. In the field of social policy it manifests itself as a group expression of need. A present-day example may be the various statutory consumer watchdogs established to monitor the recently privatised public utilities. These are bodies expressly set up to articulate people's views about prices and standards of service. In the travel and tourism industry, one could consider that the expressed need manifests itself through the market mechanism. A decline in UK visitor traffic to Spain at the end of the 1980s, coinciding with the increasing popularity of other Mediterranean destinations and long-haul travel, sent signals through the market. The result has been increased provision, by the industry, of long-haul packages; and significant investment by Spanish resorts such as Magaluf and Benidorm in the quality of their product.

4 *Comparative need*   This definition applies more exclusively to the publicly funded social services than any of the three others. It involves examining bodies of people in receipt of a service which meets a need, and then looking to see if similar people elsewhere are in receipt of that service; if they are not, then they are in need. One controversy which affected the world of UK visitor attractions was rooted in the implementation of this kind of thinking. The 1988 Education Act made it illegal for schools to levy a charge from parents for compulsory school outings; the intention was that the children of parents unable to pay should not be disadvantaged.

The most that could be demanded was a voluntary contribution. Visitor attractions, theatres, and other day-out destinations feared that the consequence would be a dramatic reduction in group visitor traffic from schools. In fact, it now appears that the consequences have not been so dire as had been anticipated.

The interrelationships between Bradshaw's four definitions can offer some interesting insights into aspects of holiday 'need'. For example, consider a young couple, 23 years old, born and bred on a diet of Mediterranean package holidays: initially holidaying with their parents, then in their late teenage years with friends, most recently together, always booking at a High Street travel agency. They now have a young child; for financial and logistical reasons they do not wish to take the baby abroad; they have a 'need' for a holiday, they have some money available, they want to be by the sea, but they are thoroughly unfamiliar with British resorts and with booking procedures. Their travel agent, of similar age and upbringing, is aware of a limited range of prepackaged commissionable holidays for the domestic market (Mintel 1992, p. 17) but is otherwise nonplussed. In terms of Bradshaw's definitions they have a felt need, which may well coincide with a real need, for a holiday; but their ability to provide for that need is limited by their own perceptions. The person to whom they usually turn for a normative definition of what a holiday can be, the travel agent, can offer only limited help on this occasion.

Consider a very different example. A middle-aged middle manager, German, male, wife at home, children having flown the nest, is told by his family doctor that the consequences of years of stressful hands-on management responsibility, plus the parallel demands of rearing a family, are catching up on him. The prescribed programme includes a six-week *Kur* – a break in a Spa resort – in Switzerland. The visit will be supported financially by his *Krankenkasse*, which provides his medical insurance scheme, and German employment law allows him time off work for the purpose (Bundesminister für Arbeit und Sozialordnung 1976, p. 146). In terms of Bradshaw's definitions, the need for this holiday has been prescribed by an expert; the subject has felt need, having visited his doctor in the first place; the situation carries no aspects of expressed need, since the means of identifying this need are present in the culture of German society; and his need has been recognised as a comparative need, since employment law recognises the prescribed *Kur* as attracting an entitlement to absence from work.

Other social policy researchers who have addressed the problem of defining needs include Doyal and Gough (1984) who build on Bradshaw's definitions. They argue that there are such things as *basic individual needs* which are necessary preliminaries for individuals to achieve other goals. They define these basic needs in two 'pairs': survival/health, and autonomy/learning. There are also, they argue, two pairs of preconditions which society must fulfil, termed *basic societal needs*, without which individuals within that society cannot satisfy their basic *individual* needs. They define the *basic societal needs* as: production, reproduction, culture/communication and political authority. Detailed exposition of these ideas lies slightly outside the present remit and reference is recommended to Doyal and Gough's paper for further explanation. However, the idea of individuals having to satisfy certain basic needs as preliminaries for achieving other goals has much in common with those parts of the body of psychological theory which have most to offer the quest to understand and explain tourist needs and motivations, and which are the next subject of examination.

Maslow's hierarchy of needs

The 'hierarchy of needs' was first advanced by its originator, the psychologist Abraham Maslow, in a paper published in 1943. It was further expanded in his book, *Motivation and Personality*, first published 11 years later. The present writer has made use of the second edition of the book, revised by Maslow and published in 1970, in the preparation of this chapter. Maslow suggested that human beings were motivated by the quest to satisfy an ascending range of needs: *physiological* needs, such as food, and air to breathe; *safety* needs, in the form of a roof over one's head and insulation from threats, real or feared; *love and belongingness*, that is to feel loved and valued as part of a family or group; *esteem* needs which are represented by the desire and search for respect in the eyes of others; *cognitive* needs, being the search for understanding and meaning; *aesthetic* needs, by which is meant having the opportunity and understanding to appreciate beauty of the natural and artistic kinds; and *self-actualisation* which is, in Maslow's own words, 'everything one is capable of becoming' (1970, p. 46). Maslow theorised that the individual would first seek to satisfy the 'lower' needs: 'For our chronically and extremely hungry man [*sic*], Utopia can be defined simply as a place where there is plenty of food.' (1970, p. 37). That person, in such extreme circumstances, is unlikely to be concerned about his other needs unless or until his or her need for food has been satisfied. The gist of the theory is that the human being seeks to satisfy the needs in some kind of order, first satisfying the 'basic' needs before addressing the 'higher' needs. Maslow makes the point that preoccupation with a certain need can change a person's philosophy for the future. One thinks of the businessperson who, having achieved a level of material and societal success which many would envy, directs all his or her efforts towards the acquisition of a civil honour, such as a knighthood, regarding this as the pinnacle, perhaps, of the satisfaction of esteem needs. One thinks of a whole crop of popular musical groups in the late 1960s, such as the Beatles, who, having achieved the pinnacle of aesthetic success in terms of their art, turned to eastern religion in pursuit of 'self-actualisation'.

Maslow's hierarchy can in no way form a law of human behaviour, and Maslow himself takes pains to emphasise this. Conscious motivation differs from culture to culture, and most behaviour is 'multimotivated'; indeed, he observes that 'it would be possible (theoretically if not practically) to analyse a single act of an individual and see in it the expression of his physiological needs, his safety needs, his love needs, his esteem needs, and self-actualisation' (1970, p. 55). If, for example, the 'Lear' episode is examined in terms of Maslow's hierarchy, we see that his daughters are offering to meet his physiological needs, and not much more; they are scarcely offering to provide in full for his safety needs, since the withdrawal of his retinue would deprive him simultaneously of psychological support and security. Lear for his part is already, as far as he perceives it, self-actualised; he has been king, has exercised power and needs only to maintain his esteem needs by keeping his title and 100 followers. But his daughters' attack on his esteem is not, as we have seen, the assault which causes his 'wits to turn'; it is rather the withdrawal of the powerful and, to use Maslow's term, 'prepotent' drive to receive and give love, and feel a sense of belonging within a family. Lear's prepotent need was for *love and belongingness*, rather than for his 100 followers.

Applying Maslow's hierarchy to different tourist types affords some interesting insights. Consider, for example, the expectations of a participant in a 20s/30s type holiday, sold on the sun-sea-sand-and-fun principle. The holiday-maker is promised, and expects, his or her physiological and safety needs to be fulfilled in excess of the standards enjoyed at home: a surfeit of food, drink and enjoyment, plus the added sense of belongingness acquired through being a member of a like-minded group of similar age. But it would be a mistake to suppose that having had these needs satisfied, this particular holiday-maker then pursues the higher needs. Quite the reverse, in fact. The whole point of such a holiday, and it should be said that there is nothing wrong with it, is to experience *escapist fun*. Talk of politics, sensitivity to other cultures and the meaning of life may be considered out of place, when the overriding purpose is to *have fun*. As a second example, consider the tourist who chooses to go trekking in the Himalayas. Choosing to forsake a comfortable bed, and with the near certainty of some form of digestive trouble in prospect, he or she forgoes certain aspects of the first two levels of need in pursuit of higher things: cognisance of an alien culture, the breathtaking aesthetic beauty of the world's highest mountain range, possibly even a flirtation with Buddhism in the quest for self-actualisation. The contrast with the 20s/30s holiday-maker could not be greater, and yet both are tourists.

Tourist typologies

Some writers have developed terminologies and typologies to assist in understanding motivations of 'types' of tourist. Gray (1970) offered two terms: *sunlust*, referring to those who, on vacation, seek to experience the same kind of leisure experiences as at home, but in greater quality and quantity. The 20s/30s holiday-maker could be described as a *sunlust* tourist. The second term is *wanderlust*, referring to the behavioural type which seeks different experiences from those at home: our Himalayan trekker. Plog, writing around the same time as Gray, began to develop a behavioural typology which has subsequently been related to destination choice (discussed in Ryan 1991, pp. 30–1). Based on studies of the US population, he identified three types: psychocentric, midcentric and allocentric. The *psychocentric* tourist has an internal focus, where the pleasure is in the mind (*psyche*). The *allocentric* tourist (*allo* = 'different') relies on new, external stimuli for pleasure. Most people are mixtures of the two: *midcentric*. Psychocentric tourists may choose familiar destinations where they know they will feel comfortable. They are likely to be the kind of people who revisit the same place year after year. Allocentric tourists are more likely to choose a different destination every year, in the search for new stimuli. These types have been applied to coincide with the life cycle of a destination: the allocentrics explore, the midcentrics follow, and the psychocentrics remain loyal even when the destination declines (see Butler 1980).

However, it would be a mistake to consider that Plog's categories are immutable types. The same individual can be an allocentric tourist in terms of main holiday choice, and psychocentric in terms of an additional short break (Cooper *et al.* 1993, p. 23). Or the other way around. It would also be a mistake to equate Gray's *sunlust* tourism with Plog's *psychocentric* tourists: Gray's terminology applies to the nature of the holiday experience, Plog's to the mind-set of the tourist. It is possible to be a sunlust tourist who never visits the same destination twice, as with a young person who sets out to sample all the lively destinations of the Mediterranean on a year-by-year basis. When any of these 'types' come into a travel agency, they may look very similar in appearance. They may *say*, as an example, that they want a city break of three of four nights in Paris, a European capital which they know and love. They may not say that

they are also planning a three-week trip to Canada, a country which they have not visited before. This suggests a powerful commercial rationale for Crompton's suggestion for travel clerk as travel counsellor, as discussed earlier. Arguably there is business to be had through investing time and effort in uncovering the quality as well as the quantity of a customer's holiday needs.

Doyal and Gough's appraisal of human needs, discussed earlier, has much in common with Maslow in postulating the requirement for certain basic needs to be satisfied before other needs can be actualised. But life, and tourist behaviour in particular, is not as simple as that. The last word can be left to Doyal and Gough:

Unlike Maslow's well-known hierarchy of individual needs, in which the most basic needs must be satisfied before higher needs can be met, we therefore argue that human needs are systematic or interwoven like a web. (1984, p. 11)

Satisfactions in the mind

Urry, basing his comments on the ideas of Campbell, offers the following thoughts on the subject of satisfaction:

Individuals do not seek satisfaction from products, from their actual selection, purchase and use. Rather, satisfaction stems from anticipation, from imaginative pleasure-seeking. People's basic motivation for consumption is not therefore simply materialistic. It is rather that they seek to experience 'in reality' the pleasurable dramas they have already experienced in their imagination. (1990, p. 13)

It can be argued that the purpose of exposure advertising (see Chapter 10) is precisely to create a series of 'pleasurable dramas' which consumers can link with their anticipated consumption of the product. At this point it can be recalled that one thesis of this book is that tourism is largely psychological in its attractions, and some writers have addressed the extent to which the satisfactions of leisure and tourist activities are 'in the mind'. Mannell suggested that leisure is 'an experience or state of mind, is uniquely individual and that the quality rather than the quantity of leisure in our lives deserves attention' (1984, p. 13). Mannell and Iso-Ahola examined both leisure and tourism from a psychological perspective and their principal observation was that 'the psychological benefits of leisure and tourist experience emanate from the interplay of two motivational forces: to escape from routine and stressful environments and to seek recreational opportunities' (1987, p. 314). Developing their discussion and quoting other researchers, they suggest that tourist experience is of distinct and exceptional importance to the individual, can be a 'religious-like experience' and can be potent as a force for personal development. It has a parallel efficacy as an escape from the everyday, and presents opportunities to re-establish, or establish for the first time, intimate personal relationships. In all of this, the activity of the mind is paramount:

Though general satisfaction certainly constitutes one important experiential concept, the stream of associations that occur during an episode (imaging, daydreams, emotions) are equally important experiential aspects of leisure and tourist behaviour. (1987, p. 323)

Quoting research by Wahlers and Etzel published in 1985, Mannell and Iso-Ahola (1987) report that it is tourists whose everyday lives are relatively less stimulating who tend to seek greater stimulation while on holiday. Not surprisingly, the converse was also found to be true: those leading stimulating lives placed a higher value on peace and tranquillity in holiday choice. The relevance to this of the psychological theory and tourist typologies discussed earlier is clear: as but one example, the 'religious-like' nature of some tourist experiences has unmistakable parallels with the 'self-actualisation' need postulated for the highest level of Maslow's hierarchy. But the most significant conclusion to be drawn from this contribution from Mannell and Iso-Ahola is that the satisfaction *takes place in the mind*. Thus, whether the main holiday motive is escape or recreation, tranquillity on a beach or windsurfing, both are goals formulated in advance by the tourist, the achievement of which contributes to the satisfaction. Perhaps this expresses itself in

the tourist's mind as not just, 'Isn't it wonderful, enjoying the sun here on a Mediterranean beach?', but 'Isn't it wonderful *that I am here*, enjoying the sun here on a Mediterranean beach?'

The 'existential dimension'

The notion of control and achievement, having got there, and being there, opens up the whole field which Hamilton-Smith has described as the 'existential dimension'. He outlines four major determinants, the presence or absence of which he identifies as contributing to 'the existential dimension of human behaviour': (1987, pp. 333–4)

- feeling that an experience is truly satisfying
- feeling free from external constraint
- feeling free to choose or take action
- feeling personal involvement in, or commitment to, action

He cites sunlust tourism, or to use his words, 'tourism-as-escape', as a type of tourism where the existential dimension is highly positive. There is no wanderlust-type quest involved, but the personal rewards are achieved by not straying far from home surroundings: 'tourism-as-familiarity'. Aptly he observes that this kind of tourism tends to be neglected by scholars in favour of international travel, whereas domestic holidays form the major part of tourism. He cites the tourist behaviour of the affluent working classes of the USA as an example of attachment to domestic destinations. This is equally true of a country like England, where seaside resorts, often derided by scholars and the media as a spent force, still attract nearly 40 per cent of domestic holiday trips and over 50 per cent of domestic holiday spend (English Tourist Board 1992a). This can be a salutary reminder to those who are smitten with travel-glamour tourism, that for the majority of their compatriots, an effective holiday break can mean visiting the same, familiar, domestic destination year after year. As Hamilton-Smith puts it:

Tourism-as-escape is often scorned by both those who prefer to identify themselves as travellers . . . It is seen as mindless diversion, and as low status behaviour. Such an attitude, of course, ignores the reality and the importance of personal satisfaction, which may well be extremely high. (1987, p. 339)

In an uninhibited examination of the nature of western holiday activity and the society which generates it, the Swiss academic Jost Krippendorf, like other writers, seeks to define travel motivations through a list of qualities. For Krippendorf (1987, pp. 24–8) travel is: *recuperation and regeneration*, restoring body and soul; *escape* from familiar environments and/or working life; *compensation* for what everyday life does not offer; *communication* either with host populations (wanderlust) or with one's own compatriots in a different environment (sunlust); *mind-broadening* (mainly wanderlust); offering *freedom* and *self-determination* (Hamilton-Smith's existential dimension); and presenting the opportunity for *self-realisation* (Maslow's self-actualisation). The thread which runs through all of this, observes Krippendorf, is the notion of 'going away' and 'I decide' (1987, p. 29).

Krippendorf considers the nature of work in present-day society and its role in generating tourism; for example, he quotes data suggesting that between 1900 and 1940, three-quarters of achieved increase in productivity went into shorter working hours; after that date, between 80 and 90 per cent of it was used for wage increases (1987, p. 78). Thus were created the twin requirements of discretionary time and discretionary income, without which no tourist can travel anywhere. His concluding chapters advocate changes in attitudes to achieve what he describes as the 'humanization' of travel. In particular, he advocates the use of holidays as a time for 'self-communion' (1987, p. 129). This is an unmistakable parallel with Maslow's self-actualisation, and Krippendorf's question, 'Does happiness for me lie only in extremes, in the exotic, in prestige? Am I already sceptical about happiness? Can I find happiness in small things?' (1987, p. 132), uncannily mirrors a principal finding of Maslow's research into self-actualising people, who 'have the wonderful capacity to appreciate again and again, freshly and naively, the basic goods of life, with awe, pleasure, wonder, and even ecstasy, however stale these experiences may have become to others' (Maslow 1970, p. 163).

Two theses about the 'need' for a holiday

So, do people 'need' a holiday? Is it a 'want' induced by the consumer society? Or can western society, in some way, create a genuine 'need' for a holiday? Two theses are suggested, based on the insights assembled in this chapter:

THESIS 1   INTENSIVE LIFESTYLES DEMAND INTENSIVE RECREATION

It seems that, to some extent, the increasing complexity and intensity of western life has created a need for intensive repose as a means of maintaining physical and mental well-being. For many, this is achieved through a holiday. An analogy can be drawn with an intensively used building, such as a school: it may be cleaned daily, it may have its floors washed and windows polished on Saturdays, but there is a need for more intensive cleaning, known as 'deep cleaning', which occurs during a two-week shut-down in August of each year. Krippendorf expresses the same idea by referring to the servicing of a motor engine, or the summer grazing of milked cows (1987, p. 24).

THESIS 2   CELLULAR LIFESTYLES DEMAND COMMUNAL VACATION TIMES

First, an explanation of 'cellular lifestyles' is necessary: the term: 'cellular society' became widely used during the 1980s, describing the way in which changes in patterns of consumption led to the differentiation of lifestyles within the household and consequent erosion of contact between household members. So, for example, the wine box enabled the individual drinker to drink wine when he or she liked, whereas the opening of a traditional bottle might have demanded more of a corporate decision. The relative lowering of the prices of all things electric, such as televisions, telephones, and music reproduction equipment, made possible the acquisition of multiple examples of these goods so that several family members could pursue their own interests simultaneously. The proliferation of personal computers introduced a new dimension into home entertainment. All of this could be enjoyed by each household member in his or her own room, or *cell*.

Arguably, *something* involving communication and group activity was being squeezed out of this society, and it is suggested that this is the *something else* which western society seeks to rediscover, and for which holidays are one vehicle. The proliferation of holidays designed to bring people together, such as activity holidays and the peer-group experiences offered by 20s/30s holidays, are evidence of the holiday performing this function. As society becomes more cellular, as more women acquire and maintain employment, as relocation for job or other purposes increasingly creates geographical divisions between family and friends, so the need for time to recover communication and belongingness increases, as does western tourism. An overt motivation for a holiday may be to achieve self-esteem by visiting exotic places and acquiring new aesthetic experiences such as observing beautiful environments; the covert agenda may be to rediscover belongingness to a lifestyle, a peer group, a generation.

Is a holiday the only means of recovering love and belongingness, or achieving the 'deep cleaning'? The role of the holiday as the sole means of meeting that need is open to doubt. Krippendorf observes that taking holidays itself involves stress (1987, p. 62) and advocates extended periods of anticipation and recuperation pre- and post-holiday, not travelling too far afield, looking afresh at what traditional resort destinations have to offer, and poses the ultimate question: 'Why am I going away? And we would then have to admit that we don't necessarily have to go on a trip to recuperate or get a change of scene, both of which may be done equally well or even better at home or in its immediate vicinity' (1987, p. 136).

It is not really credible to suggest that vacational tourism as a phenomenon may, or will, die out. Holidays are a suitable object for spending discretionary income, for satisfying the urge to travel and explore, and for responding to fashion and peer pressure, which is the subject of the next chapter. But neither is it credible to project a continued, unabated growth of tourism. The marked rediscovery of interest in native natural environments, the marked resurgence of many western cities as places of culture and leisure as well as places to work and live, are but two contemporary indications of a rediscovery of what has been called 'a sense of place'; an awareness of the character, assets, and potential of the domiciliary area, and a feeling of belongingness toward it. This theme will recur in Chapters 13 and 14. Human needs can be satisfied in different ways; fashions can change. Acquiring the hospitality instinct means understanding, remembering and recognising that tourists have a place called home, to which they like to return and where for 40 per cent of the UK population each year, they remain.

Chapter 7
Society's attitudes

*Don't look down on me because of my colour,
because the sun has tanned me. My brothers
were angry with me and made me work in the
vineyard. I had no time to care for myself.*
                              (Song of Solomon 1:6)

*A tanned complexion is still read as an
unmistakable sign of youth and vitality, and
even the proletarianisation of Mediterranean
travel has failed to diminish the allure of the
tan.*   *(Bayley 1991, p. 155)*

Times change

The *Song of Solomon*, also known as the Song of
Songs, is a collection of love poems written during
the first millenium BC, and recorded in the Judaeo-
Christian Bible. In the first poem, the woman
meets her lover and, early in the encounter,
splutters an apology about her appearance: she
has acquired a suntan. The contrast with the
significance of a suntan in present-day western
societies could not be greater. There are
indications that the value of the suntan's
apparently unassailable position in the west as a
signifier of health, wealth and happiness, and as a
powerful motivator to holiday in a warm climate,
is under threat because of an increased incidence
of skin cancer. But suffice it to say that times
change. Fashions are not immutable.

The focus of study in this chapter is the effect of
cultural change, fashion and peer pressure on
holiday choice. The study will include reference to
the nature of 'culture' and how structural changes
in economy and society have created cultural
shifts which have been recognised and described
by some as a condition of 'post-modernity'. The

chapter will examine the contribution of
researchers into the role of prestige as a motivator
in vacation choice and the effects of cultural
evolution and fashion-influenced motivations on
the evolution of destinations. The focus of this
chapter contrasts with that of Chapter 6 in that it
concerns what can be called the *apparent*, as
opposed to the *real* reasons for holiday choice. An
understanding of what society's current attitudes
and fashions are, why they have evolved in the
way they have, and how they are likely to develop
in the future is arguably central to the
understanding of the personal rationale which a
particular tourist adopts in choosing a particular
kind of trip, and has implications for the effective
practice of the hospitality instinct. A marketeer's
rationale for such a study would be to understand
consumer behaviour, which is rooted in
consumer culture: this is further considered in
Chapter 11. For the present purpose, the study
begins with an examination of 'culture'.

The nature of 'culture'

'Culture' is one of those abstract words which
means different things in different contexts. An
archaeologist, who studies society through its
material remains, may describe a culture as 'a
consistently recurring assemblage of artefacts'
(Childe 1929, p. vi). An anthropologist may find
such a definition too limiting, since culture as it is
lived and experienced contains not only material
things but abstract artefacts such as knowledge,
learning, religion, ethics, indeed all the material
and non-material devices which human beings
create or acquire in order to adapt to and make
sense of the world in which they live: in short,
'man's extra-somatic means of adaptation' (White

1959, p. 8). A definition suited to the present purpose is provided by Thrift (in Hamnett *et al.* (eds.) 1989, ch. 1) where he talks of 'maps of meaning', a term whose first use is ascribed to Stuart Hall writing in 1980, as a group term for the ways in which different social groups within society evolve interpretations for the social phenomena and social changes that they see around them. Thrift makes a number of points about 'maps of meaning' and the way they are observable in society.

1 *Maps of meaning are transferable* They are 'learned, handed down or otherwise picked up' in a variety of ways through parents and friends, the media, social and educational institutions and so on. Maps of meaning could be likened to organisms which spread infectiously or contagiously, thriving or otherwise in the cultural atmosphere in which they move. For example, the blue jean, with origins in nineteenth-century America as durable workwear, has become an enduring feature of late twentieth-century leisure-wear whose cultural power has extended to the four corners of the globe. Bayley suggests that the wearing of blue jeans by Marlon Brando in *The Wild One* (1954) and James Dean in *Rebel Without a Cause* (1955) were seminal influences in their global popularisation (1991, p. 168).

2 *Maps of meaning are complex* Maps of meaning, as cultural concepts, are affected and influenced by many different factors. Different groups within society are apt to view the same social phenomena in different ways. Thus, for example, the habit of paying for goods and services by credit card, originating (again) in North America and having acquired very rapidly a place in UK consumer culture, did not take hold in Germany. The Economist Intelligence Unit reports that in that country, in 1992, cards issued were only one-tenth of the number in circulation during the same year in the UK. Reasons given for the reluctance of Germans to assimilate the credit card included easily accessible cashpoint machines, and promotion by German banks of the Eurocheque system. But in the end, there was a cultural factor present: 'the average German consumer is wary of credit' (1992a).

3 *Maps of meaning are negotiated* People, and groups of people, do not generally assimilate others' ideas in an unmodified form. A certain process of modification, or to use Thrift's term, 'negotiation', takes place. For example, Africa and South America are rich in indigenous communities which have embraced the Christian faith, 'originating' from the continent of Europe, but with a vibrancy and vitality which many European churches may lack. The vibrant forms of worship they adopt, in terms of expression and music, may owe more to their own pre-Christian traditions than to those from Europe. Indeed, the sight of (say) Africans acting out unmodified European rituals can seem odd; there is the expectation that cultural meanings will be negotiated and modified.

4 *Maps of meaning can constitute a cultural 'hegemony'* The idea of cultural 'hegemony' is adapted from Marxist theory, principally in the works of Gramsci, and can be successfully applied in explaining cultural conflict in the non-work areas of life, for example in leisure (Heron 1991). 'Hegemony' is intended to describe a situation where certain cultural concepts – maps of meaning – become dominant or predominant, and are used consciously or unconsciously by those groups associated with them to impose a 'hegemony' on other groups, so that these meanings are perceived as 'the natural order of things' (Hamnett *et al.* (eds.) 1989, p. 15). A key feature of this is that the other groups may be generally unaware that they are being dominated. For example, the notion that foreign holidays are inherently of greater worth than domestic holidays has some of the characteristics of a hegemony. When such a notion is portrayed as axiomatic in the context of mass-market popular culture, then arguably a hegemony may be said to exist. For example, during the episode of Channel 4 TV's comedy game show *Don't Forget Your Toothbrush* broadcast on Saturday 18 February 1995, game contestants stood to earn a holiday in Montserrat if they won, and a holiday in Margate if they lost. The studio audience readily accepted the parameters of the game, roaring respectively approval and disapproval

as the name of each resort was mentioned. Cultural predisposition demanded conformity; peer pressure excluded dissidence.

Post-modernity

The last twenty years have witnessed such a range of cultural changes within western societies that many commentators consider that a fundamental change has taken place, the manifestations of which are evident in architecture, work, leisure, culture and consumption habits, including the 'consumption' of holidays. This phenomenon has been described as 'a regime of signification whose fundamental structuring trait is de-differentiation' (Lash 1990, p. 11) whose effect is 'a dissolving of the boundaries, not only between high and low cultures, but also between different cultural forms, such as tourism, art, education, photography, television, music, sport, shopping and architecture' (Urry 1990, p. 82). The phenomenon has been termed *post-modernism*, a concept for which a detailed exposition does not serve the present purpose[2] but for which a characteristic trait is the eclectic borrowing and mixing of images from other cultures, and particularly from the past. For example, the effects of the enterprising Bridlington hotelier in equipping his hotel with a 'Spanish Bar Lounge' and a 'Manhattan Coffee Lounge' as mentioned in Chapter 5 could be argued to demonstrate the eclecticism of a post-modern approach. This is something of which the hotelier may not have been aware, but as with many cultural fundamentals, these are features which are not consciously imbibed during the routine of everyday life. The affection for decorating homes with prints from yesteryear as reproduced and marketed by Laura Ashley is an example of how culture becomes, quite literally, part of the wallpaper of life. It is perhaps as well to inject a cautionary note. *Post-modernity* is not a tangible and universally accepted phenomenon. Jackson cites this observation: 'The meaning of "post-

modernism" is shrouded in uncertainty. A recent dictionary entry declares: "This word has no meaning. Use it as often as possible"' (1989, p. 175). The relevance of *post-modernity* to tourism is significant inasmuch as it can be argued that there has been a fundamental change in fashionable attitudes toward tourist consumption. The following paragraphs attempt to demonstrate the casual linkages whereby this change has occurred.

Economy, culture and the rise of the service class

Many commentators attribute the origins of these cultural changes over the past two decades to economic changes which in turn have changed the structure of employment. Principally, this concerns the shift from secondary industries (manufacturing) to tertiary industries (services). In 1971, 11.6 million people in the UK were employed in service industries; this had increased to 15.9 million by 1990. By contrast, the 8 million employed in manufacturing in 1971 had shrunk to 5.1 million 19 years later (Central Statistical Office 1993, p. 56). This is not solely a reflection of a decline in UK manufacturing. The increasing complexity of government, a massive expansion in banking and financial services and in higher education opportunities (which began in the 1960s), the maturing of retailing as an industry, increased discretionary income which spawned an expansion of the leisure and tourism industries, and an expansion in the media all produced an expansion of the number of people employed in, managing and directing these new industries. They are professionals, working in the media, arts, government, advertising, the professions, education, and as managers in mature private sector concerns and have been termed the *service class*. Urry differentiates them from other white-collar workers by their possession of 'educational credentials' and 'well-defined careers' (Urry 1990, p. 89), that is, they can expect to advance in their jobs in terms of the quality of their work and its financial rewards. Thrift (in Hamnett 1989, ch. 1) has identified the service class as having given rise, in pursuit of a pedigree, to two powerful cultural traditions,

[2]*Post-modernity has been the subject of study by many commentators. The study by Harvey (1989) has been widely regarded as one of the most comprehensive and would reward further reading.*

readily identifiable within society, which he refers to as the *countryside* and *heritage* traditions.

Thrift suggests that the service class has largely succeeded in creating a national culture which is dominant and to some extent hegemonic, particularly in the south of England where, during the 1980s in particular, the working classes were seen to adopt, albeit in a negotiated form, some of the consumerist and cultural attitudes of the service class. One of the features of 'Essex Man', as he came to be called, was a move away from the working-class values of East London and the adoption of Conservative voting habits. Thrift suggests that the service class has successfully created a dominant national culture by borrowing from and adopting select aspects of existing national culture; as he puts it, 'tapping into some important traditions of a specifically English cultural life' (in Hamnet *et al.* (eds.) 1989, p. 23). The *countryside* tradition is said to draw on a nostalgic vision of an English rural ideal. Manicured by eighteenth-century landowning 'improvers' and romanticised by writers and poets of both the nineteenth and twentieth centuries (Wordsworth and Betjeman, to name but two), the vision is one of mankind in harmony with nature, roses climbing up cottage walls, 'bluff and manly squires and elegant ladies' and 'rosy-cheeked milkmaids cavorting in the fields' (in Hamnett et al. (eds.) 1989, p. 27). Clearly this is a select memory since, in common with all nostalgia, unpleasant features are suppressed or excluded, and enhanced features are either promoted or invented. Rural squalor in its various forms does not make an appearance.

The *heritage* tradition is defined by Thrift as the way in which, more and more, preoccupation with and images of the past 'are gradually intruding more and more into the present'. This takes the form of a developing fixation not only with established examples of what could be termed 'hard' heritage (such as great country houses) and 'soft' heritage (for example the monarchy, ceremonial, the parliamentary tradition) but all aspects of the past and with a particular eye for those aspects which can be regarded as 'quintessentially English'. Thrift's examples are public school choirs, punting on the river at Oxford and Cambridge, events regular and special such as cricket and the Henley Regatta (in

Hamnett *et al.* (eds.) 1989, p. 28). Additional examples could be morris dancing, cask beer, but probably not, for reasons which will be discussed later, fish and chips.

Evidence of the rise of these two traditions is abundant. Thrift documents the use of countryside and heritage images in 'lifestyle advertising', that is, advertising which makes use of images with which its target audience are known to identify, in order to establish a similar identification with the product. His chosen illustrations include a British-made car parked in front of a *patisserie* in an obviously francophone country; and images and vocabulary of rural England to sell units on a new residential development in the Home Counties. Also cited are the increases in membership of bodies engaged in the preservation and conservation of heritage and the countryside – in the case of the National Trust, from 278,000 in 1971 to 1,404,181, and new museums which were, at the time of a survey in 1987, opening at the rate of one per fortnight (in Hamnett *et al.* (eds.) 1989, pp. 27 and 29). Indeed, a whole new commercial industry has grown up around 'heritage', of which the opening of the Jorvik Viking Centre in York in 1982 was a seminal event. The word 'heritage' now features in the title of a cabinet minister presiding over the *Department of National Heritage*.

The consequences of this for the tourism industry are quite profound. Part of Thrift's definition of the heritage tradition is 'the way that the government, the media retailers, and other institutions are generating more images of the past' (in Hamnett *et al.* (eds.) 1989, p. 25). There is no better example of this than the way in which the national tourist boards, for England, the English Tourist Board (ETB) and, marketing the whole of the UK to the overseas market, the British Tourist Authority (BTA), have used countryside and heritage images to market the national product. Beefeaters, Buckingham Palace and Anne Hathaway's cottage are the kinds of image by which the BTA has defined Britain abroad; at home, the ETB, since its formation as a consequence of the Development of Tourism Act 1969, has relied heavily on imagery of the country house, cathedral, cottage and so on to define the product which was available to English people on their own doorstep. Of course, one result of this has been a surfeit of tourists visiting cathedral cities and certain country areas, and an ETB report from 1991 entitled *Tourism and the Environment* discussed the problem of excess visitation of historic towns, heritage sites and the countryside. This attracted a media response to the effect that the Board had spent 20 years encouraging tourists to do precisely that which it was now declaring to be detrimental.

A less publicised but nevertheless sustained complaint from the nation's seaside resorts had been that the Board's activities failed to support, adequately, those very places which were equipped to handle visitors, and which owed their very living to tourism. Since the beginning of the 1990s, however, the Board has pursued a modified strategy which has very much focused on the needs of seaside resorts in terms of regeneration, investment and marketing. The English Seaside Campaign of 1992, to which one-quarter of the Board's marketing budget was dedicated, and special reports on renewal and regeneration issues (see Middleton 1991 and English Tourist Board 1993 as examples) are evidence of a change of perspective.

A paper by Urry (1988) examined the effect of the dominance of the service-class culture on contemporary holiday-making habits, and in particular its effect on the traditional English seaside. Identifying mass seaside tourism as a feature of industrial 'modern' society, he relates forms of tourism which could be described as 'post-modern' to a post-industrial society. For example, modernist thought would regard a visit to a coal-mine, or working on a farm, as experiences exclusively relating to the world of work. By contrast, the 'post-tourist', living in a de-differentiated post-modern society, sees nothing unusual in regarding either of those activities as potential tourist experiences. The range and variety of new 'post-tourist' experiences not only reinforce, but feed, the thirst for 'cultural capital' by which the service class define themselves. The Henley Centre for Forecasting expressed it thus:

Individualism, or a desire for personal control, is growing in importance as a key social attitude. This is reflected in consumers' increasing tendency to manifest their social and material success by distinguishing

themselves from their peers in a stylish and individualist way, as opposed to the immediate post-war manifested desire to match their peers (or 'keep up with the Jones'). This has important implications for the growth and positioning of premium brands. (1989, p. 20)

Mort, quoted by Thrift, offers a similar assessment:

Lifestyle advertising is about differentiating oneself from the Jones, not, as in previous decades, keeping up with them . . . what we can say is that the 80s have seen a hyping of the process, an explosion of individualities – of the number of yous on offer. (in Hamnett et al. (eds.) 1989, p. 21)

Therein lies the source explanation for the proliferation of niche markets in the post-modern holiday business: cultural tourism, industrial tourism, activity tourism, long-haul tourism to exotic destinations, agro-tourism and the rest are arguably responses to the 'explosion of individualities', the seekers of cultural capital whose objective is not to keep up with the Jones, but 'up and away from the Jones'.[3]

But as post-modern individualism takes hold, modernist mass tourism suffers a rejection. Urry explains it thus:

With such an elevation of taste and its social distinction the 'typical working class holiday resort' would seem the very embodiment of a particular construction of nature, 'vulgar' and 'basic', and the negation of culture. As a powerful service class possessing considerable cultural capital has developed, so it has proclaimed the tastelessness of the 'common', 'low', 'vulgar' holiday resort. Having 'good taste' would be demonstrated by not visiting such places, although contemporary cultural practices might involve using or appropriating elements in a postmodern pastiche (e.g. McGill's postcards). (1988, p. 41)

[3]Phrase used by Fiona Stewart of the Henley Centre for Forecasting during a presentation at the Entertainment and Arts Management Conference, Harrogate, October 1988.

Hamilton-Smith offers the following anecdote, drawn from a North American environment, which ably summarises the same situation:

as an illustrative example of this problem, a long experienced tourism professional recently confessed to the author that, following a period of extreme work stress, she had taken a packaged sun resort holiday. She found it intensely satisfying and appropriate to her personal preferences at that juncture, yet still felt a degree of embarrassment in discussing it. (1987, p. 339)

Thus fish and chips, although enjoying a quintessentially English pedigree and being an authentic part of English heritage, is not a product to find favour with the service class because of its association with the seaside, i.e. the 'low', 'common' and 'vulgar'. Cornish pasties, cream teas and scrumpy can all be successfully annexed to the 'countryside tradition' and thereby discussed with enthusiasm rather than embarrassment; but the association of fish and chips with mass seaside tourism, whether on mainland Britain or on the Spanish costas, sets it apart. The success story of the international operation being developed under the name of Harry Ramsden, the famous Yorkshire fish and chip restaurant, appears remarkable precisely because of the marginal official value placed on its product by contemporary fashionable opinion.

Prestige as a motivator

If the *real* reason for taking a holiday is to rediscover a sense of belongingness, the *apparent* reasons, the ones offered when plans are being justified, can be concerned with prestige and status, or Dann has termed it, 'ego-enhancement' (1977, p. 187). This has come about because of the way in which the holiday has joined other major consumables as a prerequisite for modern living. Urry suggests that 'Not to "go away" is like not possessing a car or a nice house. It has become a marker of status in modern societies . . .' (1990, p. 4).

Crompton (1979) sought to delve deeper into the characteristics of tourist motivations by undertaking qualitative research, consisting of unstructured interviews, amongst 39 respondents. His results suggested, first, that prestige motives were not involved in own decisions, but were observable in other people's. Perhaps self-consciousness creates a reluctance to admit to prestige playing a part in decisions on choice of destination, but our apparent ability to observe such a motivation in others is indicative of its presence in our own minds. Given that discussion of holiday experiences can only be of a narrative rather than interactive nature, that is, the participants to the discussion may not have shared the same holiday experiences, the scope to interpret the other person's motives as one-upmanship is considerably greater than discussion of a theme of which both parties share primary knowledge, such as the state of the weather.

Crompton's second conclusion was this: the more people get used to holiday travel, the less scope there is for using it as a status vehicle. Or as Crompton puts it, 'Prestige potential disappears with frequency of exposure' (1979, p. 417). When, as Urry suggests, holiday travel becomes a societal prerequisite, its capability to offer differential advantage in status terms becomes more limited. The other side of this is that to not undertake holiday travel is to fail to meet an accepted cultural norm; and there is also the implied assumption that the vacation will be taken at a location or destination which meets with fashionable approval.

A further point arises from an appraisal of tourist motivation by Dann. It is that ego-enhancement is 'usually associated with relative status deprivation in the individual' (1981, p. 191). The individual for whom holiday travel never loses its role as a status-indicator is said to have a particular need to reassure him or herself and others of their self-esteem by means of *trip-dropping*, a term used by Dann (1977, 1981) and attributed by him to Lundberg writing in 1971. In his 1977 paper, Dann reported results of research which, he claimed, supported a hypothesis that 'trip-dropping' as a form of ego-enhancement may be more apparent in circumstances where there is an absence of other ways in which to display and document status achievement.

But whether it is simple self-differentiation through tourist activity or a deeper psychological need to 'trip-drop', the role of prestige as a motivator has some profound implications for those who work in tourism. For one thing, prestige is linked with fashion, and fashions go in cycles. There is an inexorable self-destructive quality in this, as the implications of the following conversation which Hamilton-Smith claims to have overheard, are considered:

'It seems Nepal is the really fashionable place to go at present'.
'Not at all, that's passé. Ladakh is the place to go'.
'I don't even know where Ladakh is!'
'Of course, that's why it's now the place to go.'
(1987, p. 338)

This conversation offers frightening confirmation not only of the capacity of tourism to devour vulnerable environments, but that fashionable thought determines the building-in of obsolescence to the destination from day one. The concept of sustainability, itself bearing some of the characteristics of a fashion, has been advocated as a paradigm for the planning and development process whereby the worst effects of popularity followed by obsolescence can be mitigated. However, fashion is an inexorable component of consumer choice in a free market and there is, inevitably, the pressure to 'commoditise' tourism to a new destination once incipient popularity has been achieved. The tourism professional needs to understand this, and perhaps the greatest challenge is to marry the concept of sustainability with commercial objectives.

Some effects of fashion and social trends

The most profound effects of changing socio-cultural attitudes have been seen in the decline of the domestic seaside. This has been particularly noticeable in the mass-market coastal resorts of the UK. This is considered in Chapter 12, but in summary the decline of domestic resorts in the 1960s and 1970s can be largely attributed to changing domestic holiday patterns occasioned, in part, by the failure of resorts to invest in and upgrade their product. An Indian summer was enjoyed in the 1950s, when post-war austerity inhibited the growth of international travel. As in many traditional UK industries such as textiles, there was a failure to invest, so that the resorts' product continued to be based on facilities and infrastructure dating from the Victorian and Edwardian eras and, at the very latest, from the 1930s. More particularly, cultural changes during the 1960s exacerbated the problem. The era witnessed an explosion of youth cultures as the products of the post-war 'baby boom' came of age: near-full employment made these young people financially independent, and as western nations broke away from the austerity of the previous two decades, new music, new clothes and new lifestyles appeared, contrasting with and challenging those of their parents. The so-called 'generation gap' appeared.

It is not surprising that the seaside resorts, still positioning themselves for the traditional family holiday, did not enjoy the same rapport with this new, younger generation. Some standard-bearers for the new youth cultures found the beaches and seafronts of resorts such as Margate and Clacton more suited to internecine conflict than traditional seaside pursuits. The mods and rockers beach battles of the 1960s created image associations from which, even today, some resorts consider they have not entirely distanced themselves. It was at the end of the 1970s, when overseas package travel from the UK began to rise sharply, that a direct link between overseas holiday-taking and domestic seaside decline can be observed. Decline was followed by a slight recovery near the end of the 1980s fuelled in part, ironically, by the growing unfashionability of the UK's main outbound destination, Spain. Resorts which had been built in the 1960s and 1970s were beginning to look jaded, and compatriot excesses – the lager lout was to 1980s Spain what mods and rockers were to 1960s Clacton – accelerated the process of obsolescence. Nights spent in Spain by non-resident tourists declined by 11.4 per cent between 1988 and 1989; and Spain's share of travel receipts declined, during the same period, from 24.6 per cent to 22.7 per cent of the European total (Eurostat 1992).

A second outcome of the effects of the socio-cultural trends of the last two decades has been the *growth of segmented products*. As service-class lifestyle-images characterised by individ-ualism, heritage and countryside came to dominate consumption habits, holiday products which targeted a mass-industrial market whose idea of social climbing was to keep up with the Jones, ceased to attract general approval. Caution must be exercised here, because the notion that the mass-market seaside holiday, often written off as dead by the educated media and some academics, is still vigorous: Spain was still in 1991 the most favoured overseas holiday destination of UK tourists, attracting 23 per cent of the total UK outbound market in that year, despite having dropped from 34 per cent in 1987. Any suggestion of long-term implications should also be interpreted with caution, because as a consequence of the recession of the early 1980s, a similar peak of 34 per cent in 1974 reduced to 23 per cent in 1980 (Devas 1993). Obviously it is percentages rather than volumes which are being discussed here, but it is the mass-market which tends to be the most recession-vulnerable. Domestically the English seaside still attracts 40 per cent of domestic holiday trips, and half of domestic holiday spending (English Tourist Board 1992a). Mass-market tourism continues; what has happened is simply a trend which represents a move away from, rather than a replacement of, the mass-market holiday.

The growth of the domestic short break, and in particular the city break, is a third indication of changing consumption patterns impacting on holiday behaviour. The short holiday has been a growth sector since the 1970s and in particular since 1980, but for obvious reasons this holiday tends to be of a domestic rather than international nature: Beioley reports that in 1989, only 7 per cent of short breaks taken in the UK originated from overseas; the number of short holidays taken by the British increased from 31.7 million to 34.2 million trips between 1980 and 1988; and of these, 'short breaks' (i.e. paid trips in commercial accommodation as opposed to visiting friends and relatives) increased from 12.5 million to 16.9 million (1991b). The number of long holidays also increased over this period, but was represented by a dramatic jump in long holidays overseas and a contraction of long holidays taken in the UK. In 1989, short holidays accounted for 47 per cent of the UK domestic holiday market; and though

commercial short breaks represented fewer than half of the total, they accounted for 62 per cent of spending (Beioley 1991b).

Explanations for the growth in short breaks could include higher disposable incomes for those in work, particularly for those in professional and managerial jobs; increases in holiday entitle-ments; the emergence of a class of early-retired well-off persons, equipped with personal pensions and children who have flown the nest and hence time and money to travel; and in particular, the opening up of rural areas and cities as tourist destinations in response to the growing fasci-nation with countryside and heritage. At the time of the publication of the ETB's development strategy for rural tourism, the most recent figures then available (1986) showed that just over 20 per cent of visitor nights by British people in England were spent in the countryside, which included one-quarter of the buoyant short-break market, which was growing at 20 per cent per annum with significant continued growth predicted (English Tourist Board 1988, p. 4).

The pressure to find new kinds of industry to supplement farming, now all the more urgent in view of the European Union's set-aside policy for farmland designed to contain the productivity of the Union's agricultural industries, has accelerated the development of a range of new holiday products: farm holidays in the UK, *gîtes* in France. One of the clearest forms of secondary evidence for contemporary cultural trends affecting the social and economic life of communities can be seen in the radio or TV soap opera. For example, farm tourists made an appearance in BBC Radio's countryside soap *The Archers* and found the rural idyll lacking when woken early in the morning by cockerels. A plot in Yorkshire TV's country soap *Emmerdale* involved one of the principal characters, who had already established a 'holiday village', seeking a partnership with an established farming family to establish a 'heritage farm'.

Evidence of the cultural shift is also identifiable on a European scale. There has been a significant growth in packages specialising in mountains, natural forests and natural lakes (Euromonitor 1992a, p. 24). Independent travel, and the purchasing of tailor-made packages which use scheduled rather than charter flights, has clearly increased; between 1987 and 1989, an examination of outbound holiday traffic from the UK reveals the following: inclusive tours rose from 12 million to 12.6 million, holiday trips by air rose from 14.2 million to 15.5 million, but the flight package market declined from 11.8 million to 11.1 million (Economist Intelligence Unit 1992b, p. 3). That inclusive tours rose, while the flight package market declined, is evidence of a further segmentation of product: the increase in tours which use a sea crossing, either on a self-drive or coach-inclusive basis. And very noticeably, there has been an increase in long-haul holidays. This can be attributed to increased airline capacity, the opening up of new destinations in response to some consumer dissatisfaction with established Mediterranean resorts, and to the growth of individualism in holiday choice. It should be noted that long-haul holidays are of, to use Gray's terminology, the *sunlust* as well as the *wanderlust* variety. Florida, with its mass-market attractions of heat, beaches and Walt Disney World, is a destination whose product attributes are primarily defined by fun rather than exploration. Destinations such as Bali, which became available to holiday-makers of the midcentric (using Plog's typology) persuasion around 1985, also provide the recreational product attributes required for a sunlust holiday but with added exotica, so that the visitor can consider him or herself participating, if only in part, in a voyage of exploration.

The post-industrial city as a tourist destination

But it is the emergence of the post-industrial city as a tourist destination which, in many ways, is the most remarkable response to the changing cultural tastes of the 1980s and 1990s. In the widest context, cities as destinations for pleasure visits have been a feature of world tourism for some time: the Grand Tour for the offspring of the well-born British of previous centuries included the cultural splendours of the cities of Renaissance Italy. Capital cities, from ancient Rome to modern London, have been and are visitor honeypots for travellers both domestic and foreign; and provincial cities, such as York, Chester, Bruges, and Aix-en-Provence, have a long

pedigree as sightseeing destinations. What has changed has been the discovery of innate visitor-worthiness in industrial cities whose primary role until very recently, was to provide places to work, to manufacture things and to make money, and little else. Even living in the centre of them was considered a breach of taste. The middle classes had joined the 'flight to the suburbs', leaving the inner city to take on an industrial, non-residential character. The changes which have occurred are complex and discussed by this author elsewhere (see Voase 1994) but are rooted, it is suggested, in economic change which in turn impacted on social and cultural values wrapped up in the earlier-mentioned concept of post-modernity. What follows is an attempt to bring together various strands of change in an attempt to provide a basis for explanation.

One of the consequences of the economic restructuring mentioned earlier in this chapter was not only a shift in patterns of employment from manufacturing to service industries, but an impact upon the morphology of cities in advanced industrial nations, as manufacturing industries contracted or closed. Large areas of urban landscape, often within or immediately peripheral to the urban cores, became disused and, within a short space of time, derelict. These physical changes did not just result from the contraction of manufacturing in the inland industrial cities as traditional industries such as textiles and car manufacture contracted. Maritime cities found themselves with redundant dock areas as foci of trade changed, and developments in the technology of shipping, such as containerisation, made existing infrastructure redundant, and traditional sea-based industries contracted or disappeared. For example, ports on the western seaboard of England, such as Liverpool, saw their business contract as the focus of UK trade changed from west to east following the UK's entry into the (then) EEC in the early 1970s. The city of Hull was located on the eastern seaboard and therefore well located to benefit from increasing trade with the countries of the European mainland, but still had to accommodate the consequences of containerisation, roll-on roll-off freight ferries and the contraction and near-extinction of its deep-sea fishing industry following the so-called Cod Wars with Iceland of the late 1960s and early 1970s.

These changes took place throughout the developed world. In Europe, municipal authorities, national governments and the now-named European Union developed policies and funding schemes to address the problem. Regeneration schemes would, not surprisingly, seek to develop new kinds of industry which were known to have growth potential. It is debatable whether, when the UK Government's Urban Programme was launched in the mid-1970s, creating 'tourism' *per se* was frequently an objective of schemes that secured approval and funding, but within a very few years its potential had been realised. It can be viewed thus: during the early 1970s, attitudes to old infrastructure began to change. People, amongst whom the opinion-formers were arguably the new 'service class', ceased to view redundant docks, factories and warehouses as outdated inconveniences to be replaced with modernist monuments. There was a re-evaluation of their potential for alternative uses such as shopping, leisure, even residency. The Urban Programme made it possible to translate such dreams into reality. For example, in the city of Hull a sequence of docks dating from the eighteenth and nineteenth centuries, and conveniently located within the urban core, were converted to leisure use as a marina. A former warehouse nearby, a survivor of the twilight days of demolition zeal of the late 1960s and early 1970s, was converted to provide low-cost accommodation for young single people, but soon found its units changing hands at commercial prices. Trusthouse Forte, interested by the success of the marina, constructed a new hotel adjacent to it. The example of Hull is discussed in more detail in Chapter 13.

Thus it was that in this particular city, but also in many others like it, the pump-priming effect of leisure-based urban-programme-funded projects created the basis of a tourist product to which the commercial sector reacted by providing new accommodation, and other secondary resources such as public houses, restaurants and bistros.

Obviously a new hotel built in a commercial/industrial city will expect the bulk of its visitors to be business rather than leisure tourists, but there lies the opportunity: empty bed capacity, where it exists, will occur at the weekends, conveniently suited to the development of the fastest-growing sector of domestic tourism, the *short break*. Thus equipped with the basis of a tourist product and a growth in services to support it, the governing authorities of post-industrial cities started to market themselves as tourist destinations. Success breeds success, and national governments, not to mention the EC, were keen to encourage and support cities in their new role as post-industrial tourist destinations.

One of the most celebrated UK successes was Bradford, which in the early 1980s succeeded in attracting an out-station of the Science Museum, the National Museum of Photography, Film and Television, which with other ingredients formed the basis of a tourist product which was vigorously and conspicuously marketed as a short-break destination. To build on the success, the English Tourist Board together with the tourist board for the Yorkshire and Humberside region, the local county council and Bradford's municipal government established a Tourism Development Action Programme (TDAP) to further develop the product and broaden marketing activities. The EC supported the initiative with grants, totalling £2.6m., from its Regional Development Fund toward the photography museum, and the refurbishment of the nearby Alhambra Theatre. It is claimed that the 'strategy has paid off; £4.5m. was generated by tourism in 1985 from zero in 1979' (Walsh-Heron 1988). Given that the definition of tourism includes business visitors, a 'zero' claim must be treated with caution because without a doubt, Bradford received business tourists before 1979 and probably some leisure tourists as well, for that matter. If the claim is considered to refer to measurable sales of short breaks, then it makes more sense.

Bradford is but one example of an English provincial city which, during the course of the 1980s and after the incipient wave of urban-programme-supported regeneration had taken place, looked to the arts, museums and the media, the *cultural industries*, to further consolidate their positions as visitable destinations. EC structural funds, in particular, were applied to the cause of cultural regeneration, with tourism benefits now as an identified objective. Birmingham's International Convention Centre (ICC) was opened in 1991 having had one-third of its £150m. capital costs provided by the European

Regional Development Fund; and though primarily a facility to develop the city's potential as a conference destination, the development included a new 2,240 seat concert hall (Griffiths 1993). Refurbishments and enhancements of the Hull New Theatre, Hull Museums, Newcastle Theatre Royal, the construction of a National Fishing Heritage Centre in Grimsby and the reopening near Wakefield of the former Caphouse Colliery as a mining museum are a few examples of projects which have benefited from the support of EC structural funds. Additionally, government and quasi-government bodies have further assisted cities in their quest for visitor identity by offering themed titles such as the rotating 'City of Culture' designation, which perhaps was exploited to greatest effect when in the hands of Glasgow, Scotland. The UK's Arts Council of Great Britain offered themed designation on the basis of open competition to UK cities. Birmingham became the 'City of Music', Swansea in 1995 will bask in the attention derived from being 'City of Literature', and at the time of writing (1994) Manchester is 'City of Drama'.

Griffiths (1993) observes that cultural regeneration is not simply about endowing a post-industrial city with the visitable qualities which it hitherto lacks. Its residents, or at least those who set the agenda, have their own lifestyle and consumption demands which they wish to see addressed; and attracting more citizens like them, and the wealth which they have the capacity to create, becomes a business in itself. Griffiths includes the following amongst the motives:

the emerging need for cities to equip themselves with new (post-industrial) 'images' in order to compete with one another for new investment, and the political demands of the new middle class of professionals and managers, who have come to recognise that 'quality of life' depends on more than private consumption standards. (1993, p. 39)

Griffiths observes that this is not the first time that cities have sought to demonstrate economic success through cultural expression. The magnificent municipal palaces of the north of England, for example the town halls of Leeds and Bradford, built respectively after classical Greek and Italian renaissance models, are Victorian examples of this. An American contemporary of the Victorian era, Jessup W Scott, writing in *Hunt's Merchant's Magazine* in 1843, observed that 'the increasing tendency to reside in towns and cities . . . is manifested by the inhabitants of all countries, as they make progress in the arts and refinements of civilisation' (quoted in Short 1991, ch. 3). What is different this time, as Griffiths points out, is that on this occasion the cultural industries are viewed as a condition of the city's wealth, not, as in Victorian times, as simply a reflection of it (1993, p. 43).

The argument can be summarised as follows: economic restructuring beginning at the end of the 1960s and accelerating during the 1970s caused dereliction within urban areas and at the same time created a mass middle-class, the *service class*, whose consumption habits included more holiday trips, supported by their increasing wealth, and an interest in lifestyle imagery associated with heritage. Governments responded to the urban crisis by funding regeneration initiatives based on the new service industries. This whether by accident or design created a tourist product out of erstwhile industrial cities. The market for short breaks grew, caused in part by more paid holiday leave, early retirements on occupational pensions, and a general increase in disposable incomes. The increased availability of short-break destinations to visit, of which cities are a prime element, further fuelled the development of both market and product, instilling further life into urban regeneration. By the mid-1980s, cities not only had discovered the market sector to serve (the short-break market), they had a clearer idea of what their product was: *cultural tourism*, as old as the hills and the *raison d'être* of the Grand Tour, had been reborn.

The emergence of the post-industrial city as a tourist destination has not been without its consequences for traditional resorts. Although on the surface they are not competing for the same market, the reality is that the existence of the cultured city serves to reinforce the heritage lifestyle aspirations of the 'service class' and thus assist in proclaiming, to echo Urry (1988) quoted earlier, the 'vulgarity' of the holiday resort. There are a number of ways in which this notion can be said to have been reinforced, and which are advanced by Urry: first, that resorts can no longer claim to be the places where entertainment and pleasure opportunities are concentrated; secondly, that television has further eroded the power of live entertainment as an attraction; and thirdly, that resorts, often run by Conservative councils, are reluctant to spend on collective facilities (1988, p. 49). To these could be added a fourth factor: improvements in transport networks, with the result that faster trains and the construction of motorways tend to have favoured cities and not the resorts.

The post-modern city is above all things a leisured city: its facilities exceed resort facilities in just about every way. This is particularly noticeable when the 1980s wave of 'Leisure Pools' is considered; cities are able to construct much more substantial facilities than those which were opened in Bridlington in 1987, and in Great Yarmouth and Rhyl earlier in the 1980s, and thus visitors find that even the best and most recent efforts of the resorts fail to eclipse the level of provision which they encounter in the conurbations where they live. The issue is not just that coastal councils, whether conservative with a small or large 'c', are unwilling to spend on collective provision. In fact some of the most ambitious municipal tourism development projects of the 1980s, such as Harrogate Conference Centre, were built by Conservative administrations. Rather, it is that the sheer size of available budgets is greater in urban areas. For example: in the early 1980s, Bradford allocated £100,000 for its first year of tourism promotion (Channel 4 TV 1986); at that time, Bridlington's advertising budget was *circa* £80,000, considered generous, and the seventh highest of any resort in the country. What was a speculative venture for Bradford, involving a small proportion of an enormous metropolitan budget, was greater than the budget in a resort in which 30 per cent of direct employment was dependent on tourism. Exacerbating the problem was the fact that variety entertainment, which had long since replaced seaside repertory and seaside orchestras in the resorts as the mainstay of their entertainment programmes, was in decline. Television had created a class of 'stars' whose fees increased in inverse proportion to the number of them who could command and sustain full houses. The editor of *The Stage* (Hepple 1993)

observed that the reduction in seaside summer shows 'leaves only Blackpool, Bournemouth, Great Yarmouth, Scarborough, Torbay and possibly Eastbourne as appreciable areas of summer show business . . .'. Also, the newer stars who emerged in the 1980s, tended to be impressionists, performing no doubt with great artistry but relying on the distinctiveness of others' art as the basis of their material. This recycling process could be viewed, alongside the other factors, as a sign of an artform in decline.

The importance of the transport factor can be viewed in two ways: the motorway network completed over the past two decades tends to link conurbations rather than resorts, and although trunk road improvements have improved access to many resorts, relatively speaking they are less accessible; and the faster trains of the 1970s and 1980s, the InterCity 125s and 225s, are used to link cities rather than resorts. But as the editor of *The Stage* observed on another occasion, good transport links can be regarded as a mixed blessing for a resort:

> *as has been pointed out more than once, the building of the [M55] motorway signalled the end of Blackpool's long-stay holiday trade. Now, less than an hour from some of the biggest conurbations in Britain, its visitors drive in first thing in the morning and leave before dark. (Hepple 1992)*

An upside of this is that short-break takers prefer, for obvious reasons, to keep travel time to a minimum, so good transport links open up the possibility of tapping into a growth domestic market. Doubtless this has contributed to the success of the cities.

Paradox and change

The paradox, some may say irony, is that the resorts have become unfashionable precisely because they offer no industrial heritage and, in Urry's words, 'lack interesting, well-preserved historical sites which can be sacralised, packaged and viewed' (1988, p. 50). In a scene from the third programme of the documentary TV series, *The Marketing Mix* (Channel 4 TV 1986), a televisually recorded event is shown: it concerns the arrival of the first short-break holiday-maker in Bradford. The train draws into the railway station, and the platform is resplendent with the trappings of northern culture. The brass band plays an industrial anthem of years gone by; the Lord Mayor, complete with bowler hat, is in attendance; Union flags, and bunting, reinforce the earthy loyalty of it all. The train arrives, and the package holiday-maker, perhaps in his early sixties, emerges from the train. He is greeted by the Lord Mayor, and is handed a stick of rock. The name Bradford runs through the stick of rock.

In the language of semiology, the stick of rock could be viewed as a signifier, denoting the accomplishment of a leisure trip; the giving of the stick of rock is a sign; and the referent is the seaside, for which the giver and receiver share a common affection and approval. What has happened is that the industrial source of the tourist consumer, the city of Bradford, now presents its credentials as a post-industrial producer, signifying this by providing the stick of rock for the holiday-maker to produce on his return home as documentation of his trip. Whether the originators of the idea planned the event in terms of a semiotic interpretation is unknown, but it was certainly a masterly example of symbolic hijacking.

The conclusion which can be drawn from the issues discussed in this chapter is that, in terms of the theses advanced in Chapter 1, the evolving culture and mores of society are prepotent in their power to create predisposition in tourist choice. This is arguably a consequence of tourism being an item of essentially psychological consumption. The rather frightening consequence is that even the best practice of the hospitality instinct may face an uphill struggle to impress, when the location fails to fit with post-tourist notions of fashionability. A constructive solution for destinations which cultural change have consigned to unfashionability may lie in Urry's observation, quoted earlier, that 'contemporary cultural practices may involve using or appropriating elements in a post-modern pastiche' (1988, p. 41). This is arguably what the Yorkshire resort of Bridlington achieved in its successful 1986 entry for the ETB's Resort 2000 competition, and which is discussed in Chapter 12. The other significant change to evolve out of post-modern cultural change is the rise of individualism and the astonishing broadening of the range of experiences which can be regarded as being of interest to the tourist. This has had powerful implications for the formulation of the tourism product and for tourism marketing, and forms the basis of the next chapter.

Chapter **8**

The tourism market

The purpose of this chapter is to offer a structural model for the way in which tourist motivations can be understood and translated into patterns of demand, and to offer an introduction to the way in which the tourism industry responds to those patterns. The chapter adopts a *commercial* approach in contrast with the previous three chapters, the approach of which has been essentially *cultural*. The intended outcome is to create a body of understanding for consideration of the tourist experience from a marketing perspective. A new semantic framework, the language of marketing, is adopted for this chapter.

What is a market?

This term has two distinct meanings in the professional world. An *economist*, for example, would define a market as existing when three criteria are satisfied:

- there are buyers
- there are sellers
- there are the means to meet

The 'means to meet' can mean a physical place, such as a market-place in a historic town, or it can mean a system which permits buyers and sellers to buy and sell without physically meeting. Telephone systems, the post, televisual selling systems, out-of-town retail parks and the traditional High Street are all examples of ways in which buyers and sellers can communicate with one another. Some sellers use more than one means to reach their buyers. For example, the Next chain of clothing stores offers its products through High Street sales outlets, and through the post in response to customer orders from a

catalogue. If the means to meet do not exist: for example, if buyers know they have a need but know neither what product meets that need, nor who makes it; and if the sellers likewise are not aware of these potential buyers' requirements, then a market cannot exist. The fundamental idea behind the creation in 1958 of the EEC (now the EU) was that, by removing obstacles such as border controls, tariffs and trade barriers, buyers and sellers within the member states could create the 'means to meet' more freely, facilitating growth in the level of overall economic activity within the EU and thus increased wealth.

The practitioner in marketing, the *marketeer*, uses a slightly different definition. To the marketeer, a market is 'the set of actual and potential buyers of a product' (Kotler and Armstrong 1991, p. 673) or, more fully, 'all those actual and potential customers who do or could buy a product or service' (Foster 1985, p. 97). It is worth noting that both these definitions stress both *actual* and *potential* customers. The actual and potential customers are two very different sets of people who need to receive, in almost every respect, different treatment from the marketeer. At its most elementary, one basic principle of marketing is to find out who and where the customers are, and so arrange promotional activity so that (a) you make as many sales to them as possible and (b) you find more of the same to whom to sell. In such a case we would be selling to the *actual* market. But this does not tackle the *potential* market. It would be unrealistic to believe that anyone and everyone is a potential customer, but situations arise where potentially vigorous markets remain hidden. This was ably illustrated in a letter sent to a magazine by a man resident in Germany whose concern was to create a good lawn. His purpose in writing was to say that he was unable to acquire a good-quality hand-mower in Germany, even though German law forbade the use of powered lawn-mowers after 8 p.m. and on Sundays or bank holidays. In order to acquire one, he was planning to buy one during a visit to England. The point he wished to make was that a well-known English manu-facturer of hand-lawn-mowers was missing out on a potentially lucrative market, namely 80 million Germans (Mellor-Stapelberg 1994). While this example should be treated with caution, because there may be facts pertaining to this situation of which the letter-writer was unaware, in principle it is an object-lesson on how a lucrative potential market for a product may exist in a place where, it may be thought, domestic producers already provide for the need.

Appraising the market

The process of coming to terms with the actuality and the potential of a market can be described as an *appraisal*. What an appraisal involves depends much on individual circumstances, but it is a process of asking questions before drawing conclusions. In very simple terms, these are some of the questions that should be asked.

WHAT IS THE MARKET WORTH?

For example, we may say that the market for holiday tourism in the UK is worth £22bn., because in 1989 that was the total spent by UK residents on holidays (English Tourist Board 1990). As a stand-alone statistic, it has limited usefulness; comparison with something else makes it intelligible. So, for example, the knowledge that UK spending on business travel and entertainment in 1990 was expected, also at £22bn., to be twice the revenue paid in corporation tax (Peterson and Belchambers in Quest (ed.) 1990, p. 56) gives a better idea of the significance of the statistic. But again, the figure refers only to the *actual* market: those people who spent money.

IS THERE A WIDER POTENTIAL MARKET?

It was noted in an earlier chapter that, annually, 40 per cent of British adults do not take a holiday of four or more nights, and that the short-break-takers tended to be the same people as those who took long holidays. Therefore, it could be suggested that this 40 per cent represents a potential market. On the other hand, the statistic has remained constant for over two decades in spite of a dramatic increase in holiday-taking. That suggests, perhaps, that there is limited potential for growth. The market is already *mature*. This contrasts with (for example) Germany, where the taking of holidays of four or more nights rose from 42 per cent to 66 per cent between 1970 and 1989 and was, so it appeared at the time, still rising (Euromonitor 1992a, p. 9).

WHAT IS THE MARKET'S FUTURE POTENTIAL?

Tourism within the UK for business purposes grew around three times as fast as all tourism between the early and mid-1980s (Beioley 1991a, table 2). Rapid growth continued, if somewhat abated by the recession of the early 1990s. But how will falling telecommunications costs, the prospect of personal televisual communication and the consequences of the introduction of fibre-optic cables as a means of transmitting messages affect the volume of business tourism in the future? This begs a number of further questions regarding business tourism: to what extent is personal contact important, and to what extent does this vary within the different forms of business tourism? Such factors may influence the market's future potential. It is not our purpose to answer these questions now, although the process of researching markets will be examined in more detail in later chapters.

Sectors, segments and niches

These are terms whose meanings are at the same time flexible and precise. They share a common purpose in that all three define part of a market, usually qualified by a suitable adjective: for example, the *business tourism sector*. Another purpose which they hold in common is that they all differentiate one part of the market from the rest. Therefore, if we are talking about the *business tourism sector*, common sense tells us that business travellers use (to some extent) means of travel and accommodation in common with holiday tourists. But as a part of the *market*, their purpose and motives in travelling are distinct. As will be seen, 'segments' and 'niches', widely used terms in the vocabulary of marketing, seek to do the same. The difference is essentially one of scale.

A MARKET SECTOR

This can be defined as a slice of the total market identified by one particular feature, for example business tourism. It is not to be confused with the term *industry sector* which is applied to the various contributing sectors, principally transport, accommodation, visitor attractions and destinations, which make up the tourism 'industry'. A *market sector* will generally be of a large scale, and may have only one distinguishing feature in common, as in the case with business tourism. People travel on business for a whole host of reasons, but the fact that they do it as part of their employment separates them from other tourists and, very broadly, unites them in certain behavioural characteristics which distinguish them. An example would be business tourists' purchasing decisions which may often be less price-sensitive than those of holiday tourists. People travelling on business may have little choice as to whether they make the journey, and may be less fussy about how much the trip costs, particularly if their employer is paying. There may also be sectors within sectors: when we talk of the holiday tourism sector, we may need on occasions to draw a distinction between customers who, within that sector, choose to stay in hotel and guest house accommodation, the *serviced sector*, and those who do not, opting to cater for themselves and falling into the *self-catering* or *non-serviced sector*. Notice again that it is just that one factor in common which characterises the sector. Other examples of sectors may be the *long-haul sector*, the *domestic holiday sector*, the *conferencing sector*, the *general business travel sector* and so on.

A MARKET SEGMENT

The term *segment* is, like its companion term 'sector', prone to being used flexibly to refer to a part of the market. The crucial difference is that a *segment* is smaller in scale than a sector and is differentiated by having several features in common. So, if we are discussing those travellers whose three distinguishing features are (a) travelling from the UK independently to the near continent, (b) taking their cars with them and (c) staying in farmhouse or rural bed and breakfast accommodation, we are discussing a *market segment*. At the very least, the contents of a *segment* will have two distinguishing features, but usually more.

The *segmentation* of markets is very much the story of the 1980s, and the story continues into the 1990s. The socio-cultural changes of the last two decades as discussed in Chapter 7, in Mort's words the 'explosion of individualities . . . of the number of "yous" on offer' (Thrift in Hamnett *et al.* (eds.) 1989, p. 21), has led to a proliferation of *segmented products* to match the requirements of the explosion of individualities. This is a trend which has had a general if not universal effect on industries selling products and services to the consumer, not least the tourism industry. The response of the industry has been to *segment their products* and thus, to take the overseas sector as an example, tour operators produce brochures with titles such as CityBreak, Small and Friendly, FlyDrive, A la Carte. Outside the tourism industry, *segmentation* can be observed in the proliferation of magazines targeted at special interests, and consumer edibles such as chocolate bars, where variations on the basic 'Yorkie' bar have appeared.

A MARKET NICHE

A niche is a highly specialised segment, small in scale, but which owes as much to the way in which it was identified, as it does to the many features which the contents of the *niche* hold in common. The use of this term, which normally refers to a recess in a wall or a hollow gap of some sort, is quite deliberate. As the segmentation of demand precipitated the segmentation of products to meet those needs, marketeers became adept at finding gaps between segments and developing them. The identification of these gaps, or niches, formed the basis of much of the expansion in the more specialised tourism products which have appeared over the past dozen or so years. Thus a company such as Prospect Music and Art Tours Ltd identified an opportunity to present to a wealthy, aspirational clientele, in their words 'a present-day version of the Grand Tour, taking small parties of people, accompanied by a knowledgeable guide to travel to many of the same destinations . . .' (Prospect Music and Art Tours Ltd 1992). Prospect is a small company serving a small and very specialised segment of the market, the development of which is in part due to the activity of the company itself. Prospect Music and Art Tours Ltd is a *niche operator*.

The growth of niche markets is by no means confined to the holiday tourism sector. Within the business tourism sector, in particular the conferencing and incentive travel sectors, niche operations are found. For example, close to the village of Birchington on the northern coast of Kent is a country residence known as Quex House. Within the house is the Powell-Cotton Museum, established by Major P H G Powell-Cotton during the last century and claimed to be the first example of wildlife from the jungles and savannahs of Africa and Asia displayed in the form of diorama, which has since been reproduced by (amongst others) the British Museum of National History in South Kensington, London, and the Natural History Museum in New York. The present director of the museum, Mr Christopher Powell-Cotton, now makes the diorama galleries available for the meeting and banqueting requirements of small conferences, meeting the needs of a conference organiser whose needs demand an unusual venue. In the conference business, Quex House in a niche operator. Likewise, the top end of the incentive travel market thrives on unusual and exclusive tourist opportunities: the practice of the late Earl Spencer, father of the Princess of Wales, of receiving and entertaining select gatherings of American visitors at the family home at Althorp is an example of the most exclusive end of the commercial incentive travel business and is another example of a niche operation.

Market segmentation

There is no single way to segment a market. A marketeer has to try different segmentation variables, together and in combination, hoping to find an insightful way to view the market structure. (Kotler 1984, p. 254)

Determined tourism practitioners need to have a clear idea of the market sectors which their businesses serve, and in which parts of those sectors, in terms of segments and niches, they operate. Some, like Prospect Art Tours or, to take another example, PGL Adventure who specialise in outdoor activity holidays, have built up their businesses by developing a particular niche. Just as a politician finds it impossible to please all of the people all of the time, so a tourism operation cannot be all things to all people. Even nowadays, vapid sloganry pops up in some holiday brochures and in travel journalism. Phrases such as 'something for everyone', 'fun for young and old alike' and 'entertainment to suit all tastes' may have had some meaning in pre-generation gap days when the extended family took its holidays together, but nowadays such language is anachronistic if not downright silly. Practitioners of the hospitality instinct know which part of the market they are serving, and their passion for service is *targeted* at those particular customers.

There are many ways of segmenting a market and a detailed look at the relevant chapters of generic marketing texts such as Kotler (1991), Baker (1991) and those specific to tourism (Middleton 1988, Holloway and Plant 1992) will repay study. A later chapter examines how the practice of segmentation is applied in the active marketing of tourist products. For the present we are going to examine three ways in which markets segment themselves. Markets, we should remember, consist of people, customers, who because of the socio-cultural changes discussed in Chapter 7 are much more diverse in their tastes, preferences and interests than was the case in previous decades. Three principal ways in which people segment themselves will be discussed: by age, income, occupation and related factors, that is *demographics*; by their actual preferences for product use as demonstrated in the market-place, that is, their *behavioural characteristics* as consumers; and by their chosen lifestyle as an expression of their personality characteristics, termed *psychographics*.

DEMOGRAPHIC SEGMENTATION

Demographics is the study of population change. Factors such as the number of people in particular age groups, the number of children in households, the jobs they do, the amount of money they earn are all *variables* which influence the behaviour of the market. For example, during the years following the Second World War, a so-called 'baby boom' occurred as, with the onset of peace and the return home of that part of the male population engaged in the hostilities, relationships between the sexes were renewed and pursued. The baby boom has been a potent force in shaping patterns of consumption. At present the baby-boomers are in their mid-forties, approaching their peak earning capacity, and in addition are inheriting wealth from their parents who were the first generation of post-war home owners. During the 1960s the baby-boomers' influence on society in economic and cultural terms was described as a revolution, as, during a period of near full employment, their earning capacity created a capacity to consume which begat success for new expressions in music, clothes and pastimes. This was the genesis of a new social order in which people segmented themselves by *lifestyle*, creating the need for a new way of identifying segments and giving rise to *psychographics*, of which more shortly.

However, one method of segmenting the population which is time-served and still forms the basis of much segmentatory work in the UK is the system of socio-economic classifications administered by JICNARS (the Joint Industry Committee for National Readership Surveys) and which is maintained through the National Readership Survey (NRS). The system was originally conceived in the years after the Second World War and is now commonly described as

NRS Social Grade Definitions (Waterson (ed.) 1992, p. 11). It uses as its basis the occupation of the head of household (see Table 8.1).

These classifications will appear somewhat anachronistic since the distinction between what constitutes a 'professional' and a 'managerial' employee began to blur in the 1960s, and more recent times have seen technology displace or alter many 'clerical' and 'unskilled manual' jobs. Attempts have been made to redesignate the categories by redescribing (for example) the Professional and Managerial categories respectively as 'Upper Middle Class' and 'Middle Class', C1 becoming 'Lower Middle Class'. This in the author's view does little to clarify the situation and in fact introduces terms whose meaning is more anachronistic than the originals they are intended to replace. Better it is to retain the original terms whose meaning can be clearly understood, always bearing in mind that the world has moved on in the meantime. Another point, concerning group E, is that it comprises those who are at the lowest level of subsistence. That would not include all of the unemployed, many of whom may be well provided for, or all pensioners, of whom many in more recent times have retired with occupational pensions. It is rather those for whom welfare payments, minor earnings from casual work or the state retirement pension are their principal means of support.

Marketeers still tend to rely on the NRS classifications as their initial means of acquiring Kotler's 'insightful way'. That, together with one other key variable, such as age or gender, can give a general picture of the consumer profile for a

Table 8.1 NRS socio-economic classifications

Social grade	Description	% of total population (all adults 15+)
A	Professional	2.9
B	Managerial	15.0
C1	Clerical	24.2
C2	Skilled manual	27.1
D	Unskilled manual	17.5
E	Welfare-dependent and state pensioners	13.2

(*Source*: Adapted from the National Readership Survey, July 1991–June 1992 (in Waterson (ed.) 1992))

particular product. So, for example, after the UK government (in February 1991) deregulated television programme information, Watts was able to offer this indication of the readership profiles of the main television listings magazines:

Radio Times	ABC1 bias, age profile neutral
TV Times	Class profile neutral, 15–44 bias
What's On TV	C2DE bias, 15–44 bias
TV Quick	C2DE bias, 15–44 bias

(*Source*: **Watts 1991**)

The choice of example is quite deliberate in that the television listings magazines are a prime medium for advertising tourist products and therefore, for the tourism marketeer, an appraisal of their readership profiles is essential.

The NRS-type classifications, though widely used by research organisations and the media outside the UK, are essentially a British invention. The marketeer of tourism who is approaching the segmentation of markets in another country will need to acquire an understanding of the local classifications used. Bennett alludes to some of these: the Dutch system appears to be similar though not identical to the UK classification; German segmentation is based on monthly household income; Greece classifies in accordance with place of residence, whether urban, suburban or rural, and France's classification combines 'senior management' with the self-employed (1993, pp. 152–3).

As segmentation by socio-economic classification alone became increasingly unsatisfactory, a demand arose for new ways of targeting, more accurately, groups of consumers whose patterns of consumption could be expected to be similar. During the late 1970s and early 1980s various new classifications were conceived, with names such as ACORN, Pinpoint, MOSAIC. These systems base themselves on the fact that people segment themselves by seeking out and retaining the company of like-minded people. Chisnall (1992, pp. 242–4) offers a detailed summary of these classifications whose founding principle, as he points out, is that 'birds of a feather flock together'. Therefore, people living in the same area are more likely to have similar consumption patterns than those who do not. In other words, it is not just the *demography* but the *geography* of the situation that is taken into account, giving rise to the term *geodemographic analysis*. For example the ACORN system, developed initially in 1977 and operated by CACI Ltd, divides the UK population into 38 ACORN types, by area of domicile; ACORN is an acronym standing for 'A Classification of Residential Neighbourhoods'. Thus, for example, residents in areas of ACORN type D14, tenement flats lacking amenities, would be expected to have different consumption patterns from those of type J34, spacious inter-war semis with big gardens. The material which forms the basis for ACORN is the Official Census undertaken by HM Government.

If income and/or social grade are one key determinant of purchasing habits, age is another. Human consumption patterns have always been to some extent segmented by *lifestage*; for example, operators of sheltered accommodation are unlikely to lose sleep over the fact that the appeal of their product is limited to elderly members of the population. However, a librarian known to the author once expressed concern that his branch libraries appeared to attract a clientele most of whom were over 65. There are three responses to such a concern: first, it is not so much the usage of particular branch libraries but the overall usage of the library service which shows whether or not the service is satisfying the broad requirements of the population. If retired people borrow more books to read than the rest of the population, then that need not be a problem; after all, they have more time and opportunity than the working population to read. Secondly, the notion that neighbourhood branch libraries, many of them in suburbs, should attract a cross-section of the resident population in their area, is flawed. The working population is likely to use, at least in part, library facilities near their place of work which is likely to be in a city centre or some other non-residential area. But thirdly and most importantly, the use of a branch library can be regarded as a *lifestage* activity: those of us who reach the age of retirement after a typical life of consumption will have moved progressively from the incipient fad purchases of teenage years through working life, marriage, childbirth, maturity and finally to a pleasant morning amble down to the neighbourhood branch library from our sheltered accommodation. If William Shakespeare's insights into human nature qualified him as an 'early psychoanalyst' (Ellison 1994), he also surely had an 'insightful way' into the segmented nature of human life:

All the world's a stage, and all the men and women merely players: They have their exits and their entrances, and one man in his time plays many parts.

(Shakespeare: As You Like It, *Act II, Scene vii, author's emphasis)*

An effort to recognise the role of lifestage in a geodemographic analysis system was made by Research Services Ltd when, in 1981, they produced the *Sagacity* classification, the basis of which is the recognition that our consumption patterns change as we pass through the stages of life. Drawing on income and socio-economic groupings, *Sagacity* groups the population into 12 classifications (see Chisnall 1992, pp. 260–2 and Waterson (ed.) 1992, p. 13). It recognises four life-cycle stages:

Dependent	Adults 15–34 living at home but not as head of household or housewife; and full-time students
Pre-family	Adults aged as above, who are head of household or housewife, but with no children
Family	Adults under 65 who are head of household or housewife, with one or more children under 21 years
Late	All other adults whose children are no longer at home or who are over 35 years and childless

'*Sagacity*' defines its occupation groups from NRS groupings, labelling the ABC1 classifications 'White' (-collar) and the C2DEs 'Blue'. Chisnall relates how Research Services Ltd demonstrated the capacity of *Sagacity* to identify an index of likelihood to consume in the case of two contrasting products, a package holiday and ownership of a cheque book. Package holidays abroad appear to be most prevalent during the *Pre-family* and *Late* stages. The relative lack of presence amongst those in the *Family* stage is caused, it is supposed, by the lower disposable income occasioned by the arrival of a young family, and the problems associated with taking children abroad. By contrast, ownership of a cheque book is more associated with socio-

economic classification than with lifestage, the white-collar groups having a greater propensity to use one. Nevertheless, the actions of the banks in recent years to encourage a wider population to open accounts appear to have brought about a higher than average propensity to use a cheque book amongst the *Pre-family* and better-off blue-collar groups (1992, pp. 261–2).

PSYCHOGRAPHIC SEGMENTATION

Where demographic and geodemographic analysis can still be seen to fall short of offering a complete model for segmenting population is that they cannot, fully, come to terms with the individualist consumerism which developed in the 1980s. Patterns of consumption can differ widely within groups which otherwise possess similar demographic characteristics. It can be hypo-thesised that the individualism of the 1980s may have positively encouraged a divergence of behaviour within demographic groupings: a positive unwillingness to visit the neighbours' holiday destination, drive the neighbours' car, or pursue the neighbours' hobby. Fortunately for marketeers, yesterday's original idea is today's trend: as one reviewer put it when describing the BMW motor car marque: 'Uncommonly good ... Now a common sight ... Individualism for the common man' ('Car' 1990). The achievement of BMW in sustaining high-volume sales and at the same time maintaining an image of individual appeal is a considerable marketing success story, considering that the number of BMWs on the UK's roads approaches half a million (Samuel 1994).

Motor cars are an interesting example of convergence and divergence in consumer tastes: as the styling of conventional motor cars converges, giving rise to concepts such as the 'hatchback' in the 1980s, there has been evidence of divergence in the explosion of interest in 'classic cars'. The classic car movement, as it came to be known, spawned a range of new businesses selling, maintaining and repairing veteran and not-so-veteran vehicles, plus a range of special-interest consumer magazines with titles such as *Classic and Sportscar* and *Your Classic*. It is significant, as well, that consumers' requirements for individuality have been met, arguably in classic post-modern fashion, by looking to the past to provide image and inspiration. The major car manufacturers have not yet responded significantly to this trend, except perhaps in the Rover group's decision to relaunch the MGB in an updated but essentially classic form and its continued manufacture of the 1960s classic, the Mini, and perhaps also in the re-emergence of the cabriolet as an adaptation of standard models. In 1994 the Rover group was acquired by BMW and its new German owners, in its public comment on completion of the acquisition, offered a hint that classic brand-names such as Wolseley and Riley may appear on new models in the later 1990s. Whether the styling of the Rover group's new models will represent a genuine departure from the converged 'Eurostyle' of the early 1990s, or little more than a badging exercise such as Rover's own 1980s revivals of some of its classic brand names such as MG, remains to be seen.

However, the present purpose is to examine how people segment themselves in terms of their lifestyles, and how psychographic analysis can identify those segments. *Lifestyle* can be regarded as a personal response to the behavioural options which society and environment present. If culture can be defined as 'man's extra-somatic means of adaptation' (White 1959, p. 8), then lifestyle can usefully be defined as a *personal adaptation* to the culture in which the person lives. The adaptation is personal in the sense of being individual, but it is very rare for the adaptation to be limited to the individual and unseen by others. Human beings are social animals, and lifestyle adaptations are designed to be shared, creating subcultures. One of the objectives of punk hairstyle and attire may be to defy convention, but they also create a bond of identity with other punks. How do lifestyle and consumption interact? Bennett offers this comment:

It seems . . . that consumers often buy goods they feel they ought to purchase in order to pursue a particular lifestyle, rather than the products they objectively need. 'Vicarious participation' in a certain desired way of life (e.g. healthy, sophisticated, man-about-town etc.) is sometimes possible via consuming goods mentally associated with the lifestyle to which the individual aspires. (1993, p. 154)

So in other words, it may be real, or we may be playing at it. Urry introduces the theme of *playfulness* in the context of a discussion about post-modernity and in words undoubtedly influenced by those of Shakespeare quoted earlier, observes that 'the world is a stage and the post-tourist can delight in the multitude of games that can be played' (1990, p. 100). This was said in order to set a context for a discussion of the buying of souvenirs by tourists, as discussed in this book in Chapter 5.

The identification of lifestyles is more complicated than it might at first seem: consumption reflects not only chosen lifestyle needs, but lifestyle aspirations. Consumption of tourist products probably, in many cases and very often, reflects aspiration rather than need, as discussed in Chapter 7. What psychographic analysis attempts to do is to link personality factors to the decision-making process in which purchases and opinions, interests and motivations, are associated with groups of people in a way that makes it possible to identify like-minded individuals as future prospects. There are many approaches to lifestyle (psychographic) analysis but the technique owes much to some initial studies of human behaviour characterisation, of which the work of Riesman *et al.* is an example: in the early 1950s they identified three types of characterisation: *tradition-directed behaviour*, which changes little through time; *other-directedness* in which the individual submits or adapts to peer pressure; and *inner-directedness* where the behaviour of others does not appear to influence decisions (see Wilson *et al.* 1992, p. 212). Bennett offers his own list of common characteristics which psychographic research would aim to uncover. This includes additional factors which would be associated with contemporary society: are people's motives materialistic or non-materialistic? Are their concerns to survive and subsist, or to consume conspicuously? (1993, p. 154).

The British Market Research Bureau (BRMB) produces a Target Group Index (TGI) which identifies usage levels of products and services, and the nature of purchase decisions, amongst a population sample. An analysis of TGI data based on almost 200 statements of consumer attitude and opinion produced six 'Outlook' groups, named as follows:

Outlook group	% of sample
1 Trendies	15
2 The indifferent	18
3 Social spenders	14
4 Pleasure seekers	15
5 Working-class puritans	15
6 Moralists	16

(*Source*: **Chisnall 1992, pp. 241–2**)

The names of these groups are sufficiently evocative for the reader to form a view of how Riesman's and Bennett's factors may be represented in their personality make-up. In practical terms, a company specialising in psychographic analysis will maintain a computerised database of lifestyle types and associated known consumer behaviour. A marketeer wishing to have his or her own database of customers 'profiled' in this way will have his or her database 'run' against the company's database revealing the 'profile' of that set of customers, that is, the particular consumption characteristics that apply to them. Other potential customers with a similar profile can then be identified from the database owned by the psychographic analysis company, and rented to the marketeer for an agreed fee.

As an example, a coastal resort submitted a database of 25,000 names and addresses, representing the responses to an advertising campaign, for lifestyle analysis. The analysis profiled the addresses against an existing geodemographic/lifestyle database and yielded a picture of who these people were. The two greatest lifestyle 'likelihoods' were reading the *Daily Mirror*, and holidaying in the UK. The two least 'likelihoods' were reading the *Financial Times*, and holidaying in South America. Such results are perhaps unsurprising for a resort whose primary market, that is those people who form the mainstay of the visitor clientele, is C1C2D. Gardening featured above the average as a pastime, perhaps not surprisingly, but there was also a significant interest in the environment, which it is otherwise tempting to write off as a fashionable feature of middle-class liberalism. In fact, concern for the environment has percolated up and down the socio-economic groups. The determination of producers of food and personal consumer toiletries to persuade us that their products are free of additives, or ozone friendly, the evidence for which proliferates on supermarket shelves, emphasises the point.

What was both intriguing and useful about the analysis was that the resort seemed to be underperforming in attracting families with very young children, perhaps missing out on a market to which it was suited in terms of product and price. But interestingly, there was a matching trend of relative overperformance in attracting a younger class of elderly person, and older 'young' children in the 6 to 10 year age range. It could be hypothesised that, as children grew a little older and more manageable, still-spritely grandparents would take them on holiday to the UK seaside while their still-young parents took a break by themselves, perhaps abroad, as they might have done before the children were born. If this hypothesis were to be tested out through other forms of market research and proved valid, then it could be accurately said that a *niche* had been identified. A 1994 UK television advertising campaign by Disneyland Paris featured a grandparent and young granddaughter visiting the park, the child remarking that she did not know how old her grandfather was, but he became younger during his visit. It can be concluded that Disneyland Paris had identified the selfsame niche and was targeting this particular advertising campaign at both child and grandparent.

A good example of a segmentation of the domestic holiday market was achieved by MEW Research using data collected during a Holiday Destination Choice Survey undertaken in 1991, commissioned by the ETB and the regional tourist boards of England (MEW Research 1992). Applying multivariate analysis to *quantitative* and *qualitative* data (see Chapter 11 for more details), MEW defined five segments based on the factors considered important in selecting a destination for a domestic holiday of five nights or more in paid accommodation:

Segment	% of total
'Bucket and spade'	19
'Sun and fun'	27
'Get away from it all'	12
'Heritage and hikes'	22
'Sights and service'	18

(*Source*: **MEW Research (1992), A-24**)

The segments' labels evoke a picture of the people involved. Most of us will have little difficulty in imagining the types, in terms of people of our own acquaintance, who match the descriptions. To choose just two of the segments and compare and contrast them reveal similarities as well as differences. 'Get away from it all' and 'Sights and service' holiday-makers are respectively aged 65+ and 55+; they are both retired; neither takes children away with them; the party size is two; the former go away in May or June, the latter June or September. The key difference is the socio-economic variable: 'Get away from it all' are AB, 'Sights and service' are DE. A picture emerges of 'Sights and service' holiday-makers perhaps showing an interest in organised coach holidays with an eye on low cost, whereas 'Get away from it all' tourists perhaps have their own transport and are able to spend more; in fact, a feature of this segment was the likelihood of taking two or more holidays in 1991. It is important to understand that this is not the only way in which the domestic holiday market is segmented; there are as many ways of segmenting a market as there are of cutting a cake. The nature of the segmentation ultimately relates to the needs of the marketing operation for which the marketeer is responsible.

BEHAVIOURAL SEGMENTATION

This is an altogether simpler concept resting on little more than applied common sense. It is segmentation by *product usage*, based on the principle that people segment themselves in accordance with the purchasing decisions they make in the market-place. So, for example, if the above hypothesis that 'Sights and service' tourists have a low budget and regard a coach tour as the service which delivers the sights, then there is little point in trying to sell fly-drive holidays to them. People's purchasing decisions, and more especially the records of them, are valuable guides to the *actual* markets in which they are active as consumers, although they are not such good guides to the *potential* market unless, as a group, their type can be shown through the methods described earlier in the chapter to be potentially active in other markets.

Marketeers' response to behavioural marketing data drops through the letterboxes of most houses, on most mornings. An adult whose purchase of a product involves giving a name and address, and virtually all travel and tourism products involve this, can expect to be approached through the post, or exceptionally by telephone, with invitations to purchase more of the same. The use of names and addresses together with known profile information of individuals, termed *database marketing*, is subject to voluntary and legislative restrictions. Most database users subscribe to the mailing preference service, by which individuals who do not wish to receive direct mail can register and have their names and addressed 'cleaned' from subscribers' lists. Database marketing is also subject to legislative restrictions under the Data Protection Act 1984, which requires all users of computer databases that contain information about individuals to register with the Data Protection Registrar. The permission of individuals must be obtained before their names and addresses are used for repeat offers or invitations to make other kinds of purchase. Usually this permission is sought through an invitation to the customer on response forms to tick a box if they are unwilling to receive, through the post, information on similar or other products. The perception of the general public may be that some marketeers overplay the field, to the extent that the volume of offers becomes an irritation. Nevertheless, it is a proven fact that repeated mailings often secure a purchase in the end (Newman 1977, ch. 17).

In markets where there is perceived to be a large, latent, potential market to be tapped, some marketeers may use *direct mail*, writing to people directly in their own houses, as a very blunt instrument, engaging alongside their competitors in an excess of activity, a sort of saturation bombing by mail. This was noticeably the case in the UK during the 1980s and into the 1990s, where the consequence of the deregulation of the financial services markets was a plethora of approaches from banks, building societies and other financial services firms, aiming to sell products such as life assurance which is not the kind of service that people need to purchase regularly. This kind of activity has given rise to the label 'junk mail' and at one time caused a former UK Secretary of State for the Environment, Chris

Patten, to consider legal restrictions on direct mail activity on the grounds of conserving resources. To the great relief of the industry, the idea was not taken any further. Practitioners in the travel and tourism industry have the benefit of knowing, first, that holidays and trips tend to be a regular feature on the household calendar for the majority of adults, and secondly, that approaches presenting holiday options are likely to command a greater welcome than yet another attempt by the bank to sell them yet another endowment policy.

It is worth making the point that the increasing self-segmentation of society has been matched by the means to *model* that segmentation. This has come in the form of information technology. The arrival of computers made it possible to manipulate and use large volumes of data, with many variables, on a scale which would have been otherwise impossible. The proliferation of cheap computer technology in the 1980s put the capability to hold and segment a customer database into the hands of the smallest businesses. It also made possible the manipulation of multivariate data applying to millions of names and addresses, and the capacity to store and update that data systematically. It is not surprising therefore that expenditure on direct mail advertising rose from £474m. to £895m. in the UK between 1986 and 1991, an increase of almost 100 per cent, and exceeding the rates of growth of expenditure in all other advertising media. The actual volume of items sent increased over the period from 1.4 billion to 2.1 billion. (Waterson (ed.) 1992, pp. 72 and 81).

The primary focus of this chapter has been the market, by which is meant the body of actual and potential tourists whose preferences, aspirations and dreams translate into the segmented diversity of consumption habits that can be identified and understood through the techniques of analysis which have been described. The response of marketeers of tourism to this diversity is to create a range of experiences and opportunities to fulfil those preferences, aspirations and dreams. The terminology of marketing describes these experiences and opportunities as *products*, and it is these which form the theme of the next chapter.

Chapter 9

The tourist product

What is a product?

The general purpose of this chapter is to conduct a select appraisal of the principles of marketing as a prelude to Chapter 10, where the application of those principles in tourism is discussed. Its particular purpose is to acquire an insight into the meaning of the word 'product', and specifically what it can mean when used in tourism. A concise definition can be found in any glossary of marketing terms (see Kotler and Armstrong 1991, p. 676), but in this chapter it is proposed to devote some extended attention to the subject. This is because, as will be argued, the true definition of the 'tourist product' is in the mind of the tourist. By implication, there can be as many definitions of the 'tourist product' as there are tourists. This is a daunting prospect, but an examination of experiential definitions from a customer perspective can yield insights into how the tourist experience which is on offer can, at different times in different places and to different people, vary very considerably from the provider's perspective.

'Product' is, after all, a term which by tradition has referred to a manufactured good, a thing that can be seen, touched, eaten and so on. It implies a degree of inherent simplicity, the value or effectiveness of which can be easily observed or measured. Thus, soap powder companies advertise on television to persuade us that their product is best: apparent housewives, accosted in their domestic surroundings with apparent spontaneity, are invited to conduct an anonymous comparison between two washing powders. Some time later, it is the powder which the advertisers are keen to promote that emerges in the judgement of the apparent housewife as the better buy. In this scenario, there is little scope for confusion. There is an underlying assumption that agreement exists on the need to get shirts really white.

Defining the tourist product is not so simple. The use of the word 'product' is problematic when applied to service industries in general. For example, to what extent can a university degree course be described as a 'product'? What is the 'product' that the student acquires? It is an education or a degree? The conceptual difference is important. A student may set a higher value on actually getting the degree certificate than obtaining full educational value from the course. It is like buying an expensive car with the intention of framing the receipted invoice and placing it on the wall for all to see; whether the expensive car actually exists or not is incidental. A place at university may also be an opportunity to live in a certain locality because the girlfriend or boyfriend is there, it may be an escape from home or from unemployment, or it may be an opportunity to live in a certain town and enjoy financial support and some discretionary time to rehearse and play with a rock band. The author, in a tutoring role, has known all these advanced as primary reasons for attending university. So the *product attributes*, the features of the product that influence the student's decision to buy, can be very diverse.

By contrast, the product attributes of a manufactured good like a pair of shoes are specific and the subject of general agreement: in the end, a pair of shoes is a pair of shoes, a fact about which there is little scope for disagreement. Given the range of *informal* product attributes that can be ascribed to services as opposed to manufactured goods, it is not surprising that service industries seem to be the butt of so many complaints. It is not so much that things are always going wrong, but that people's expectations differ. What is excellent service to one person may be deficient in some way to another. For example, a very conscientious student may wish to have more tutorial time from teachers; by contrast, the student whose primary purpose is to rehearse with a rock band may view all the attentions of tutors as unwelcome intrusions.

This is where quality assurance initiatives such as the UK's Citizens' Charter risk being inadequate. They are expressions of *normative need*, that is need prescribed by experts who may not be fully in touch with what the citizens actually require (see Chapter 6). For example, rail commuters may approve of a target of (say) 95 per cent of trains arriving on time, but may prefer to exchange a five-minute delay for a seat to sit on. Product attributes, from a consumer perspective, can depart from the primary attributes of the product from the normative view of the provider. For example, a senior local authority leisure manager once had to be persuaded that the bad language used by a comedian on the stage of a municipal concert hall was the primary attribute of the performance. A normative view might suggest that customers are offended by bad language, but on this occasion the customers were present for the express purpose of being offended. The comedian, for his part, made his living by being offensive.

Introducing the tourist product

The effective practice of the hospitality instinct relies on insight into the formal and informal attributes of the tourist product: not so much what is being sold, but why it is being bought. Some tourist products acquire an informal attribute by accident, such as an association with celebrity. For example, the Hotel Formentor on the northern coast of Mallorca was visited by the late Princess Grace of Monaco. The hotel knows the value of such an association (it is mentioned in promotional literature), regarding it as a positive attribute to attract visitors who seek a certain style, in addition to location and service, for their holiday break. Identifying in advance what the

customer may consider to be positive attributes may involve looking at the existing product to identify under-used attributes; it may involve managing the process to acquire the right attributes, just as Glasgow in 1990 convinced the world of its status as a City of Culture, and the tennis player André Agassi was drafted in to endorse a brand of instant coffee in television advertisements. Below are some examples of how the attributes of a tourist product may be viewed from the differing perspectives of provider and customer.

A two-week break in the sun at an established mass-market destination can be:

Provider's perspective	Customer's perspective
(a) *The product*	(a) *The product*
A package holiday	Our honeymoon
(b) *Product attributes*	(b) *Product attributes*
Cheap and cheerful	It took years to save for it
A familiar resort	First time abroad
An ordinary resort	I fell in love there
Watersport opportunities	Scared of water
Flights from provincial airports	Scared of flying

Two recent works of the cinema ably demonstrate the way in which what is on the surface a tourist trip becomes, experientially for the tourists, a life-event of considerable import. The first and perhaps best known is *Shirley Valentine*, based on the play by Willy Russell and featuring Pauline Collins in the title role. Escaping from the blandness of suburbia and a husband obsessed with routine, she takes herself on holiday to a Greek island. Through a fleeting but romantic encounter with a Greek restaurant owner, played by Tom Conti, she experiences an awakening which equips her for a reconciliatory meeting with her husband on her terms and on her new adopted territory.

The experiential outcome of the second of the two examples is in some ways very similar, although the scene, action and setting are very different. *Sirens* (1993) is set in Australia in the 1930s. A young English clergyman and his wife, played respectively by Hugh Grant and Tara Fitzgerald, are asked by a bishop to visit the Blue Mountains studio of a liberal artist to persuade him to withdraw a controversial work of art from an exhibition. On arrival, they encounter something resembling a bacchanalian paradise.[4] The events of the visit present too robust a challenge for the clergyman, but something of a liberation for his wife. The concluding scene of the film, set in a railway carriage after the conclusion of the visit, suggests that the experience of the clergyman's wife, like that of Shirley Valentine, is expected to bring qualitative enhancements to the couple's relationship.

Neither of these films was about tourism as such, but in both cases a tourist visit was the facilitator by which different characters were brought to the same place, with apparent life-enhancing results. In the recollection of the protagonists, the memory will not be simply of a trip to Greece or a trip to the Blue Mountains; the memory of the place will be identified with and synonymous with their experience there, and unique to them as individuals. Profound personal experience, particularly of the romantic kind, is not uncommon on tourist trips and the point is that such experience frequently features in the advance expectations of the tourist. In other words, like students who have a variety of reasons for accepting a place on a university degree course, tourists have a variety of expectations which may be based on the desire to recover or repeat past personal experience or an aspiration to achieve something as yet unexperienced. It is in his way that the product attributes of the tourist trip are as potentially numerous as the tourists themselves.

Fortunately, the actual range of aspiration tends to fall into predictable categories, of which romance may be one example. Even straightforward travel products such as a trip on a train can be the subject of very different customer aspirations, and the paragraphs which follow seek to analyse the different product attributes which a train journey may have for different customers, and demonstrate how marketeers working for British Rail have segmented their product to serve these different customers.

[4]*An expression used in a résumé of the film issued by the Pictureville cinema, Bradford.*

Example: product attributes of a trip on a train

On the surface, buying a trip on a train is a simple purchase: the traveller buys a ticket, and travels on the train to the desired destination. On closer examination, the motives and background to the decision to travel vary considerably. A business-person probably has little choice as to whether to make the journey, and is in all likelihood not paying for himself or herself. A commuter has even less choice. A person travelling from the provinces to London on a pre-Christmas shopping expedition does not have to make the journey, but will do so if the trip is comfortable and the price is right. An enthusiast may travel on a historic and scenic route such as the Settle–Carlisle line for sheer pleasure. Some travellers are able to plan their trips well in advance and know which train they will take. Others, particularly business-people, may not have the same advance notice and may not be able to commit themselves to particular trains because of the unknown length of time required to transact their business.

British Rail (BR) has over the past few years evolved a flexible pricing structure which has not only been successful in increasing revenues, but has taken account of the different product attributes of a trip on a train taken by different kinds of customer. The key to understanding customers' perceptions is to remember that travel is very often a means to some other end, as discussed in Chapter 3. The product attributes of a train journey in the eyes of the pre-Christmas shopper differ greatly from the attributes viewed through the eyes of a businessperson. The alternatives for the former are not to make the trip at all, and complete the shopping either locally or at some nearby regional shopping centre; alternatively, to make the trip but travel by coach. The alternatives for the businessperson are to travel by private car, or, exceptionally, to fly. Until the mid-1970s, product differentiation on the railways was determined by the level of physical comfort and facilities provided. First class offered peace and quiet and some additional services for those able to pay for them; standard class offered similar standards of comfort, but without exclusivity. There was some further price differentiation based on type of journey: the Cheap Day Return has been a feature of BR pricing for a long while. What BR did from the mid-1970s onwards was to recognise the widely differing perceptions of product attributes amongst its customer base, and create new 'products' around the basic concept of a 'rail journey' to develop each segment of the market.

Student Railcards were introduced in the mid-1970s: these were followed by Senior Citizens' Railcards and subsequently by a range of differentially priced tickets which are on regular offer to all customers. First class is still available at considerable expense and is taken up primarily by business users. A standard class open return is still available, offering the use of any train and valid for return within one month. Special tickets are available which offer considerable discounts in return for some usage limitations: the *Saver* and *Supersaver* tickets are described by BR respectively as 'our flexible leisure ticket' and 'our off-peak leisure ticket' for journeys of over 50 miles (Intercity East Coast 1993). The difference is that *Savers* can be used on virtually all journeys, while *Supersavers* are not valid on Fridays and are subject to some other restrictions. The *Apex* ticket, introduced in 1991, offers yet further generous discounts in return for booking at least seven days in advance and making a commitment to specific trains for the outward and return journey. Further product variants include *SuperApex* tickets which are offered tactically to fill seats on particular services, for example overnight holiday-maker trains from Yorkshire to the South West (Intercity Derby 1993), and *SuperAdvance* which is a hybrid of a *Supersaver* and a *Saver*, priced similarly to a *Supersaver* but offering Friday travel if a commitment to travel is made at least one day in advance (Intercity East Coast 1993). The whole range of flexible fare opportunities is now quite complex and has attracted criticism, particularly from infrequent travellers, who experience difficulty in understanding the system. While one can have some sympathy with this, it is no different from air travel where discounting of fares to fill vacant seats is widespread and far less formalised. At least in the case of British Rail, the principles of discounting are consistent and published and anyone who wishes to can study the fares and plan their travel to gain maximum value. The recognition that the product attributes of a rail journey are defined in the consumer's mind more by price and convenience than class of travel has proved to be a successful strategy and contributed to an increase in passenger journeys of 11.1 per cent between 1985 and 1990 (Euromonitor 1992c).

Perceived attributes of common tourist products

Applying this kind of thinking to three common forms of tourist product, we can make discoveries of factors that influence the way the product is presented to the purchasing public.

1 *Two weeks in the sun* is precisely that. The attribute which the customer values is the sun. Whether it is to be found in Spain, Portugal or Greece is of secondary importance. The recognition of this during the early 1980s, when recession hit the UK, enabled travel agents and tour operators to fill up holidays at the last minute, because it was the sun rather than the place which mattered. The place was of secondary importance. A by-product of this tactic, which the industry probably now regrets, is that holiday-makers found the last-minute bargain in the sun to be a very attractive product, and late booking and discounting are now a permanent feature of the industry.

2 *Particular destinations*, such as Torbay, are also products. The product on offer is a particular place with all the attributes associated with that place, in the case of Torbay an image of continental exotica which has been so ably developed by the English Riviera advertising campaign with its imagery of palm trees and associated 1930s chic. The product on offer by the Torbay Tourist Board is a particular place, which may have place associations (honeymoon, family holidays etc.) in the perception of individuals within the target market. Alternatively, it may be positioned as an option alongside other fashionable resorts in its market sector, such as Bournemouth.

3 The *short break* is precisely that. The customer's objective is to travel away for two or three nights, and many short-break takers take multiple short breaks in any one year (Beioley 1991b). Thus, the fact that it is a break is more important than where it is. In the perception of the customer, the limited duration of the holiday offers the opportunity to experiment and thus opens the field widely to a whole host of emerging domestic destinations.

Fashioning the link between product and market

The principles of marketing are well covered in specific texts on tourism marketing such as Middleton (1988) and Holloway and Plant (1992) and in generic texts such as Baker (1991) and Kotler and Armstrong (1991). Middleton observes that, 'In its principles marketing planning is no more than a logical thought process ... it is an application of common sense' (1988, p. 128). It is in that spirit that the following paragraphs are offered, the purpose being to offer a practitioner commentary, and complement rather than duplicate the treatment of marketing in existing texts.

This common-sense process can be divided into three sequential stages: *situational analysis, marketing strategy* and *marketing plan*. The first stage can be thought of as a sort of reconnaissance venture, where the environment of operation, attributes of products and all other factors that could have a determining influence on the performance of products in the market-place are identified and analysed. The second stage, *marketing strategy*, represents a set of strategic decisions based on the results of the *situational analysis*. By 'strategic' is meant long-term: deciding which business the organisation is in, and where it expects to be in 5 or 10 years' time. Thirdly, the *marketing plan* concerns the implementation of the strategy: how the strategic objectives will be achieved, and what will actually be done on a year-by-year basis to achieve them.

SITUATIONAL ANALYSIS

The core of the situational analysis has two parts to it: an appraisal of the organisation's products and delivery systems, that is, what is on offer, who buys it, and how it is promoted and delivered to its customers; and a parallel examination of everything else outside the organisation and its products which may impact on performance and effectiveness. Marketing theory offers two methods by which such information can be arranged, presented and considered logically, and both are identified by acronyms: the SWOT Analysis (Strengths, Weaknesses, Opportunities, Threats) can be applied to the product itself and its delivery systems; the PEST Analysis (referring to the Political, Economic, Social and Technological environment in which the organisation and its products operate) is applied to the external environment. There follow examples of these techniques in application, the first a hypothetical PEST analysis, the second a real SWOT analysis. The first concerns a hypothetical tour operator whose primary business is mass-market short-haul tours from the UK to Spain and other established Mediterranean destinations.

Table 9.1   PEST analysis* by a hypothetical tour operator whose primary business is mass-market short-haul tours to the Mediterranean from the UK

(a) *Political environment*
- Implications of EC Package Holiday Directive
- Implications of European airline deregulation
- Effects of EU Social Charter on labour costs at destinations

(b) *Economic environment*
- Long-term trends in relative currency strengths
- Effects of business cycle (recession etc.) on UK target markets
- Fluctuations in discretionary income (interest rates, tax regimes etc.)

(c) *Social environment*
- Effect of demographic change on present UK target markets

- Attitudes and actions of receiving (host) communities
- Market consequences of endemic discounting

(d) *Technological environment*
- Competitive challenge presented by computer reservation systems
- Lower telecommunications costs, proliferation of credit cards
- Opening of a land-link with the European mainland (Channel Tunnel)

***Note*: this is a hypothetical example which is not an exhaustive treatment. Issues have been limited to three in each category.**

Interpreting this hypothetical PEST analysis reveals business over which there may be question marks in the medium- and long-term future. We know from earlier chapters that mass-market sunlust tourism is still a preferred option for the mass of holiday-makers, but the contemporary cultural agenda applauds individualism and independent travel. As the cultural agenda percolates through the markets, fashion will be affected and indeed has been affected as far as some Spanish destinations are concerned. Traditionally low labour costs in southern Europe may be pushed up by a combination of the requirements of the EU Social Charter and the general relative strengthening of their currencies, as the economies of those countries develop faster than those of the already developed economies of northern Europe.

Fluctuations in the business cycle may affect some markets more severely than others, as was the case with the most recent UK recession where the C1C2 groups tended to cut back on leisure spending more than the AB groups, who tend to enjoy a higher level of residual financial security. The demographic contraction of the number of young single persons could cause, and has caused, problems for certain kinds of mass-market holiday products such as the 'twenties holiday'. And crucially, if southern European accommodation providers were to take to accepting credit card bookings by telephone, and to marketing themselves directly rather than relying on tour operators to do it for them, then

customers could book accommodation and transport separately. Travel agencies are already known to offer a 'flight only' service using their access to airline computers via CRSs (computer reservation systems). There are few signs of Mediterranean accommodation providers establishing their own marketing consortia at present, but if that were to happen it would challenge the traditional role of the tour operator.

Constructing and interpreting the PEST analysis requires diverse and creative research, plus a wide knowledge of events in the world and the ability to spot the way in which apparently unrelated events can impact on each other. For example, a tour operator running low-cost holidays for persons who are largely dependent on the state retirement pension as their main means of support may have been alarmed by the imposition by the UK government's 1993 budget of VAT (value added tax) on domestic fuel. Such a move obviously has a greater effect on the discretionary income of those for whom the payment of domestic fuel bills takes a large slice of overall income than on the disposable income of those on a high salary. Making connections such as that is the essence of effective PEST analysis and, incidentally, is the skill which employers expect from graduate recruits. To contruct a PEST analysis such as the one above, the sources to be consulted would include public sources of information which in the UK are listed in the *Directory of HMSO Publications*, and sources produced by private research organisations such as Euromonitor, the Economist Intelligence Unit and the Henley Centre for Forecasting.

The second example is a real SWOT analysis compiled by a manager on taking up an engagement to review and develop a resort area's marketing function. Because the product was a *destination*, the product (the resorts) and the environment in which they operated were to some extent one and the same, and so this exercise combines features of both the SWOT analyis and PEST analysis. This is a good opportunity to remember Middleton's (1988, p. 128) comment that marketing planning is the application of common sense, and if it makes sense to present all the information together, do it. Marketing principles exist to serve rather than to lead the process.

Table 9.2 SWOT analysis of the prevailing situation on taking up a marketing post in a UK coastal resort area

(a) *Strengths*
- Tourism Strategy produced by consultants in 1987 and incorporated into resort policy
- Effective members of staff with potential for development
- Respectable budgets available
- Group identity and logo and composite Holiday Guide for the three resorts established by immediate predecessor
- A large multi-auditorium venue available for conferences
- Excellent sandy beaches, well maintained and with water safety service
- Some recent market research data available
- Participation with neighbouring districts in a Tourism Development Action Programme
- Supportive Economic Development and Tourism Unit at County Council level

(b) *Weaknesses*
- Tourism Strategy remained largely unimplemented
- History of ambivalence and inconsistency in local authority members' support for tourism
- Staff demotivated by the above, and by several changes of manager in recent years
- Marketing operation very basic, e.g. no customer database, and key markets (e.g. conferences) unaddressed
- Built environments of the resorts have a tired, run-down air
- No readily available information on the economic impact of tourism
- Local tourism industry demoralised and cynical. Accommodation quality patchy
- Reverberations from the failure of a recent high-profile special event

(c) *Opportunities*
- 1980s recession in seaside tourism bottomed out, with modest growth predicted
- Key target markets to grow in size and spending power
- Evidence of investment in accommodation product by owners

- Brand-names of the resorts still strong and recognised
- Evidence for acceptance and recognition of recently established group identity
- Large population (including London) within two-and-a-half hours' travelling time
- Proximity to near continent, including a passenger ferry link
- Potential for recovery of conference business from a low baseline

(d) *Threats*
- Continued ambivalence of local authority members toward tourism and toward their responsibilities for destination marketing
- Legacy of lack of investment in private and public facilities over two decades
- Large multi-auditorium venue subject to competitive tender and operating 'commercially'. No first-call arrangement for conference usage
- Cynicism of local tourism industry exacerbates ambivalence of local authority members and vice versa
- Competing resorts have invested and upgraded during the 1980s
- Continued talk of special events to regenerate tourism, in spite of past failures

(Adapted from Voase 1992)

The operational response to this SWOT analysis is outlined later in the chapter as an illustration of marketing planning.

MARKETING STRATEGY

The formulation of a marketing strategy is simultaneously one of the easiest and the most difficult jobs in the organisation. Easy, because the ultimate strategy of the organisation usually hangs on two or three key decisions, in comparison with the myriad of detail involved in assembling the diverse targets of a marketing plan. The concept of the *mission statement*, now adopted by a wide range of organisations both private and public, is in essence a very simple and short sentence. If it is done properly, its brevity belies the amount of thought, consideration and discussion which has gone into formulating it. And herein lies the reason for marketing strategy being difficult: it is largely synonymous with the whole process of strategic planning, as Kotler and Armstrong (1991, p. 37) point out, and those simple decisions, if wrong, can be catastrophic for the organisation. Therefore, decisions on marketing strategy are taken by the most senior people in the organisation because of the experience, knowledge and insight which seniority ideally affords. Public bodies frequently seek the counsel of outside specialists when determining a tourism strategy. Private bodies receive advice from their advertising agents and other retained specialists. The marketing strategy, which may be updated every five years, is also likely to define a series of *strategic objectives* toward which progress is to be made within broad specific time scales. These objectives may be further categorised as long term, medium term and short term.

Essentially the purpose of a marketing strategy is to set a direction, to determine the business that the organisation is in and the shifts in emphasis between different parts of the business and to set objectives for the future: at least five years ahead, maybe a lot longer. For example, the hypothetical tour operator in the earlier example may, on the basis of the PEST analysis shown in Table 9.1, decide to develop long-haul holiday packages, known to be a growth sector, in order to diversify away from the short-haul packages on which it at present depends, and which may be expected to contract for all the reasons detailed in the PEST analysis. This is the strategy which a number of tour operators have adopted. For example, the Managing Director of British Airways Holidays expressed his expectation at the time of the launch of his company's 1995 long-haul brochure, which included 15 new destinations, that 'in 1995 more people will be travelling further field in search of new experiences' (*Yorkshire Post* 1994a).

Noticing the way in which demographic change is eroding the significance of the young single person as a powerful market for mass-market breaks, the operator may choose to target the expanding family formation group; or alternatively, continue to target the young singles with a more specific and highly segmented product. Any situational analysis produces a range of options: decisions may not be a question of right and wrong, but a decision between alternative courses of action which in turn influence the character of the company's business. The response of some traditional UK manufacturing industries to new trading environments has been to change from mass producers to small-scale manufacturers producing for specialised markets. An example is the textile industry, and to some extent the motor industry. Will some mass-market tour operators take similar decisions in the face of changing market demands?

MARKETING PLAN

By the third stage of the planning process, the strategy has been determined and the next challenge is to put the strategy into action. Once again, it is not necessary to be hidebound by textbook techniques, but approaching the planning process in a rational and logical way will normally involve a formal *marketing plan* which is updated on a yearly basis. The starting point for the plan should be the mission statement and strategic objectives of the organisation. It is a good idea to set these out at the beginning of the plan so that all who read it can see how the plan's proposals fit in with overall strategy. Generally speaking the plan will set a series of *targets* within each objective, for achievement during the interval between the production of the plan and its next yearly update. These targets should be set out clearly and linked with the strategic objective to which they relate.

For example, the operational response to the situational analysis as detailed in Table 9.2 involved a recommitment to the original Tourism Strategy and its strategic objectives as established in 1987, and the formulation and implementation of a marketing plan which set up a range of targets to be achieved during the initial 12-month duration of the Plan. The targets included:

- conceiving and implementing a programme of visitor research to update earlier data and aid identification of target markets
- completing a study of the economic importance of tourism within the local economy and publicising the results as a means of restoring confidence
- achieving the relaunch of the resorts as a conference destination by identifying target

segments and approaching them through direct mail

- reworking promotional materials by the creative use of copy and photography to 'speak' more effectively to key target markets
- creating an enquirers' database on computer to acquire intelligence through lifestyle analysis and for future database marketing applications
- preparation of a short-break product to be directly bookable through the Marketing Office and the success of which would be directly measurable

Marketing plans should be reviewed and updated annually, with progress reported with respect to each target. Where the target has not been fully achieved, which in even the best of organisations occurs from time to time, an 'exception report' should be included to explain why. Progress can be impeded for a variety of good reasons such as valued members of staff leaving for other jobs, recruitment freezes, budgetary constraints applied half-way through the term of the plan, or external factors such as the onset of economic recession. Achievement of the targets will be delivered by applying the techniques of marketing; the selection of techniques that are brought together has been described as the *marketing mix*. Within the marketing mix there are four basic elements, which have been termed the four Ps: Product, Price, Place, Promotion. These are discussed below in terms of their meaning, scope and related concepts and terminology.

Product, Price, Place, Promotion

PRODUCT

Already substantially discussed earlier in this chapter, a product could be a destination, or a package tour, or any number of any other things. Knowing what the product is, in the customer's eyes, is important. The product occupies a *position* in the market-place: that is, how it is perceived by consumers in relation to other competing products. A simple example may be the perceived difference between Bournemouth and Blackpool. Bournemouth may be perceived as

somewhat upmarket, restrained, middle-class and sedate. Blackpool is bold, brassy and extrovert. The reality is that there is a fair amount of Blackpool in Bournemouth and vice versa, in the same way that a Ford Mustang and a Daimler both have four wheels and an engine. But the resorts, like the cars, are perceived in the public mind as different, despite their similarities. It is desirable to locate the product in the market in relation to its competitors, and by means of promotion to ensure that the purchasing public have accurately understood how the product relates to others of a similar type. This is known as the art of *positioning*.

For example, the Hotel Formentor, mentioned earlier, positions its product by a number of signals which are present in its promotional activity: one will be price, another may be its geographical location, a third may be the desirability of wearing a jacket at dinner. Colloquially, this hotel could be described as significantly 'upmarket'. A less exclusive hotel in the centre of Palma Nova would be making a mistake if it attempted in its product and promotion to charge too much, and insist on the wearing of jackets at dinner.

Usually the marketeer will search for one particular product attribute which makes his or her product stand out from the competition. This is not the same as the product position: it is a particular attribute which can *differentiate* the product from other products in the sector: in other words, it is the product's *differential advantage*. The same product can have a different differential advantage for different market sectors. So, if the Yorkshire coast resorts of Bridlington and Scarborough are compared, Bridlington is flat, and Scarborough is hilly. For holiday-makers of advanced age, the absence of hills is attractive and in respect of the elderly market, could be said to be a *differential advantage* possessed by Bridlington. The comedian Ken Dodd, whose frenetic schedule of live performances includes seasonal visits to both resorts, includes in his comic description of Scarborough a verbal picture of pensioners, roped together, hauling themselves back up the hill after an evening in the theatre.

Differential advantage can be obtained or created in a number of ways: through inherent quality, additional levels of service, price, or whatever other attributes are appropriate. To return to the earlier railways example: on some early-morning trains, passengers paying the full standard fare are treated to service in the form of light refreshments at their seats, complimentary coffee, free advance seat reservations and cloth covers on the headrests of their seats. This is called *Silver Standard*, and is not quite first class, but it serves to *differentiate* by level of service the full standard fare from the much cheaper 'leisure' tickets.

PRICE

The role of price is a prime determinant of market position, although the way pricing works is highly complex. Before British Rail introduced flexible pricing structures, conventional street wisdom, as expressed in local radio 'phone-ins and the like, frequently held that if rail fares were halved, double the number of people would travel, thereby doing us all a favour. The kernel of truth in this is that it is possible to over-price a product so that customers are deterred, but to simply drop prices is to ignore the range of other factors which consumers take into account when making a purchase.

For example, practitioners in theatrical management know that it is always the most expensive tickets at the box office that are sold first. If they have not, this can mean one of two things: either the expensive seats were too expensive, or the *perceived value* of the expensive seats was not sufficient to warrant the price differential demanded. A particular auditorium where the author noted this phenomenon was built in a modern fan shape and the explanation was probably a mixture of the two: the highest-priced seats did not offer a location or view particularly superior to those of other seating areas. The question of *value* as opposed to *cheapness* is crucial in the pricing of luxury purchases such as a night at the theatre or a holiday. The purchaser is buying not only for himself or herself but in most cases for other people who will normally be those closest to him or her – spouse, boyfriend/girlfriend, children – and the goods have to be of good quality. Consumers rely on price, alongside reputation and certain other factors, as a guide to quality. The

author clearly recalls the astonishment of colleagues when some perfectly acceptable but habitually unsold seats in a concert hall proved more attractive to customers when the purchase price was doubled.

In the pricing of holidays, the psychology of the consumer is complex. The consumer has high expectations of a holiday, which would normally induce him or her to buy in accordance with perceived value and reputation rather than low price. But the action of tour operators and travel agents in engaging in seemingly annual price wars has amounted to the issuing of a psychological invitation to the consumer to participate in a search-for-a-bargain game. Certainly, the holiday has got to be right, of good value, and of a quality that can be justified in conversation with friends and neighbours; but when those same friends and neighbours are as interested in how good a special deal was obtained as in the holiday itself, then the pressure to be influenced by a bargain price is that much greater. Psychologically, booking at the last minute is easier on the consumer in terms of *post-hoc* justification: 'Well, what do you expect for £300 at four days' notice?' is salve to the soul when an impromptu booking results in a poor-quality holiday.

Different approaches to pricing are described by marketeers in different ways. *Cost-plus pricing* is a very standard approach in which the costs of producing and delivering the product are calculated and then a profit margin is added. The days are long gone where this form of pricing has much relevance to the marketing of modern consumer goods and services, as the railway example demonstrates. *Going-rate pricing* is very much the current practice of the overseas travel industry, that is, following the pricing of competitors. When the race to introduce discounts becomes too intense, profit margins either are eroded or disappear completely and this places some companies at risk of bankruptcy. The travel industry is pulled in two directions: while companies are keen to beat their competitors, they are not keen on the negative effects on the image of the industry which bankruptcies entail, nor are they particularly happy about having to slash their prices and profit margins as soon as their brochures appear, as happened with the launch of the summer 1995 brochures (*Yorkshire*

Post 1994a). Going-rate pricing does not necessarily involve discounts: the higher average price of cars in the UK, in comparison with the European mainland, has been the subject of government scrutiny and allegations that an informal cartel is being operated by motor manufacturers.

Perceived-value pricing involves pricing the product in accordance with what people think it is worth: for example, the concert tickets that people were happy to buy when the prices were doubled, the trains that people were happy to use for leisure purposes once a cheap leisure ticket was available. *Pure monopoly pricing* occurs on occasions when there is no commercial competition. A public utility such as gas or water, whether publicly or privately owned, potentially has the power over the consumer to name its own price. In the UK, a range of regulatory bodies such as OFTEL and OFGAS have been established by statute with the object of ensuring that the private service-industry monopolies do not take unfair advantage of their position. *Market-penetration pricing* may be used tactically to make inroads into a particular market by setting an initial low price for the product, possibly below cost price, in the hope of securing or increasing *market share*. Supermarkets advertising baked beans at an attractively low price are attempting to entice shoppers to buy, not just the beans, but their other provisions in the store. Even if a loss on the beans is incurred – the *loss leader* – they will gain from profits made from the other purchases. Because holidays tend to be luxury, occasional purchases in contrast with baked beans, this kind of tactical pricing may be less useful since low price may be taken by the customer to denote low quality. The annual last-minute holiday bargains are not loss leaders, they are surplus holidays which, because of the particular economics of the travel and tourism industries, it is better to sell at a low price than not at all.

To conclude our discussion on pricing: when there are many buyers and many sellers of a product, it is then that a vigorous market exists and the more creative of the pricing techniques described above are employed. The pricing in such a market is described as *elastic*, a term intended to convey the range and flexibility that pricing policies can be expected to demonstrate.

The sale of overseas holiday products is a good example. Where either the product is in limited supply, supplied by a monopoly producer, or price is a product attribute which is not of primary importance to the purchaser, then *inelasticity* is the result. Business tourism is a case in point: business hotels, first-class travel on trains, and business-class travel on airlines are priced at a level which is generally beyond that which a traveller will and could pay out of his or her own pocket. A businessperson may think nothing of staying at a three-star hotel at his or her employer's expense, but would seek something cheaper for personal use. Airlines, trains and business hotels compete with one another for the custom of the business tourist, but on levels of service rather than price. There is not much point in a sales message which offers to undercut competitors on price, when the decision-takers are not footing the bill. Promising to deliver the businessperson across the Atlantic in a fit state to do immediate business has a more powerful appeal.

PLACE

To *place* a product concerns the way in which it is delivered to the target market. It is not to be confused with *position*, which is the product's perceived attributes in comparison with other products. So, for example, most overseas package holidays are placed in the market-place via the retail travel trade. UK destinations place themselves using direct response advertisements in suitable publications. Placement policies for a range of products can vary considerably in the present world of highly segmented markets and segmented products to match these needs. There is no reason, for example, why package holidays should not be placed by establishing a direct link between the producer and the consumer. This is exactly what the tour operator Tjaereborg achieved in the 1980s, by advertising directly to the consumer and mailing the brochure on receipt of customer responses. Customers booked from the brochure directly with the company. The company claimed that by cutting out the retail travel agent as middleman, it was possible to make savings which were passed on to the customer. A holiday in a Tjaereborg brochure, when compared with the same holiday at the same hotel in the same resort with an operator which placed its products via the retail trade, did generally turn out to be significantly cheaper.

What muddied the waters somewhat with this particular type of operation in the UK was the annual discount wars at the time of brochure launches, and the offering of last-minute bargains as operators struggled to fill up empty seats and beds. In such an operating environment, the *differential advantage* of offering structural reductions by selling direct to the public lost its attractiveness. Buyers preferred to visit their easily accessible High Street travel agent and witness the travel clerk, employing the mesmerising power of the computer reservation system, obtain a variety of quotations out of which the sought-after bargain would emerge. There are tour operators which sell directly to the public but these tend to be niche operators whose low volumes make them unattractive to the retail travel trade; the High Street travel agency is very much a commodity supermarket rather than a delicatessen. *Placing* the product also includes policies on location – not just how it is delivered to its target market, but where. Depending upon the product, the nature of the market and the marketing mix, national coverage may be inappropriate: it may be promoted and made available in select geographical areas.

PROMOTION

The term *promotion* is used in marketing terminology in two separate senses. Here, it refers to those elements of the marketing mix which combine to make the target markets aware of the product and how to buy it. These elements include *advertising*, which is any form of communicating the availability, attributes and attractions of a product to its target markets, and for which the promoter pays. This distinction is important because another element is *public relations*, by which similar objectives are achieved by means of influencing the media to portray the product in a favourable fashion as part of their editorial coverage. The public are not always aware of the difference: it is not uncommon in a travel agency to hear a customer talk of having seen a resort 'advertised on the *Holiday Programme*' when in fact what was seen was an editorial feature. On most occasions it does not matter whether the public know whether they have been influenced by a paid-for advertisement or editorial coverage, except that it is useful to have a clear answer when marketing research is being carried out, and on those occasions when an editorial feature includes inaccuracies and consumers regard the tour operator as responsible.

A *sales promotion* is another element of generic 'promotion' but with a specific and particular meaning: it is a particular initiative, usually of a short-term nature, to boost sales. 'Buy one and get one free', 'Keep this voucher and get 50p off your next purchase' are examples. In cases like this, which are price-led promotions, the aim may be to increase sales at the expense of competitors, in the hope that some durable increase in market share will result. Sales promotion can also involve drawing attention to the product in ways other than mainstream advertising and public relations: taking a holiday exhibition around indoor shopping centres in target market areas, staffed by persons of suitable appearance and attired in the T-shirt livery of the resort or the holiday company in question, is an example. The aim in this case may not be to secure immediate sales, for holiday booking is a considered process involving all the family or friends, but to create a level of awareness which may influence the family discussion when it eventually takes place, especially if one member of the family has retained holiday literature given out by the staff of the exhibition.

Each industry has its own particular requirements from the discipline of marketing. This chapter has discussed the principles; in the next chapter, the practice of marketing in tourism is considered; some further concepts are introduced and there is a discussion of how different techniques can be usefully applied in different sectors of the industry.

Chapter **10**

Marketing tourism

The role of the marketeer

Marketing is the process of bringing product and customer together, and securing the purchase of the former by the latter at a satisfactory and mutually agreed price. The Chartered Institute of Marketing offers this formal definition: 'The management process responsible for identifying, anticipating and satisfying customer requirements profitably.' In everyday conversation, marketeers tend to use the term with two distinct meanings.

First, marketing is a philosophy of business which puts the customer at the centre. So, to take a real example from a few years ago: at a local authority management meeting, an accountant argues against the introduction of payment by credit card for the sale of orchestral concert tickets, because setting up the system would be messy and difficult to manage. The marketeer argues that the customer's convenience takes precedence, and that administrative systems should fit in with the needs of customers, rather than vice versa. In this sense, marketing is a philosophy of business: that the business orientates itself to satisfy and change with the needs of the customer. Failure to adapt to changing customer needs will lead in the long term to loss of competitive advantage. To practise the hospitality instinct is to adopt a marketing-led approach, in which the customer comes first and administrative convenience takes second place.

Secondly, marketing is the use of a mix of techniques to announce and deliver products in the market-place. Thus, it is possible to talk about 'marketing the orchestral season', meaning how the orchestral season is going to be promoted and the desired ticket sales secured. Although marketeers use the term to convey both meanings in common parlance, and the context of discussion makes it clear which meaning is being used, it is a somewhat risky business to use 'marketing' in the second sense too liberally since it is easily misunderstood by lay persons. Being asked by senior management to 'market' some product which is in trouble, and after due situational analysis, responding that there are no customers for the product and it should be killed off, can cause offence. After all, marketeers are supposed to market things, aren't they? It is worth remembering that the real meaning of marketing implies getting the product right as well as the promotional mix. Trying to sell a product for which there is no demand is a pointless exercise. Artists from the world of show business who fail to draw an audience commensurate with their expectations will invariably refer to 'poor publicity' by way of explanation. One theatre publicity manager, antagonised into argument by the attitude of a well-known but ageing celebrity who had attracted only a half-full house, caused offence to the performer by pointing out that he was past the height of his popularity and his ability to draw audiences was reducing. Technically speaking, the 'product' was over the hill.

The centrality of the brochure

The brochure is central in the whole process of tourism marketing. This is not just because the brochure is supposed to do the best possible job of depicting the product, whether it be a portfolio of holidays or a destination, in the best possible light. After all, the producers of virtually all consumer durables, plus many service industries such as banks and building societies, also produce printed material which offer facts and figures about their products, some background information, and carefully worded copy of a persuasive nature to convince prospective customers of the products' worth. The difference with brochures for tourist products is that for the potential customer, until the trip actually takes place, *the brochure is the embodiment of the product*. This is because the customer normally does not have the opportunity to inspect the tourist product before purchase, especially when the holiday or destination is overseas. When selling the dream, until the trip actually takes place, the brochure for all intents and purposes *is* the dream.

This has quite profound implications for brochure design. An examination of a range of brochures will reveal that holidays that are sold on price, such as basic mass-market packages to the Mediterranean, tend to make fairly basic use of photography. Straightforward pictures of people in swimsuits on beaches, on windsurfers, at nightclubs, convey the simple message that it is a sun, sea and fun experience that is on offer. Flashes may be applied to the front cover making offers which reinforce the price as the main product attribute and selling point, such as '10% off if booked by [date]' and 'Children go free'. By contrast, brochures for long-haul upmarket packages may make use of evocative photography and feature, if only superficially, local culture and heritage as attractions, while still maintaining the basic character of a holiday brochure. In the end, package holiday customers of whatever price bracket have been schooled by the industry and television feature programmes to focus on price. The prevailing trend toward independent travel, and cultural as opposed to material consumption, argues in favour of brochure producers seeking to place more emphasis on speaking to the heart rather than to the head through their selection of photography and copy. The annual scramble of holiday companies to bring out brochures whose prices are immediately discounted in pursuit of market share is in danger of becoming a barren pursuit, as the marketing and placement mechanisms of the industry increasingly depart from what has been suggested to be the 'real' purpose of holiday-taking, and as discussed in Chapter 6.

Marketing tourist products

Broadly speaking there are two different placement policies for marketing tourist products: the first applies primarily to overseas holidays, the second primarily to domestic destinations. The objective of each is to get the brochure into the hands of the potential customer so that it can do its selling job, and hopefully attract a booking. Overseas holidays are generally sold via the retail travel trade who 'rack' the brochures produced by the tour operators and who are paid a commission for selling the tour operators' products. Tour operators are naturally keen to ensure that the retailers are kept supplied with brochures and that their brochures are racked in a suitably conspicuous location. Sales representatives are employed to maintain this function and surveillance. Retail travel agents rely on their High Street locations to attract potential customers, who enter the shop either as a planned or casual visit, and collect brochures. Both tour operators and retailers raise public awareness of their services by advertising: the form of advertising generally regarded as the most effective at raising awareness is television. Memorable slogans such as 'Don't just book it, Thomas Cook it' sink into the human psyche if heard often enough and can be shown to be recalled and translated into purchasing behaviour.

TV campaigns tend to be launched at key times of the year when customers are known to be in the booking vein. This used to be primarily the Christmas and New Year period, when families were together and available to consider holiday options. Bumper issues of publications such as the *Radio Times* and *TV Times* would be full of holiday advertisements, and television holiday feature programmes provided support for the process. It is still a prime time for booking, but recent trends have spread the booking season. Heavy discounting at launch time during late summer the year before, and an increased tendency toward late booking encouraged by the availability of bargain offers have meant that companies have to spread their advertising efforts more widely.

The second placement policy, most commonly used by domestic destinations, does not involve travel agents or any other middleman: the destination advertises itself in publications and in places where potential customers are known to look; the advertisement makes an appeal to the customer to write or telephone for the brochure, which is sent as soon as possible after the customer contact has been received. The brochure draws attention to the positive product attributes of the destination and contains advertisements of hotels and other tourism businesses. To book, the customer telephones or writes to the accommodation of his or her choice and makes the booking directly. Most commonly, he or she will contact a number of establishments and receive their own individual brochures before making up his or her mind. He or she must then arrange transport to the destination, which for most people within their own country is an accustomed task: either driving there, booking a rail journey, or a coach. The distinction between these two placement policies, in the UK at any rate, remains basically intact. There have been diverse attempts to encourage UK destinations and tourism businesses to sell their products via the retail travel trade, but with mixed success. Mintel, drawing on British Tourist Authority data, suggest that 26 per cent of holidays taken in Britain in 1989 were booked as packages, compared with 58 per cent of overseas holidays. The domestic package market was made up principally of tours inclusive of coach or rail travel and operated by Golden Rail, Wallace Arnold and similar companies (1992, p. 2).

The public perceive travel agents as dealing in foreign rather than domestic holidays, and the travel agents themselves prefer to use their time to harvest the greater rewards and volumes offered by overseas products. One other problem of placing domestic holidays via the retail trade is that even if the public pick up a UK brochure in a travel agency, they are very likely to use the brochure to choose a hotel in their chosen resort and then book directly. A few years ago, the managing director of one holiday company justified his company's withdrawal from commissionable UK holidays by referring to research which showed that, of all those customers who had booked their holiday from his brochure, 80 per cent had collected the brochure from the travel agent and then booked directly. It was only during the 1991 recession in outbound holiday business from the UK that retail travel agencies, Thomas Cook as an example, actively advertised themselves as offering UK holidays for sale. In recent years, however, the actual techniques and technology available to marketeers has advanced considerably and this has begun to influence the way tourist products are promoted and placed. It is proposed to tackle this by offering a general discussion of the key marketing concepts and techniques involved.

Concepts and techniques for tourism marketing

The two product placement methods outlined above rely on advertising to communicate the availability of the products to their targeted publics, their ultimate aim being to get the brochure into the public's hands. We say ultimate, because two principal modes of advertising are used, only one of which aims to secure an immediate, active response from the public: this is known as *direct response advertising*, and forms part of a marketing technique which has been termed *direct marketing*. A direct response advertisement seeks exactly that: a response from the customer in the form of a telephone call, a letter, or a coupon returned, asking for more information (i.e. the brochure). Direct response is a mode which is more suited to certain kinds of advertising opportunities than others. Television advertising, for example, is by definition confined to a few seconds' duration. Conveying a telephone number, let alone an address to the watching public during that time places expectations on the customer which border on the unreasonable. Not everyone has a pen and paper to hand, or is able or willing to jump up and write down a telephone number at the behest of an advertiser. Newspapers however, and magazines such as the *Radio Times*, offer no such problem. The number and/or response address appears ready, in print, and can be used or transcribed directly from the page without pressure of time.

The second mode of advertising is more suited to television and occasions when a pen and paper are not readily to hand, such as posters on a railway station, and has a different objective: its purpose is to raise *awareness* of the product by creating memorable images, possibly accompanied by memorable music and a memorable phrase (called a *strap-line*), so that the product and its attributes are absorbed into the customer's mind. A campaign of such advertisements is described as an *awareness campaign* and the mode can be described as *exposure advertising*, because its purpose is to generate exposure for the product. A direct response is not generally sought; but it is hoped that when a direct response advertisement for the same product is seen, the increased awareness of the product may make a response more likely. The difference in purpose between the two modes is reflected in its different character and different choices of media. Television is a good vehicle for exposure, as are large posters on railway stations and adjacent to roads. A small airship bearing an advertisement for Fuji film, travelling over the beaches of resort areas, is also an example of exposure advertising: there is no immediate way of knowing the effect on sales of such a venture. But given the extent to which people at leisure are almost guaranteed to observe a low-flying object, particularly a seldom-seen sort of craft, it can be safely assumed that the number of people exposed to the name 'Fuji', at a time when they are in the business of buying films for cameras, is equal to the population of each beach overflown. Also, people may become more favourably disposed to the company because of the apparent trouble taken to create an interesting diversion on the beach, giving their children something to talk about and a cue for elderly relatives to relate memories of pre-war airships.

Large two-page advertisements in Sunday supplement magazines, known as *double-page spreads*, are another example of exposure advertising, but one which may include an element of direct response: an atmospheric photograph is accompanied by a modicum of copy and a telephone number for a brochure. By contrast, the advertisement whose sole function is to create direct response tends to be small in size, usually monochrome in quality, and appears normally in the *Classified* section of a newspaper or magazine. There will very often be a section of the Classified columns dedicated to holidays and travel. The idea is to inform rather than to convince: the reader looking at the Classified section has at least some specific purpose in mind, and in this case the objective is to put forward the minimum possible amount of persuasive copy with the objective of getting the brochure into the hands of the customer, which is when the real selling job begins.

Between 1975 and 1991, the volume of advertising to which the UK public is exposed doubled. Expenditure rose from £2.7bn. in 1975 to £5.4bn. in 1991, at constant 1985 prices (Waterson (ed.) 1992, p. 71). This came about in part as a response to the increasing wealth and consumerism of western society, and the increasingly segmented nature of consumer choice. It was made possible and further fuelled by a proliferation in the media advertising opportunities available. In 1970, there was one television channel in the UK which accepted advertising, and no commercial radio stations. There are now two terrestrial commercial TV channels, plus numerous opportunities to advertise on satellite TV channels and commercial radio. The number of magazines on sale in this period also proliferated, with most of these new titles targeted at specific age groups, such as those in their twenties; women and men separately, as specific gender groups; and segments of the public specifically as lifestyle peer groups or shared-interest groups.

The same period witnessed dramatic progress in computer technology whose two-fold contributions to the tourism industry have been computer reservation systems, plus the facility to retain and utilise, with great dexterity, the names and addresses and associated known information about customers as commercial assets: this is known as *database marketing*. The practice of retaining the names and addresses of customers and writing to them in their own homes, known as *direct mail*, a component of *direct marketing* as discussed earlier, is not new; what is new is the potential offered by computers to organise direct mail campaigns on a scale and of a complexity which would have been impossible without them. For example, consider the 25,000 names and addresses which were referred to in Chapter 8 as the sum total of direct responses to a UK resort area's advertising campaign in a particular year. It is possible to ascribe lifestyle and demographic classifications to the names and addresses by applying some of the techniques of psychographic analysis discussed in that chapter. If it is possible using bought-in knowledge to link, for example, the taking of short breaks with certain kinds of demographic and lifestyle groupings, those parts of the database which meet such criteria could be selected, and, of those, the ones living in certain geographical areas (say within two-and-a-half hours' drive of the resort) could be isolated by postcode. The resultant names and addresses are thus known to bear some of the characteristics of short-break takers, and are known by their previous behaviour, that is by writing in for the holiday guide, being aware of and interested in the resort. They could be good prospects for a direct mail campaign. Writing to them in their own homes, enclosing a leaflet and inviting a response requesting a full short breaks brochure, logically should elicit a good response.

This hypothetical example shows the power of database marketing to *target*, very precisely, potential business prospects. That is why, in a world of fast-segmenting markets, database marketing has grown so quickly. In comparison, other forms of advertising can be very inefficient. It is true that media such as newspapers can be selected by title and thus associated with certain kinds of reader, and terrestrial television advertising can be selected in the UK by ITV region thus targeting viewers in certain geographical areas: but in each case there is the inevitability that the advertiser is paying to communicate with people who are not within the target market for the product. This does not matter too much in the case of large generic products such as the holiday portfolio of a major tour operator, but it does matter to a niche operator which is launching a new magazine which is targeting, for example, English people with francophile interests. In such a case, the better option is to rent from a database owner names and addresses of people for whom francophile interests can be identified from previous purchasing behaviour. Such people may have a record of interest in food, buying car-ferry trips to France, subscribing to travel magazines, taking French language courses, or other pursuits which could indicate an interest in Gallic culture.

Commercial burglary?

Occasionally there is a need to stand back from technique and terminology and find an everyday concept which illuminates what marketeers are trying to do. A group of students was once shown an illustration of a close of houses as a stimulus for identifying all the various entry points available to the marketeer for establishing communication with the occupants inside. One student coined the phrase 'commercial burglary' to describe the process. In a very real sense, marketeers send large volumes of unsolicited messages into people's homes, with the intent of parting people from their cash. In that sense, a kind of burglary-by-consent is taking place. Entry points are numerous: down the TV aerial, through a radio set, through the satellite dish, through the letter box, via the telephone. Access through the letter box can take a variety of forms: advertising in a newspaper or magazine, feature articles in the same which result from effective public relations activity, direct mail letters, advertising in free newspapers, leaflets inserted into free newspapers, or delivery of leaflets covering all residences in whole postcode areas, a service known as household delivery and offered in the UK by the Royal Mail. A subtle and very effective way is word of mouth: most people talk to their friends and neighbours, and it is a commonly held belief in the industry that up to 50 per cent of holiday choices are principally influenced by personal recommendation.

Communicating with people in their homes has an added value in the marketing of tourist products. The holiday, as discussed before, is not an impulse purchase. It is generally taken in the company of other people, and they need to be consulted. Those others are usually family, and so the communication is best established when the family are present together. The marketeer's aim should be, first, that his or her brochure is present when the family discussion takes place; and secondly, that one or more members of the family argue the case for his or her product. Different members of the family have different requirements from a holiday and may represent those views in the form of different destination preferences. A powerful influence can be the views of children. For instance, television advertisements for theme parks may well be placed at viewing times which coincide with family meals or programmes which are known to enjoy a family audience. The children, attracted by the idea of a visit to the theme park, begin their own campaign of persuasion on the adults who may seek peace by making some form of commitment, however tenuous. The children can be relied upon to renew their campaign of persuasion at some opportune time, converting a tenuous commitment into an actual visit. If this all seems rather elementary, it is nevertheless the essence of effective marketing. The next chapter examines the English Seaside campaign as a case study and shows how the primary decision-takers within the campaign's target market tended to be female, and how the campaign was constructed to ensure coverage of this market, conveying the right message at the right time into the home.

Marketeers do not have to wait until the targeted customer is at home. Another strategy is to wait until they come out. Journeys to the shops, travel to work, visits to the cinema, all provide opportunities to establish communication. The High Street travel agent is a prime example of reliance on a shopping location as a means of reaching customers. Sales promotions in indoor shopping malls, even leaflets left on car windscreens, are means of accosting potential customers while they are out and about. Transport networks offer various advertising opportunities such as on underground trains (on the stations and actually on the trains), buses and large posters located adjacent to roads. The question which the marketeer needs to address is what elements of each are likely to be the most effective for his or her particular holiday product, that is, what to include in the *promotional mix*. The other dimension to this communication with the potential market is ensuring that the product is clearly identifiable from its competitors: indeed, in a world which is now sated with advertising messages, that it stands out at all. Having a product with a good differential advantage and positive attributes for its target market is one thing; communicating those values to the target market, so that they are recognised and ingested in the flicker of an eyelid as a train passes a poster on a railway station, is quite another. A useful solution to this challenge is the technique of *branding*.

What is a brand?

A *brand* is a product whose differential advantage and product attributes are recognised and agreed upon by consumers in the market-place. It is a product which has established itself and has acquired a reputation. The *brand image* is the set of beliefs about the brand that are held, and agreed upon, by customers. A brand can be recognised by a variety of features: Kelloggs' cornflakes are recognised by their name, and to a lesser extent by a packet illustration of a cockerel. Kentucky Fried Chicken is identified by an illustration of Colonel Sanders and is said to be identifiable by its individual taste. Coca-Cola relies on its name depicted in a particular way, and uses a certain shape of bottle to maintain its brand image. Some brands are known as generic brands: they achieve such a hold over consumers that a brand name becomes synonymous with the product itself, irrespective of who has manufactured it. Many people, will say, quite unconsciously, 'Pass the *sellotape*', or 'Who's got the *blu-tack*?'

Kotler and Armstrong offer this definition of a brand:

A name, term, sign, symbol, or design, or a combination of these, intended to identify the goods or services of one seller or group of sellers and to differentiate them from those of competitors. (1991 p. 668)

Not all products are suited to branding. Mass-market holiday products offering two weeks in the sun are difficult to differentiate from one another, and the tour-operating industry itself is too young for individual companies to have established authentic brand images. One exception of course is Thomas Cook, whose long pedigree conveys a brand image of good quality and reliability, underpinned by the foreign exchange side of its business which affords an image of institutional trustworthiness akin to that of a long-established bank.

Perhaps the British Airways subsidiary, British Airways Holidays, is showing some signs of emerging as a brand. The holding company has retained some of the institutional kudos of having once been a blue-chip government-owned national airline and has deliberately traded on this, as evidenced in advertising messages such as 'Fly the Flag'. Since its privatisation, it has achieved the image benefits of exceptional commercial success in comparison with competitors which remain in state hands, such as Air France. The company has invested continually in establishing a brand image as a leading airline offering the pinnacle of customer attention, as embodied in advertising messages such as 'We take good care of you' and 'The world's favourite airline'. When an umbrella brand such as ICI or British Airways has a positive brand image, subsidiary operations tend to benefit from the same image and it could be considered that the purchasing public perceive British Airways Holidays as differentially distinct from other operators.

It is important to note that time and expenditure, as well as the right product, are central to the process, and subtlety is important. Overt attempts to achieve generic status for brands will generally fail: 'Don't say brown, say Hovis', dating from the 1960s, scores on honesty for revealing the advertiser's intention, but is unlikely to work because of its didactic approach. 'The world's favourite airline' represents an attempt to foster brand dominance and is highly presumptuous, but at least avoids the flagrancy of a direct instruction. It is only when a product is new and genuinely unique in its sector that the rapid establishment of a brand image becomes possible. Rowntrees, during the 1970s, spotted a market opportunity for a chunky chocolate bar targeted at males, and the resultant product, the Yorkie bar, became one of the branding successes of the decade, sustained and enhanced by creative television advertising featuring masculine consumers such as lorry drivers.

It is difficult to create brand images for specific holiday products, but destinations offer much more scope. Iconography has a lot to do with this and many resort and city authorities will adopt the outline of a conspicuous landmark building as its logo, letterhead and advertising symbol. Recently constructed mass-market destinations find it difficult to do this because the built environment offers little in the way of identifiable icons, and the presence of a natural icon such as Sugar-loaf Mountain in Rio de Janeiro is a rarity. One successful destination branding exercise of recent years has been the award-winning English Riviera campaign which was launched by the Torbay Tourist Board in 1983 and has been published in the form of a case study (Travis Davis and Partners 1989), from which the following summary is drawn.

The situation facing the Board in 1982 was one of declining visitor volume to the three coastal resorts of Torquay, Paignton and Brixham, which are located around Torbay on the south Devon coast of England. The decline had been documented in a situational analysis, of which a tourism study completed in 1981 with the assistance of the ETB has been a central component. The findings included an identification of under-performance in attracting AB visitors, and under-performance in attracting visitors from the prosperous south-east of England, in comparison with competing resorts. A strategy was determined involving a range of marketing objectives, in which advertising was to play a major role. The advertising campaign was to create a stylish brand-image which would convey product attributes redolent of stylish Continental resorts; raise awareness of the resorts with the aim of attracting more first-time visitors; and increase the reach of the resorts into the AB market in the south-east of England. The result was a creative strategy which has become a celebrated success as an example of successful branding on a comparatively meagre budget: use was made of the term 'Riviera' which had been used in previous campaigns, with its connotations of Continental chic, warm climate and high quality; coupled with this was the use of a stylised palm tree as a visual symbol of the brand. Palm trees, though not indigenous to England, grow quite successfully in the mild climate of south Devon and south Cornwall and share with the term 'Riviera' similar exotic connotations. Year by year, the basic image has been adapted and updated so that while the core image of the brand remains intact and identifiable, its execution reflects the freshness of a new season and a new visit. The brand image was launched by employing it in direct-response advertisements in the national press and television listings magazines. It also featured in colour double-page spreads in selected magazines, offering inspirational exposure as well as a direct-response facility. The initial campaign also made use of ten-second television advertisements to raise awareness in selected ITV regions, but TV was replaced by posters in later campaigns because of the escalating cost of television as a medium. The question of the campaign's effectiveness will he discussed in the context of *marketing research*, in the next chapter.

Product image and the news media

In modern society, repeated images in the media and televised news can radically affect public perceptions of reality. The media attention which tourism and tourist destinations generate can be both a pleasure and a pain for those working in the field. The willingness of television companies to run programmes featuring resorts and holiday opportunities is matched by their willingness to run consumer complaint programmes on the same subject, washing diverse examples of dirty linen in the most public forum possible. This can lead to the public perception of a product being skewed with unwanted attributes, much in the way that a virus infects a computer programme. It is the nature of the news media, particularly in the popular press and the televised equivalent, to repeat established news themes with new material as it becomes available, thus reinforcing the suggested veracity of the theme adopted. An interesting example occurred when, in the UK early in the 1990s, one or two incidents of dogs inflicting injuries on children were highly publicised and led to the passing of the Dangerous Dogs Act. In the wake of the initial incidents, the media took to reporting new incidents as they occurred, but it soon became apparent that dogs injuring humans was such a frequent and daily occurrence that it ceased to be interesting. There is a paradox at the heart of this kind of news reporting: incidents are news, because they are exceptional and outside most people's experience, such as arriving on holiday to find the hotel half-built. Yet the repeated use of such a theme, that is reporting further incidents, conveys the implicit assumption that such incidents are by their nature commonplace or at the very least, part of a significant trend. Provided subsequent incidents

are *not* commonplace, further examples of a like kind maintain their news value and contribute to the creation of an elaborate, and widely believed, illusion.

It has to be said that there are no effective defences against this kind of media activity and the objective has to be one of damage limitation. A useful strategy is to regard the negative situation, however improbable, as an opportunity that can be turned to positive effect. Some situations can be so dire that it is difficult to see any positive benefit in them, and the well-worn slogan, 'Any publicity is good publicity' is seriously flawed. The kernel of truth contained in it is that media attention has its own value: to be talked about presents opportunities. Tactics need to be specific to the situation, but if the problem is genuine, it is best to admit it and be generous in recompense. If the problem is technical or disputed, such as bathing water quality, for the short term find an outside expert who will endorse a line that is favourable to your business, and for the long term join in the chorus which demands that the government assist water companies to rectify the problem quickly. To be seen to identify with the feelings of wronged customers is to demonstrate a level of concern which may attract approval.

Problems such as bathing water quality arise out of environmental factors which are usually outside the control of tourism organisations. Coastal resort destinations are not usually in charge of their own effluent disposal and are certainly unable to influence the discharge of effluent from passing ships. Tour operators are as much the victims of striking air-traffic controllers as their customers. Crime against tourists in Florida and acts of terrorism against tourists in Turkey are not inspired by the tourism industry itself. Such circumstances nevertheless are taken up by the media in the way described and can inflict damage, as in the reluctance of American tourists to visit the UK in the aftermath of the US air strikes launched against Libya from the UK in 1986.

The other kind of circumstance which causes embarrassment and negative media exposure is the one which is self-generated, where the company or destination pursues a policy that does not work. The celebrated Hoover free-flights promotion, which offered customers two free transatlantic air tickets in return for an expenditure on Hoover products of more than £100, is a case in point. The offer was too attractive, resulting in the company having to issue upwards of 220,000 free flights (Adburgham and Summers 1994). The equally damaging consequence was copious negative media exposure and threats of litigation from dissatisfied customers. One tactic which is often best avoided in the aftermath of negative publicity is a specific public relations effort to counter the negative image. As Ashworth and Voogd put it: 'A promotional message intended to counter an existing negative image runs the risk of inadvertently propagating that image' (1990, p. 114). For example, the use of weather statistics by some UK resorts to convince their publics that they enjoy a good climate is of limited usefulness, since it is well known that they all share the same unpredictable British climate and that there is a better alternative elsewhere in Europe, and, some say, at less cost. Drawing attention to climate simply serves to remind people that they may have a week of rain. It is only where there is some demonstrable difference, such as a climate which enables palm trees to grow as in Torbay, that such protestations can be taken seriously.

The three stages of marketing planning have been described in linear terms as situational analysis, strategy, plan, in that order. The process has to be sequential in that strategy is determined by situational knowledge, and detailed planning cannot take place unless some kind of strategy is clear. It may be more apt to consider this a cyclical process in that, except in the case of brand-new ventures, a marketing operation may already be up and running. Products, strategies and plans may already be in existence and when the marketing plan is updated, say on a yearly basis, the results of fresh research will be used to revise the situational analysis, with consequent impacts upon planning and, taking a longer-term perspective, upon strategy. In the next chapter we return to the beginning of the process and examine the role of research in the marketing process.

Chapter **11**

Finding the facts

Marketing research

Whether research should be considered at the beginning or the end of an exposition of the process of marketing is a moot point. The more common situation facing a person working in tourism is the inheritance of an up-and-running operation whose strategic direction needs to be reviewed at intervals, rather than a brand-new concept for which research may be conducted before any decisions are taken. The process of situational analysis as exemplified in the SWOT and PEST analyses discussed in Chapter 9 relies on information being available, and that is where marketing research is required. People being what they are, it is quite possible to conceive and launch a product without conducting proper research or ignoring the results of research. The effects of cutting corners in this way can range from the negligible to the disastrous, depending upon the particular situation and the level of innate intuitive knowledge possessed by the marketeer. It is as well at the outset to understand the difference between the terms *marketing research* and *market research*. The former is the whole process of gathering information for the situational analysis, including analysis of the effectiveness of existing marketing campaigns, lifestyle and geodemographic analysis of database information as described in Chapter 8, and information on the marketing environment. The latter, market research, is a specific technique within the field of marketing research.

Market research

Market research involves seeking and analysing information obtained directly from the customer by means of either personal or telephone interviews, or self-completed response forms. It can be applied to discrete sets of customers: either those who fall within the actual target market for the product, or those who represent what may be a potential market. The design of questionnaires, conducting of interviews and analysis of the data are subject to a range of procedural and analytical technicalities and it is not the purpose of this text to discuss these in detail, but to select some perspectives on the process as a means of gaining insights into its overal usefulness.

TOURISTS ARE RELATIVELY WILLING PARTICIPANTS IN THE MARKET RESEARCH PROCESS

Most readers will have had the experience of visiting a shopping centre or high street and glimpsing a forlorn individual, clipboard in hand, vainly attempting to stop shoppers in the hope of completing a market research interview. The typical shopper is under pressure of time, burdened with the carrying of goods, and generally unreceptive to invitations to spend several minutes answering questions. Visiting people in their homes or telephoning them in their homes at least gives the targeted interviewee the opportunity to offer the required information in more convivial surroundings, but the research costs increase dramatically and the interviewees may still regard the request as an intrusion. The activity of religious and pressure groups in the town centre and on the doorstep, and the use of the telephone to sell one-off purchases such as double glazing, have tended to cause many consumers automatically to adopt a dismissive attitude to unsolicited approaches.

By contrast, conducting market research amongst tourists can be an easier task. The tourist product is one of the most important consumer purchases and one in which great expectations are placed and from which, as we have seen in Chapter 6, significant psychological satisfactions result. Talking about their experiences comes naturally to tourists. This can apply equally when talking to a market researcher or when relating stories to family and friends. People actually *like* talking about their choice of holiday, why they chose it, what kind of people they are that they should have made such a choice, and so on. What is more, the delivery of the tourist product provides opportunities to conduct the research while the tourist is in a state of preparedness. Whether at ease in an aircraft seat, seated in a hotel bar lounge, or strolling along the seafront, the tourist is not only willing to talk but has time to do so. Compare this with the frenetic pace of the crowded shopping centre or high street.

SAMPLE SIZE IS IMPORTANT

Specialist texts on market research offer advice on the statistical usefulness of different *sample* sizes, but the general point to bear in mind is that a sample of at least 1,000 individuals is the minimum necessary if the results are to be useful. It should be borne in mind too that a sample of 1,000 individuals may represent a much greater *population*, since tourists generally travel in groups with other people. It is also as well to bear in mind that, depending on the nature of the research being undertaken, the value of the results may still be questionable if the information sought is only obtainable from a small proportion of the total sample. Holloway and Plant demonstrate this with a hypothetical example of market research to test satisfaction levels amongst holiday-makers renting apartments in Spain. The sample is of a good size, 2,000 individuals within the general population, but any information on self-catering apartments was of limited usefulness because only 25 of the total sample had taken holidays in Spain in this particular kind of accommodation (1992, p. 38).

If research is being undertaken at a destination, the actual interviewing would need to be undertaken in a variety of locations chosen for their likelihood of yielding a sample which includes the full range of visitors to the resort. For example, simply choosing a location adjacent to a funfair would be an unwise move, since the sample would in all likelihood include an exaggerated proportion of young families and teenagers. Choosing a location adjacent to bowling greens would be likely to have an opposite effect. Seasonality also needs to be taken into account since most resorts, across a range of countries, attract different types of visitor at different times of the year. During the peak season, families with school-age children can be expected to be the prevalent grouping, whereas older visitors and conference delegates are a feature of the shoulder months.

NOTE WHAT THEY DO, RATHER THAN WHAT THEY SAY

One of the traps in social research is to believe that people say what they think. Opinion pollsters spent the days following the 1992 UK General Election in self-critical mood, because their craft had seemed to predict a win by the Labour Party. In the event, the Conservatives won quite comfortably. One theory was that voters were being less than truthful with the researchers. It was suggested that certain sections of the electorate, for reasons of fashion, were not prepared to admit to their intention of voting Conservative. It is also a mistake to assume that people *know* what they think, or have an opinion on issues which hold no importance or interest for them. One teenager, on a day-trip to a resort and interviewed by a researcher on a beach, was asked for suggestions for improvement in the town. 'More cinemas' was the reply offered. It was only on moving to live and work in that resort, ten years later, that the erstwhile teenager actually visited a cinema there.

There is a role for *qualitative* research, that is, people's opinions and views on a range of issues, but to be useful the questionnaire must be designed carefully. The best approach is to adopt a mixed approach and decide on a range of issues to be tested *quantitatively*, that is, simple facts that can be counted, and to seek *qualitative* views at the same time, perhaps offering a multiple-choice range of qualitative options. So, if views on the need for cinema screens in a resort are sought, the question 'How many times do you visit the cinema in a year?' could be supplemented with a question along the lines of, 'Here is a list of leisure facilities: please indicate which you consider to be the most important in a resort.' The list of options would include the cinema and it would be possible to correlate the cinema-goers with those who regard the cinema as a resort facility of importance. Respondents could also be asked to indicate the extent to which they agree or disagree with statements on a scale of (say) –5 to +5. Open-ended questions can be quite dangerous in that respondents, having either no view or a hastily conceived opinion, are likely to answer in terms in which they are familiar. So, 'What new facilities would you like to see in the resort?' can be almost guaranteed to elicit replies based on predicable items which the respondent has seen elsewhere, such as miniature railways, Punch and Judy, flowerbeds, a leisure centre, and the like. These may be seized upon by laypeople as evidence for the maintenance of a traditional *status quo* to the detriment of progress. Market research should be used for testing, rather than supplying, new concepts.

SELF-COMPLETION AND ITS LIMITATIONS

There are problems in expecting respondents to provide market research data unassisted by an interviewer, in that there are limits to what the public can be expected to undertake by themselves. This became obvious on one occasion when market research questionnaires, left in a destination's hotel bedrooms for self-completion, revealed a remarkably high incidence of visitors in the AB socio-economic category. This defied common sense for the resort in question, whose primary market was C2, and differed greatly from the results of formal market research carried out in the same resort by interviewers during the same period. People, unassisted, do not always know whether to describe themselves as professional, managerial, clerical or whatever. Not only are boundaries between job fields increasingly blurred, but confusion sets in with the use of terminology. For many people, 'professional' means the opposite of 'amateur' and thus if they are in full-time paid work, they will describe themselves as 'professional'. The rules for self-completion are: keep it brief, keep it simple, and keep the data sought of a *quantitative* nature,

supplemented by *qualitative* data acquired through multiple-choice response format, perhaps with one open-ended 'Have you any further comments about your visit?' question to conclude.

Consumer culture

Consumer culture is the way in which purchasing behaviour is influenced by the beliefs, precepts, values, fashions and morals of a country. It is the way in which different countries, and different regions within those countries, exhibit different behaviour in their consumption habits. It is worthwhile to look at just how much the behaviour of the purchasing tourist can vary. American and Japanese tourists are familiar sights in European capitals, the complexity and extent of their photographic equipment equalling the zeal and determination with which they make the most of a long-haul travel opportunity. The apparent urgency with which they take in and photograph their surroundings with barely a pause before moving on to the next sightseeing stop is not without reason: annual leave entitlements in those countries are generally far lower than the European norm, and in the case of Japan the workplace culture exerts strong pressure to not take the full entitlement as leave. And yet, the amount actually spent on leisure by Americans and Japanese far exceeds European levels, as can be seen in Table 11.1. American and Japanese visitors are work hard, play hard tourists.

Table 11.1 International comparison of annual leave and leisure spending

Country	Annual leave (weeks)	Household leisure spending (%)	(ECU)
USA	2	9.9	1,089
Japan	2	10.3	1,134
France	5 to 6	7.4	645
Germany	5 to 6	9.1	896
UK	5 to 6	9.2	688
Italy	5 to 6	8.6	650

(*Source*: Éditions la Découverte 1992, p. 107)

Table 11.2 Income and holiday-taking in selected European countries, 1990

Country	Consumption per head (ECU)	% of population taking a holiday	% overseas holidays
Germany	10,141	68.2	73
France	9,977	59.1	36
Belgium	9,872	56.0	67
Netherlands	8,646	69.9	74
UK	8,440	61.0	41

(*Source*: Adapted from Economist Intelligence Unit 1992b, p. 6)

The countries of northern Europe are major generators of outbound tourism to the countries of southern Europe whose borders include a Mediterranean coastline, and the sight of Britons, Germans, Swedes, Finns and a host of other northern European nationalities crowding the airport of Palma de Mallorca at peak season times can easily lead to the conclusion that all are seeking the same thing in the same way. And yet, while consumption expenditure and the proportion of the population taking a main holiday differs slightly between these countries, there are very significant differences in the proportions taking their holidays at overseas as opposed to domestic destinations, as illustrated in Table 11.2.

As an example, consider the research needs of a tour operator whose intentions include marketing holidays in countries other than their country of origin. The proportion of the population which takes an overseas holiday is clearly one of the first and most significant statistics in defining the market for overseas holidays. Based on the data in the table above, Belgium and the Netherlands join Germany as apparently strong outbound markets. France and the UK look distinctly weak. However, Belgium and the Netherlands are small countries, whereas France and the UK are large: 41 per cent of 57 million people is a larger number than 74 per cent of 15 million. Notwithstanding this, the larger market in the UK or France is 'diluted' in a large population and is likely to be more expensive to segment and reach; set against that is the fact that small countries, such as the Benelux countries and Scandinavia, tend to have well-developed home-grown tour operators and distribution mechanisms creating an operating environment in

which it may be difficult for an incomer to establish a foothold and gain market share. Also, the actual form taken by outbound tourism is also relevant: 71 per cent of the UK outbound vacation tourism market books packages involving travel by air. This is only exceeded by the Finns, at 77 per cent (Economist Intelligence Unit 1992b). The mode of purchase is also significant: UK and Scandinavian holiday-makers tend to use travel agents extensively, but in other countries for whom travel by car and train to southern Europe is relatively easy, independent booking is much more prevalent. These facts merely scratch the surface of comparative consumer culture across European countries. The art of desk research is to dig deep into the available reference material and create a comparative picture which relates and contrasts specific consumer behavioural characteristics to specific products.

The notion of 'culture' is discussed in Chapter 7 and although the mass-market holiday business has subjected itself to a commoditisation process which resists individual cultural adaptations, qualitative views on issues such as the environment may influence holiday purchasing habits, if they take hold on the population in the same way as, for example, concerns over bathing water purity appear to have done. Concern over the deleterious effect of mass tourism on fragile environments is well aired in liberal and academic circles, but to date there is not a great deal of evidence that actual tourist consumption has been greatly influenced by such concerns. Table 11.3 shows that levels of concern about the negative impact of tourism on environments differ significantly from country to country. It should be borne in mind that this data refers to levels of concern, rather than intentions to modify tourist behaviour because of those concerns.

Table 11.3 Views on mass tourism as an environmental hazard, 1991

Country	No threat (%)	Large threat (%)
UK	33	6
Italy	27	5
Spain	23	10
Netherlands	22	6
France	21	7
Germany	10	11

(*Source*: **Economist Intelligence Unit 1992b, p. 9**)

Concern over the effect of tourism on the environment is predictably higher in the country regarded as the most environmentally conscious (Germany), which also happens to be the largest outbound market. The concern is shared with Spain, where concerns may arise from having had more experience than others of the effects of rapid tourism development. The two nations which tend to see tourism as a lesser threat are the UK and Italy which are reputed to view the progress-versus-environment drama with comparative unconcern. The technical issue at stake to the marketeer of tourism is the extent to which such cultural concerns translate into buying habits. The paradox is that tourists who are most concerned about fragile environments are likely to be the very ones who go to visit them. Krippendorf advocates a rediscovery of traditional resorts as a part-solution to this problem (1987, p. 126). Tourists who aspire to be authentically green could do worse than examine the merits of staying at home, or confining their visits to those locations which are already fully adapted to the needs of tourists, such as Benidorm and Blackpool. Whether the authentically green tourist would be prepared for the fashionability implications of such a choice is another matter.

The effectiveness of advertising

It has always been one of the charms of the advertising business that, while everybody knows advertising 'works', nobody ever knows for sure what makes it work. (Chisnall 1992, p. 235)

This sentiment has been expressed in other ways, for example by the company director who, in legend, claimed to know that the *Pareto principle* applied to his advertising efforts: that 20 per cent of his advertising produced 80 per cent of the business. The trouble was, he did not know which 20 per cent it was. There are occasions when it is not an easy task to determine how advertising achieves its effectiveness and to this extent, advertising is an art rather than a science. The creative stategies behind some of the great *exposure advertising* campaigns of recent years, such as Benson & Hedges, Silk Cut, Milk Tray and Yorkie, have relied on ambitious images and dramas to raise awareness of the products they are designed to promote. The campaigns are regarded as being good because they are ingenious and original, attracting approval and discussion in their own right, thereby giving rise to the notion that they 'work'. By contrast, some companies whose branded products are in the front line of a war for market share with equally well-established and branded competitors, have tended to favour campaigns whose creative strategies are rather predictable and follow a recognised formula. For example, television exposure advertising during the 1980s for cornflakes, Coca-Cola and Pepsi, tended to rely on energetic scenes involving young attractive people, beaches and water, accompanied by an equally energetic song whose lyrics extolled the virtues of the product in question.

In fact, pessimism regarding the assessment of the effectiveness of advertising is largely unwarranted because much can be done to monitor its effects on its intended target groups. Such data is central to the process of marketing research because no marketeer wants to spend money on advertising which does not work; and the collection of this data can sometimes be coupled with market research. One of the easiest forms of advertising to monitor is *direct response*. If an advertisement is placed in a publication, and a code specific to that particular advertisement is affixed to the response address, interested customers give the code in their response and the cost of the advertisement can be divided by the number of responses, giving a *cost per response*. Where the customer has the option of responding via a telephone line, the recorded message will invariably include a request to specify the publication in which the advertisement was seen, and its date. What the marketeer aims for is a low cost per response, and thus will use the data in selecting media for future campaigns.

Getting a good response rate is of course not the same as getting actual bookings: the *conversion rate* of responses into bookings needs to be known. Where the organisation placing the advertisements is the same organisation that takes the bookings, then there is no problem and each respondent who books has that data entered into his or her customer profile. It is quite possible for some publications to offer a high rate of response but a low conversion rate. Magazines catering for people with an interest in cars have been known to compete with one another for advertising revenues on the basis of the proportion of their readers whom they can prove, from research, actually *buy cars*. Apparently some people buy car magazines because they like looking at pictures of cars and reading about them; they are dreamers, rather than buyers. If the chosen mode of advertising is *direct mail*, as opposed to a direct response advertisement, the response coupon enclosed within the mailshot will be similarly coded: one way of doing this is to ensure that the address label sent to the addressee, which has come from a computer database and has a code printed on it, is located on the reverse side of the coupon so that the response can be keyed directly into the database and added to the customer's profile.

This merging of the marketing and purchasing functions has been made possible by developments in computer technology which occurred in the 1980s and has led, for example, to theatres operating an integral box office and mailing list. New customers are automatically added to the mailing list on booking and can expect to receive news of forthcoming productions, provided the formality of seeking their permission has been satisfied in accordance with the requirements of the Data Protection Act (1984). Technology is currently providing the means for a further merging of the marketing and sales functions through the convergence of televisual, computer and telephone technologies. This has been termed a 'multimedia' revolution and is being further fuelled by the potential offered by fibre-optic cables, which have attracted the media label of the 'electronic superhighway'. The impact of computer reservations systems in the travel and tourism industry has been an early manifestation of the multimedia revolution.

Where the organisation taking the booking is different from the one promoting the product, as is generally the case with destination brochures where the recipient books accommodation directly from a selection advertised in the brochure, there is no immediately available means of assessing conversion rate. Research has to be carried out if this information is required. A sample of respondents from the database can be contacted at the end of the season and asked if they actually booked a holiday as a result of receiving the brochure. A postal approach with an incentive to respond, such as entry into a Prize Draw, is one method; telephoning is more expensive but better because it offers greater accuracy. Using the postal method risks weighting the figures because the respondents who actually send in a reply are likely to be the ones with a greater interest in the resort, and consequently the ones most likely to have booked a holiday.

Exposure advertising is a more difficult case to monitor. It is here that the creativity of the advertiser enjoys its widest scope. Exotic dramas on the television and cinema screens, or on poster sites, demand no direct response. The requirement is that the potential customer simply be influenced. *Tracking studies* are the method used to monitor their effectiveness. These involve researchers showing visuals of the images and words used in the advertisements to a sample of subjects and noting the extent to which the juxtaposition of words and images, and the vital link with the product, are recalled. A typical scenario may involve some *pretesting* of the images and words which it is proposed to use.

These may be shown to subjects before the advertising campaign. The subjects would later be tested on their recall. If the combination of images, words and music is suitably memorable, then the recall rate should be good. At the same time, if the subject of the proposed campaign is an existing product or brand, research may be carried out within specific population samples to pretest levels of awareness of the brand. After the launch of the campaign, the *tracking studies* proper begin. Research is carried out within population samples which match those used during the pretest period and typically may first test awareness of the brand or product using the same methods as were employed during the pretest phase. If awareness has risen, then that *may* be a consequence of the campaign. Secondly, the same subjects may be shown visuals along the same lines as those used in the pretesting undertaken amongst selected individuals, and may be asked questions to determine the extent to which they can link the recent campaign with the product or brand in question. Of course, like market research, tracking studies are expensive in that it involves several minutes' discussion between subject and interviewer. Unlike market research, where limited self-completion of questionnaires is an option, tracking studies require the personal attention of trained interviewers. For that reason it makes economic sense to combine market research with tracking studies.

A point which is worth understanding about exposure advertising is that creativity does not necessarily equal effectiveness. Art directors of advertising agencies have a natural interest in producing advertisements which stand up well to scrutiny by their creative peers, but there is an ever-present danger that the sheer quality of the advertisement usurps the product. One televised example from the 1980s featured a drawing room social gathering in which the late Leonard Rossiter, a comedy actor of considerable ability, served a glass of vermouth to Joan Collins. The serving of the drink went awry as the vermouth ended up, not in the glass, but down Miss Collins' cleavage. As an example of comic action it was excellent and was enjoyed and talked about by many, but as an advertisement for the brand of vermouth, it was held to have been less successful.

Audiences remembered Mr Rossiter, Miss Collins and the incident, but did not remember the product. Of those who remembered that the drink was vermouth, many thought it was Martini; in fact, it was Cinzano. The brand had been upstaged by its own advertisement. 'Safe choice' advertisements involving young people leaping around on beaches accompanied by an inspiring if insistent song may not break creative frontiers, but are known to get their message across effectively.

One method of pretesting advertising campaigns which can be used in addition to or instead of using individual subjects is the *focus group*. This is a technique which has broader application in the marketing process since it also has a vital function in new product development, or determining the perceptions of the attributes of existing products. It involves bringing together a group of people who are considered to represent the target market for the product: for example, a company manufacturing toys for very young children would assemble a group of 20 or 30 young parents to represent the target market. Where the target market is very broad, it may be necessary to assemble different groups representing different segments. For example, bank accounts are held by around 85 per cent of the adult population, but the expectations and needs of those customers necessarily differ widely in terms of their lifestage, income and lifestyle. Bringing them all together in one group would not provide insights into the specific requirements of each segment. The usefulness of the focus group is that, unlike a response made by one individual to a researcher, group dynamics come into play and group perceptions become evident. Humans are social animals, and in the real world talk to their family, friends and neighbours and their perceptions of the world around them are to some extent based on what the 'group view' is on any particular subject. Of course, this does not mean that the 'group view' is more rational than the individual view; frequently, this may not be the case (see Chapter 14 on fads and fashions).

People talking in a relaxed setting in group format tend to like to establish a degree of common ground with one another, and that may involve agreeing on a commonly mentioned sterotypical perception which may or may not correspond with reality. For example, being able to agree that foreign holidays are cheaper than the domestic equivalent may defy logic to some extent, but is a view which is commonly believed and widely shared in conversation. It is precisely this sort of information which a focus group can yield. Whether it is accurate or not is of secondary interest; the fact that the view is held is the primary point. The Midland Bank actually based a television advertising campaign around staged extracts from focus group discussions. The supposed 'members of the public' were seated on a settee bearing the bank's logo in a variety of indoor and outdoor locations, and articulated their requirements of a bank and its services. Each advertisement showed responses from three very different types of customer, the action being so designed that not only was it implied that the bank was responsive to these various needs, but that the process of listening itself should be regarded by potential customers as a differential advantage over its competitors. It echoed an earlier campaign for some years previously in which the Midland had declared itself to be 'the listening bank'.

Monitoring effectiveness: two examples

The English Riviera campaign, discussed in the last chapter, achieved award-winning national recognition but owing to budget limitations, was not subjected to tracking studies to determine the extent to which it had succeeded in raising brand awareness amongst its target markets. But the awareness campaign supported a direct response campaign the results of which were measurable. Table 11.4 shows the increase in brochure responses and the consequent decrease in cost per response over the first few years of the campaign. It can be tentatively concluded that this represents raised awareness amongst the public, but it should be treated with caution. For one thing, there is no mention of conversion rates of brochure responses into bookings, which is the statistic that would reveal the real commercial success of the campaign; secondly, there may have been other mechanisms at work which

contributed to the increase. A researcher would wish to see brochure response data from other comparable resorts over the same time period in order to determine whether or not there was an underlying trend that affected the response rate.

Table 11.4   English Riviera campaign: brochure responses

Years	Responses (%)	Cost per response (%)
1981/82	100	100
1982/83	127	56
1986/87	143	70

(*Source*: **Travis Davis and Partners 1989**)

Another example of an advertising campaign conceived to promote a UK domestic seaside product, and which involved mixed use of exposure advertising and direct response, was the English Seaside campaign. This campaign was conceived by the ETB in partnership with 36 seaside resorts, and ran for the first time in the run-up to the 1992 holiday season. The advertising agency appointed to the account was Travis Dale (formerly Travis Davis) and Partners, whose previous successes had included the English Riviera campaign. The campaign's objectives, progress and results were reported in Travis (1992) and it is this account which is a principal source for the summary that follows.

A decline in domestic seaside holiday business which began at the beginning of the 1980s appeared to bottom out in 1988. This was as a result of apparent consumer dissatisfaction with the Spanish costas, generated by well-publicised and apparently endemic airport delays, bad behaviour by compatriots, and a jaded product; UK holiday business to Spain began to decline. At the same time, an opportunity was present: the family formation group, that is young couples with young children, was growing demographically as a proportion of the population and it was known that the financial pressures occasioned by the arrival of children and the problems involved in taking them abroad caused parents to reappraise their holiday-taking habits and examine domestic opportunities. It was also considered that many of these young couples would have been raised on foreign holidays and would have a perception of the English seaside influenced more by negative media images than by their own personal experience. A campaign to target this market would need to build a more positive image for seaside resorts, and at the same time convey a direct message to parents with children, in particular to the C1C2 socio-economic groups who were known from resort research to be a primary family market for the domestic seaside.

This campaign was to be essentially an awareness campaign whose core was a series of television advertisements of 30-second and 10-second duration, screened in selected ITV regions during the Christmas/New Year booking period of 1991–92, and again during March 1992. The screening schedule took into account the need for the advertisements to be seen by children as well as parents, so that the persuasive influence of the child could be brought to bear on the adult decision-makers. It was also noted that the female partner in the family was known to have more influence than the male in determining holiday-making decisions. This was apparent from the research conducted for the ETB in 1991 to ascertain the features of the market segments identified (as discussed in Chapter 8). This showed that one of the predominant characteristics in the profile of the holiday decision-maker in the 'Bucket and spade' segment was being female (MEW Research 1992). As an issue in itself, the significant power of the female partner within the power structures of families in England (in contrast with Scotland and Ireland) and other countries who share Anglo-Saxon cultural characteristics (such as the USA, Canada, Australia and New Zealand), is a theme which has attracted the attention of social geographers (see Johnston 1991, p. 89). Marketeers of tourist products would do well to pay more attention to this, both in terms of the power of the female partner in her own right, and the power of the children which will often be exercised through her. The use of *focus groups* has confirmed that the satisfaction of the young children was of primary importance in determining holiday choice: if the children were happy, the parents were happy. The economic environment was also favourable: a recession was having its effect on spending patterns and more than half of C1C2 families were planning to cut back on holiday spending in 1992, and this was thought to enhance the opportunity of winning business away from Mediterranean alternatives.

With all this in mind, the campaign was conceived and produced. Featuring a father and two young children, but (significantly) no mother, the television advertisement showed the three perambulating along a sandy beach on a sequence of days. The children were seen in the early stages to be the initiators of activity, urging the father to hurry up and participate in the active opportunities presented by the holiday. During the course of the holiday, the father not only loosens up but becomes more active himself, eventually exceeding the level of activity of the children by doing cartwheels along the beach. The scenario is surreal rather than real, but indicating to the absent (watching) mother, and accompanying children who can identify with the children in the advertisement, that there is more fun potential at the English seaside than the soporific heat and non-tidal beaches of the Mediterranean can offer. A parallel message is the suggestion that such an environment with its added activity potential can achieve a common objective for mother and child, that is the loosening up and active reintegration of the father into family life. The advertisement was also sufficiently non-threatening to male viewers: although the projected end result was a level of activity which on day one is viewed by the father in the advertisement with some weariness, his surreal awakening is accompanied by the incentive of meeting the children's expectations, which as research has shown was a prime parental concern. The brand name chosen was simply 'The Seaside' and the *strap-line*, spoken by a child as a *voice-over* at the end of the advertisement, was 'Where grown-ups grow younger by the day'. One of the original options for the strap-line was 'Where grown-ups do as they're told', but not all seaside resorts offer a product which is primarily family-orientated – Eastbourne and Worthing are examples – and so it was considered to be too limiting to target children as the sole primary market.

The effectiveness of the English Seaside campaign was monitored through tracking studies undertaken by an independent research company which tested awareness, perceptions and holiday intentions amongst the C1C2 parents in the target market. The method and results as reported by Travis (1992) involved the establishment of two control groups: one consisting of all adults in the country, and another of C1C2 parents in ITV areas where the advertisement had not been screened. The research included the extent to which respondents agreed with the proposition that at the English seaside, 'there is so much to see and do', that the English seaside is 'ideal for family holidays' and that 'families can have real fun'. In each case, a sample of respondents living in ITV regions which had been exposed to the campaign were far more likely to agree with these propositions than the samples interviewed during the pre-campaign research in the same regions. This improvement in awareness and perception can be attributed to the effect of the campaign in that the control groups showed no change in attitude between the pre-campaign and post-campaign research.

The final round of tracking studies completed in April 1992 also asked whether respondents had taken, booked or planned English seaside holidays: results showed that respondents exposed to the campaign were 60 per cent more likely to have booked or be definitely intending to book, in comparison with non-campaign areas. The English Seaside campaign continued for the 1993 season and was claimed by the ETB's Assistant Director of Marketing, quoted in a trade journal, to have created £22m. worth of extra business for domestic seaside resorts (*Marketing Week* 1993). The main subject of that article was the government's proposed cuts in the ETB's budget, to be reduced by 40 per cent from its 1993/94 budget of £13.9m. over three years, and this on top of a cut of £1.5m. from its 1992/93 level. Comment was made on the detrimental effect this was likely to have on ventures such as the English Seaside campaign. As discussed in Chapter 1, government at national or municipal level can be ambivalent about tourism, even in the face of compelling economic arguments.

Evaluating the English Seaside campaign as a whole, we can see that it has a number of virtues: first, it was an agreed partnership between the national tourist board and a large number of resorts. The fragmented nature of the tourism industry can be a weakness, but on this occasion a consensual yet incisive approach was agreed. Secondly, it was a targeted campaign: it represented a resolute departure from the notion that domestic seaside resorts offer 'something for everyone', which arguably they do not. A specific socio-economic and lifestage group was identified and the campaign strategy was carefully conceived to address that group. Thirdly, it was an exercise in *rebranding*. In its use of a common logo and the conveyance of product attributes of relaxation and rebirth for male parents, and varied fun for children, it was a first step in creating a brand image for the 'Seaside' as a generic concept.

Facts, figures and the news media

It is worth concluding this chapter with some observations on the way in which the results of marketing research into tourism can be applied with positive effect in public relations. The media have an insatiable hunger for facts and statistics, because of the potential they offer for building stories. Tourism is at a considerable advantage compared with other industries in attracting the attention of the media, because it is perceived as a subject of communal concern and one for which public bodies bear a share of the responsibility. It is connected with the self-esteem of the community: if people come to visit, then there must be something to see and experience and by inference the place must be worth living in; more ominously, it may perhaps be perceived to incur a range of costs as well as benefits, giving rise to conflict – particularly in established resort areas.

In the early stages of a destination's evolution, any tourism news is good news and even minor triumphs can attract very positive and uncritical media coverage. The growth of post-industrial cities as tourist destinations has owed much to the positive coverage of local news media, which tends to reflect on and be enjoyed by the politicians associated with it, thus securing extended support. In post-mature destinations where the views of conservative retired residents tend toward hostility, and newer interests such as residential homes compete with tourism for locations, buildings and planning permissions, the ambivalences and tensions within the community will also be reflected in the local media.

Whatever the situation, it is arguably not only useful but important to use the results of marketing research as a vehicle for effective public relations. This does not just apply to resort marketing offices who need to direct their best efforts to ensuring that the value and importance of tourism in the local economy are known and understood. It applies also to individual undertakings such as hotels, visitor attractions and carriers. These, although privately operated, are often viewed with some proprietorial regard by the local community and news stories about how they are performing are of interest. This need not involve releasing commercially confidential information: talk of volumes need not involve divulging profit margins, and increases or decreases can be just as readily expressed in percentages as in absolute figures. Creating positive news stories through the media can also be powerfully instrumental in fashioning favourable attitudes within publicly elected bodies. Politicians such as government ministers and local councillors read the papers just like everyone else, and being in the image business themselves are, if anything, more likely to react positively or negatively to what they read than is the average voter.

Although the media more often than not set out to reflect opinion rather than mould it, perceptions of tourism within a community, as a consequence of media exposure, can become uncritical to the point of becoming hegemonic. For example, such can be the body of support that builds up behind a major city's bid to stage an international event that persons putting forward alternative views can find themselves in trouble. There was the case of a senior academic who was concerned about what he regarded as the disadvantages of a 'prestige project' which was proposed for the city in which his university was located. He wrote a scholarly letter to a national newspaper outlining his concerns, after which he was said to have been 'carpeted' by his Vice-Chancellor and warned against any further publication of his views (Kirsch 1994). Similarly, championing tourism in a post-mature resort where conflicting interests are powerful can be an exciting if dangerous game. Researching the facts

and making them known, accompanied by gallons of crystal-clear logic, can win supporters but can also be expected to produce adverse reactions from individuals and groups whose personal interests do not coincide with those of the tourism industry.

Epilogue: applying common sense

Concluding this chapter presents an opportunity to review some essential points regarding the marketing function as examined in this and the preceding three chapters, and to draw conclusions which coincide with the thesis that competitive advantage is to be had through the practice of the Hospitality Instinct.

First, practising the instinct involves complementing intuition with information. Reliance on logic is not the preferred *modus operandi* of all employees, and Handy presents a convincing argument that the kind of people who find themselves in leading roles in an organisation are often those who rely heavily on impression rather than on hard information (1991a, pp. 42–4). Such people may frequently be tempted to make marketing decisions based on 'hunches' rather than undertake painstaking research. However, just as marketing research data if unaccompanied by an intuitive feel for customer service can lead to erroneous strategies, impressions can be faulty if untutored by research data. As an example, a range of quality suits launched by the makers of Levi jeans proved unsuccessful, and were withdrawn from the market. The manager responsible for the development had proceeded with the launch, in spite of a clear indication from a focus group that prospective customers may be ambivalent about buying a suit bearing the Levi label (WGBH Educational Foundation 1981). To acquire the hospitality instinct involves instinctively *asking questions*, rather than drawing intuitive conclusions which may be premature.

Secondly, the principles of marketing are relevant both to large and small businesses. Middleton observed that marketing planning 'is no more than a logical thought process *in which all businesses have to engage to some extent*' (1988, p. 128, author's emphasis). Many tourism businesses are small scale and run by owner-operators who may lack the professional marketing expertise which is more commonly found in larger organisations. Nevertheless, as an 'application of common sense' (Middleton 1988, p. 128), the basic principles of marketing are capable of being mastered by businesspeople, and their implementation can produce significant business improvements for small-scale tourism under-takings. An example is the Polurrian Hotel, Cornwall, whose 1986–88 marketing campaign led to the acquisition of an England for Excellence Marketing Award; this has been documented as a written case study (Lazenby 1989).

Thirdly, practising the instinct demands determination as well as application. Robert Heller, former journalist and now one of the UK's foremost management writers, was once interviewed for the magazine *Marketing*. Discussing his prolific output of books and his evolving thoughts and beliefs on specific marketing issues, he was finally confronted with the basic question, 'So can the British get better at marketing?' His reply was as basic as the question, and disarmingly simple:

The more I think about it, the more I am sure that it is simply a question of unremitting application and not leaving things to chance. It's a cliché, but it's about doing things properly. That means achieving results. You must have objectives and measure whether it is possible to achieve them – and then try and do it. (Davidson 1989)

When 'doing things properly' is the accepted and instinctive *modus operandi* of an organisation, this communicates itself to the customer and the result is competitive advantage. The next chapter examines the attempts of two destinations at 'doing things' and compares and contrasts their culture, methods and results.

Chapter 12

Resorts at the turning-point: two case studies

Degrees of success

Whether the progress of the resort life cycle, as described in Chapter 4, takes 20 years (as in the case of the Spanish costas) or 200 years (as in the case of Scarborough) before the resort reaches maturity, destinations eventually reach the point where turning-point decisions are necessary. The examples which follow are of two medium-sized UK coastal resorts. They are not intended to be exhaustive case studies, nor are they put forward as examples of best or worst practice; rather, they represent an attempt to chart progress and offer an indication of the way in which the turning-point has been handled. The underlying assumption is that the self-perception of the communities involved has a salient influence on decisions taken, and that this self-perception communicates itself through the media to form an image which, in its turn, has a determining influence on decision-taking. In this sense, turning-point decisions 'happen' rather than being made. First, we consider the overall contexts in which the two resorts operate.

The English seaside

The UK seaside tourism business started to contract from the mid-1970s onwards, heralding what has been termed the *decline* phase of the resort life cycle (see also Chapter 4). This demanded that *turning-point decisions* be made: investment to upgrade the product, and remarketing of the product to specific markets which had growth potential. Some resorts such as Brighton and Bournemouth invested in conference facilities to boost business tourism; others, such as Rhyl and Bridlington, in new

facilities for family holidays. Remarketing was also required and the English Riviera campaign (see Chapters 10 and 11) and the English Seaside advertising campaign (see Chapter 11) were both attempts at awareness-raising and rebranding.

The essential problem of the domestic seaside is one of a spiral of decline in which contracting business inhibits investment, which in turn contributes to the continued deterioration of the product and a continued contraction in business. The larger resorts such as Bournemouth, Blackpool and Scarborough, where the tourism industry is comparatively strong in terms of access to private capital, and possesses significant political and economic strength within the local community, fared better than the medium-sized and smaller resorts where the local authority was the main, and probably only, large investor. Consultants commissioned by the ETB (Middleton 1991) recognised the problem that faced these smaller resorts and identified the need to break the spiral of decline. Recognising that government curbs on local authority capital spending had made it all but impossible for councils to fulfil their responsibility for capital investment, they suggested that vigorous marketing of existing products should be undertaken in order to secure improvements in business, which in turn would create a more credible climate for attracting private investment (Middleton 1991).

This was a well-reasoned argument because, in spite of the decay in the physical fabric of these resorts, coupled with a decline in business and the portrayal of domestic seaside holidays by the media as unfashionable if not extinct, seaside holidays had held their position within an admittedly declining domestic tourism market, as Table 12.1 shows.

Table 12.1 The seaside as an element of domestic (English) holiday tourism

	1978	1985	1990
Nights	135m. (45%)	115m. (42%)	102m. (46%)
Trips	38%	33%	39%
Spend	£875m. (52%)	£1,475m. (48%)	£2,885m. (52%)

(*Source*: English Tourist Board *Shorelines* 1992)

This is hardly a picture of a product for which demand has expired. More vigorous marketing of existing products could well deliver the increased business which would create a credible climate for investment. There now follows a select recent history of two medium-sized English coastal resort areas which share some product similarities in terms of size and primary markets, but for which geographical location and marketing environment – political, economic, social and technological factors – are significantly different.

The political context

It is not the purpose of this text to analyse policies on party-political lines, but if the suggestion outlined in Chapter 1 is correct, that local governments bear pivotal responsibility for the development and maintenance of a tourist economy in a destination, then the health or otherwise of local government is germane to an analysis of a resort's progress. When the present government came to power in 1979, a major component of the new economic policy was the application of restraints to public spending. That included spending by local authorities, some 60 per cent of which came from central government funds in the form of the rate support grant (RSG). Resort tourism officers were already, in 1980, becoming preoccupied with the need to maintain resort services in a climate of increasing financial restraint. The value for money offered by resort facilities became the subject of increasing scrutiny, and provided an opportunity for individuals and

groups within the resort, whose personal interests did not coincide with tourism, to question the appropriateness of this expenditure. Additionally, many resorts had found themselves merged with large rural areas as a consequence of the local government reorganisation of 1974, and representatives from the non-resort areas, quite understandably, wished to see capital and revenue expenditure spread equitably.

In a remarkably prophetic article, Burgess (1980) criticised the replacement of the RSG by a block grant which would be allocated by the Secretary of State in accordance with a ministerial assessment of what particular local authorities needed to spend, and should spend. This was seen as undermining the accountability of locally elected councillors, and by implication it would be detrimental to the quality of decisions taken at local level:

The legitimacy of local government springs from two sources, one electoral, the other financial. Because they are elected, local councillors can be called to account for what they do . . . They do not have to refer the decision upwards to an area, regional or national tier of administration . . . There is a healthy tension between the services which people demand and what they are prepared to pay. To take away either election or taxing powers would reduce this independence considerably. (Burgess 1980)

The erosion of the powers of elected councils would also have some effect on the quality of people who were prepared to stand for election, thereby discouraging, perhaps, some of the very people whom the government during the following decade sought to bring into the sphere of public decision-making by appointment to the boards of quangos.

Burgess's fears were realised by the passing through Parliament of the Local Government Planning and Land (No. 2) Bill, but he can hardly have thought of the extent to which the erosion of local authority powers would continue. There followed, during the 1980s, the imposition of penalties on local authorities which exceeded the Secretary of State's spending assessment (the so-called rate-capping), severe restrictions on capital spending and limitations on the extent to which capital receipts could be applied, and the introduction of compulsory competitive tendering for a range of local authority services. The consequence of these measures was to channel much of the creativity of local councils and their staffs into introspective activity as they struggled to cope with the increasing legal and financial limitations that central government imposed upon them. Against such a background it is difficult to maintain the kind of proactive strategic vision which the leadership role in the management of a destination demands. This was the climate in which the local authorities in both the following case studies were attempting to make turning-point decisions.

Case 1: Bridlington

BACKGROUND

Bridlington is a beach resort located on the coast of East Yorkshire just below the chalk promontory known as Flamborough Head. Like many resorts, Bridlington developed as a consequence of the arrival of a railway connection in the mid-nineteenth century, although there is an older settlement two miles inland from the seafront which is known as the 'Old Town' and which is centred on a medieval priory church of cathedral proportions. The heavily cultivated but nevertheless scenic Yorkshire Wolds provide a rural hinterland of gently rolling hills. The seafront is equipped with promenades dating from the Victorian and Edwardian era and is divided into a 'north' and 'south' side by a historic working harbour which is the base for an inshore fishing fleet, plus private yachts, pleasure steamers, and smaller craft specialising in sea angling for visitors. Adjacent to the harbour to the north is a small seafront amusement park, to the south the Spa complex which includes the 2,000-seat Spa Royal Hall and 1,000-seat Spa Theatre. These facilities offer summer entertainment and also serve as a venue for large conferences. There are 4,500 serviced beds in the resort, but a much larger number in the self-catering sector such as caravans and flats, *circa* 22,000. Tourism to the resort was estimated in 1986 at 2.5 million bednights per annum (East Yorkshire Borough Council 1987). Tourism was estimated in 1988 to have generated a contribution to the local economy of £51.1m., supporting an estimated 3,627 jobs (Humberside County Council 1992, p. 5). One of Bridlington's key successes has been its ability to attract respect and positive approval from national tourism organisations. The resort attracted the attention and approval of the industry when it won, in 1986, the ETB's 'Resort 2000' competition. This in turn appears to have attracted the positive approval of the media and of academic commentators (Urry 1990, p. 36). The common source of this respect seems to reside in its consistent implementation of a clear strategy, and its successful amendment of the strategy when the operating environment was seen to be changing. It is proposed to illuminate the progress of Bridlington by relating a select history of the resort since the late 1970s, highlighting seminal events.

STRATEGY

In the late 1970s, the key element in the tourism strategy of Bridlington was to position itself alongside the major resorts as a provider of first-rank variety entertainment. The local authority was the owner of four entertainment venues: the Spa Royal Hall, Spa Theatre, 3Bs Theatre Bar (formerly the Grand Pavilion and converted to the requirements of cabaret entertainment to meet the tastes of the 1970s) and the Floral Pavilion, which was a wrought-iron-and-glass concert hall on the seafront and which was the venue for daily performances by a traditional seaside orchestra. The local authority was the major tourism operator and investor in the resort: other municipally operated facilities included a cliff-top country house and park, a golf course and, of course, the beaches themselves. The 1970s were a time when differentials between working-class and middle-class pay were at their narrowest, large amounts of discretionary income being in the hands of the still-substantial industrial work-forces of the West Yorkshire conurbation, whence the primary market for Bridlington's holiday trade was drawn. On its home ground, that market supported programmes of entertainment by international stars at venues such as Batley Variety Club and Wakefield Theatre Club. It was therefore an ambitious but well-reasoned strategy, and one which was recommended in a consultant's report of 1973, for Bridlington to invest in a high-profile entertainment programme. Success showed itself in a lengthening of the season and apparent increases in business which bucked the national trend. The trade press lauded this success (Martins 1980a and 1980b). The resort's tourism director was credited with having created it, 'backed by a convincing tourism committee and a convinced council' (Martins 1980a). The same source contains an indication of what was to become, during the 1980s, a powerful trend: the proprietors of the Shirley Hotel, one of the principal seafront accommodation establishments close to the Spa, were quoted as having 'our best season in ten years' but also alluded to their abandonment of Saturday to Saturday bookings to allow variable lengths of stay. This was an early indication of the growing influence of the flexible short break on traditional domestic holiday-taking patterns.

The product strategy was not the only respect in which Bridlington at that time was seen to be original and successful. Viewing the contemporary increase in package holiday-taking to Mediterranean resorts, Bridlington decided to place its product using similar methods and launched its own package holidays. These were first launched in 1978 and Bridlington was the first (although this is disputed by Colwyn Bay) of the very few domestic resorts which marketed true package holidays at an all-inclusive price. The initial scheme aimed to fill beds in the off-peak shoulder months, although eventually the packages ran throughout the year. There were two versions: the customer could book directly with the council in which case travel to the resort was by British Rail or National coach services, or the package minus the travel element was sold to an operator who in turn marketed the package to customers. The package included accommodation and half board at a choice of hotels with different charge bands, four nights' entertainment, a round of golf, free admission to the country house and park, a half-day coach excursion, plus a range of extras such as free deckchairs throughout the stay. Later versions of the package also included a 'self-catering' version. The package holiday scheme ran for around 10 years and produced some exceptional results: in particular, a test-marketing of the package in London, a location

way outside the resort's traditional catchment area and expected to be unreceptive to the offer, produced 200 bookings. An astonished British Rail had to lay on a special train to cope with the demand. At the same time, efforts were made to fill beds by making inroads into the conference market. Voluntary associations and trade unions were targeted: bodies which required a large meeting hall, but whose members were paying their own costs and required budget accommodation. The number of delegate nights achieved rose from *circa* 6,000 in 1979 to 29,000 in 1981; this provided further business for the 'shoulder months' either side of the peak season and served to consolidate the progress made in lengthening the season through mainstream holiday business.

PRODUCT INVESTMENT

Despite the success of the product and marketing policies of the late 1970s and early 1980s, the resort's council and its officers were aware that the destination was living off investments made during the 1930s and the previous century, and there was a need to upgrade the product to equip it to compete, not only with other larger and better-endowed resorts, but with the sunshine packages which were by now making significant incisions into domestic main-holiday tourism. A capital project was conceived and presented to the public; and, in keeping with the resort's philosophy, it was bold and very ambitious. The proposal was to create a new development on a cliff-top location on the north side of the resort, adjacent to the Bridlington–Scarborough railway line the embankment of which would serve to partly obscure the development from the view of neighbouring middle-class housing. The site was large enough to accommodate the development and its car-parking requirements, because 'Paradise Island', as it was termed, would be a day-out destination in its own right, in addition to being a show-piece attraction for staying visitors in the resort.

Paradise Island was ambitious, comprising 'a lagoon, beach, miniature harbour and a score of different environments under one roof' (Voase 1981), plus a tropical jungle, an artificial lake with a three-masted sailing vessel, and the merchandising of third world crafts and goods from 'authentic' native settings. Such a development would have retained a degree of uniqueness even by the standards of the present decade; the scheme included many of the features which, in the present decade, differentiate Disneyland Paris from other theme parks and leisure developments. However, it did not proceed. The capital cost of the scheme was estimated at *circa* £13m. at contemporary values, which was a considerable sum. The intention, as with other aspects of the resort's policy, was to create something that would have a durable differential attraction for decades to come. One problem was that the council, faced with restraints on its own spending and interests from elsewhere in the borough which had reservations about spending so much money to the apparent benefit of only one part of the district, declared publicly that no monies from local taxation would go into the project.

Arguably this was a guarantee of failure since, in a marginal resort like Bridlington, despite the fact that bold investment in entertainment and marketing was clearly keeping visitor numbers up, it was unlikely that private investors would provide capital on a sole-risk basis; if the council was so convinced of the potential of the project, why not demonstrate that by providing part of the capital funding? But the project also encountered fierce resistance from sections of the local population who saw Bridlington as a residential and retirement centre rather than as a holiday resort. The likelihood of the project being accepted was not helped by the fact that the location of the proposed development was adjacent to a middle-class residential area and, although the degree of likely disturbance and interruption of views was disputed, the implications in terms of traffic and pedestrian traffic were clear. Petitions were organised, public meetings were held, councillors were lobbied. Eventually, faced with considerable hostility from residents, which further diminished the prospects of private investors beating a path to the door, the council abandoned the proposal.

Another scheme was prepared, again to be located on the seafront on the North Side of the town, but within an area of existing intensive tourist use and incorporating the existing 3Bs Theatre Bar and an indoor municipal swimming pool. Leisure World opened in 1987, having been constructed and paid for by the council without private sector involvement, but the £5m. cost was substantially offset by a £2.25m. grant from the European Regional Development Fund, £0.25m. from Humberside County Council, and £66,000 allocated by the ETB under Section 4 of the Development of Tourism Act (Barrett 1987). The development included a refurbished version of the former 3Bs auditorium, a wave pool with flumes claimed at the time to be the longest in England and a multipurpose space whose potential applications included not only exhibition use, but activities to satisfy residents such as indoor bowls.

The construction of Leisure World marked two shifts in policy: first, the council, having reconciled itself to the need to support the development with communal funds, put money into its construction; secondly, the resultant facility was not at all comparable with Paradise Island in scale and purpose. Since inland municipalities were also building centres similar to Leisure World, the facility could not be perceived as something special and particular to Bridlington. It represented not an attempt to create an attraction which was a day-visitor attraction in its own right with some unique qualities, but a desire to match the standard of attraction already enjoyed by the resort's target market in their home locations. It can thus be argued that the Leisure World development could not have been expected to secure Bridlington's long-term future as a family holiday destination, but at best it could mitigate the effects on Bridlington of the national decline in domestic seaside holiday-taking which was in progress at the time of the facility's construction.

PRODUCT IMAGE

Nevertheless, the construction of Leisure World was seen by the industry as continued evidence of Bridlington's determination to succeed and was instrumental in the resort's success in winning the ETB's 'Resort 2000' competition in 1986, jointly with Torbay. The entry pointed to the resort's achievements in marketing and product development and offered other proposals including various niche marketing ideas such as developing activity holidays, the creation of an iron-age village in the grounds of the cliff-top country house and park, and a Guest House museum themed to the 1940s. These may seem to have little to do with the primary C2D holiday market for a resort like Bridlington, but certainly everything to do with *service-class* attitudes as reflected through the media and, no doubt, culturally ingested by decision-takers nominated by the ETB. Urry's observations are relevant here and provide an explanation involving the concept of *post-modernity* (introduced in Chapter 7):

Indeed the way in which all sorts of places have become centres of spectacle and display and the nostalgic attraction of 'heritage' can both be seen as elements of the postmodern. It is only through the analysis of such wider cultural changes that specific tourist developments can be properly understood . . . Having good taste would involve looking down on such places [domestic seaside resorts] and only passing through, to view them as a voyeur would (as an Orwell or a Hoggart), never to stay. The only permitted exception might be to appropriate elements from such resorts, such as McGill's postcards, in a postmodern cultural pastiche. The uncivilised resorts are not to be taken seriously, but can perhaps be played at (or with?). (1990, pp. 93–4)

Arguably Bridlington was also playing a game, and was rather good at it, being as adept at identifying the requirements of other players in the industry as the needs of its own customers. The prize was a Tourism Development Action Programme – TDAP – for three years, qualifying for special treatment from the ETB and pursuing a selection of business development objectives. Although the Guest House museum and the iron-age village were not built, a number of projects were pursued and achieved, including the marketing of Bridlington for a range of activity interests under the advertising strap-line 'the resort for sport'. Another project involved a resort improvement scheme, led by the Civic Trust Regeneration Unit, designed to 'make Bridlington a more attractive place' (East Yorkshire Borough Council 1987). This was to provide a part-solution to a problem which faced the resort during the 1980s, namely the contraction in demand for variety entertainment.

RESPONDING TO CHANGE

During the course of the 1980s, variety entertainment, which had proved so successful in maintaining Bridlington's profile as a destination, became subject to change. What exactly happened is under-researched and potentially a quite fascinating subject of study, but a number of factors contributed to changes which impacted on resort entertainment. For one thing, the supply of new 'talent' was unequal to demand. This has been ascribed variously to the withdrawal of various televison talent shows which had enabled stars such as Les Dawson and Freddie Starr to achieve fame, but also, in part, to the power of television itself: it created 'stars' and gradually, resorts ceased to market their main summer shows as a 'show' under a title such as 'Showtime 79' and instead equated the name of the star with the name of the show, e.g. 'The Les Dawson Show'. The implicit message to the public was that the primary reason for visiting the theatre was to see the star rather than to see the show; the reverse implication being that if there was no star, there was no show. Shortage of 'stars' and their rising importance led inexorably to a rise in the fees demanded; the inability of resort authorities to pay high fees did not result in a lowering of the fees, because in engaging star names, resorts were in competition not only with each other but with television, from which a star could earn more money, and arguably with less inconvenience, than in live performance.

At the same time, changes in the structure of the economy had their effect. The 1970s were something of an Indian summer for a large, high-wage-earning industrial work-force. The recession of the early 1980s and subsequent economic restructuring brought this to an end, creating unemployment and, for those C2D families where the head of household retained work, a relative reduction in discretionary income. Domestic seaside resorts were badly affected by this. Bridlington in particular, relying on a catchment area which included the coalfields of West and South Yorkshire, saw its market eroded. Batley Variety Club closed, signalling the end of liberal spending on entertainment by an industrial work-force. Moreover variety, as an art form, was showing signs of decay. Many of the new 'stars' of the 1980s such as Bobby Davro and Duncan Norvelle were regarded by many as gifted entertainers, but they were essentially impressionists who fed off existing material: to amuse an audience with an impression of Bruce Forsyth requires the prior existence of Bruce Forsyth himself. It could be said that the new inheritors of the variety tradition are entertainers such as Rik Mayall and French and Saunders who emerged from alternative cabaret performance in fringe venues, and more recently surreal entertainers such as Reeves and Mortimer. Variety is not dead, any more than seaside tourism; but like seaside tourism, it tends now to be concentrated in the larger resorts such as Blackpool, where audiences can be guaranteed. For Bridlington, a new strategy was needed.

The response was to shift emphasis from activity to the environment. Schemes to upgrade the harbour and seafront areas included improvements to the frontages of buildings, new street furniture and heritage interpretation panels. Partnership schemes with a private developer included a major town centre shopping redevelopment, pedestrianisation of key town centre streets, and improvements on the north side promenades which attracted an award from the Royal Institute of British Architects. The spa complex was also updated and modernised to make it more attractive to conference and business usage. Meanwhile, the entertainment programme was substantially curtailed and the main summer show has now been replaced by music-hall type variety shows without star names. The Floral Pavilion, venue for the seaside orchestra until the early 1980s, was converted for use by operators of children's amusements. An adjacent area, close to the harbour on the north side, was allocated for use by fairground rides. Thus the resort is successfully providing for a more segmented visitor base in its upgraded environment and, simultaneously, an enhanced experience for visitors seeking a more commercialised atmosphere.

Estimating the success of these measures is not easy. Reliable statistics on visitor numbers are difficult and expensive to obtain, and infrequent: the only survey which estimates visitor numbers and spend district by district on a national basis was conducted by the Association of District Councils in 1984 and published in 1987. Secondary evidence can offer some indications: for example, the number of serviced beds advertised in the resort's *Holiday Guide* in 1993 totalled 2,462, whereas in the *Accommodation List* of 1983 – for this purpose, the predecessor publication – the figure was 3,715. While allowances must be made for the fact that such figures are as much a reflection of disposition to advertise as level of business, and that the real total of bedspaces in the resort can be expected to be much higher, nevertheless they serve to indicate that in spite of some good quality strategic and tactical decisions, the accommodation base, reflecting levels of staying visitors, has contracted. Admissions to Sewerby Hall and Park, the council-operated cliff-top country house and grounds, were 232,000 in 1974/75 (East Yorkshire Borough Council 1980b, p. 7); in 1990 they were 129,000 (Humberside County Council 1992, p. 7). It is thought that this dramatic drop is primarily the effect of significantly increased prices which discouraged regular resident visits, but nevertheless the trend is clear.

The attrition of the tourist accommodation base created a body of building stock available for other purposes such as residential homes, for which planning permission for change of use was required, and occupation by DSS (Department of Social Security) clients, for which change of use permission was not (until April 1994) required. The problem that such changes of use causes is that occupants of residential homes, DSS hostels and family holiday-makers tend to have different lifestyle requirements which do not easily coexist. Though such issues have proved more of a problem in the resort area covered by our second case study, they have tended to affect virtually all resorts and Bridlington is no exception (Hickman 1994). Nevertheless, Bridlington has been effective at convincing the world, by winning the Resort 2000 competition and combining consistency with flexibility in its marketing strategy, that it is a survivor; securing, in the process, the endorsement of the middle-class liberal press:

Unlike many of its competitors who have allowed themselves to fall into decay . . . Bridlington has refused to retire from active service. Its local authority has been busy injecting new ideas, energy and money to guarantee the resort's survival well into the next decade. (Wickers, 1987)

Case 2: Margate, Broadstairs and Ramsgate

BACKGROUND

The three resorts of Margate, Broadstairs and Ramsgate are located adjacent to one another on the eastern tip of the county of Kent, south-east England. Margate can lay claim to being one of England's oldest resorts and is indeed where the bathing machine is claimed to have been invented in the mid-eighteenth century. Initially frequented by the gentry, Margate became a resort of popular character for the industrial masses of the London conurbation with the establishment of steamship links with London and the arrival of the railway during the 1840s.

It has retained this profile to the present day although the visitor base is now more diverse, and attracts significant numbers of visitors from the Midlands. Ramsgate shares Margate's profile as an essentially C1C2D resort, although the character of the town has been altered during the past 15 years by the successful establishment of passenger and freight ferry business at Port Ramsgate, a development created during the 1980s. The adjacent Ramsgate Royal Harbour is now primarily a yachting marina. Broadstairs enjoys an altogether different character, having never been extensively developed as a visitor destination on the scale of Margate and Ramsgate. Hence, paradoxically, it is better suited to contemporary *service-class* tastes and can command the approval of the quality press. The colour supplement of the *Observer* spoke of a 'vision ... of the perfect British bay-side experience' (Anthony 1994). Interestingly, the socio-economic profile of visitors to Broadstairs is slightly but not significantly higher than those of Margate and Ramsgate (Thanet District Council 1991a, p. 17). Maybe the *Observer* was right to describe the town as the 'undiscovered jewel' of the Kent coast, meaning perhaps that it had not been discovered by the *service class*.

All three resorts are endowed with sandy beaches of a high standard and thereby distinguish themselves from the pebble beaches found at other south-eastern resorts such as Hastings, Eastbourne and Brighton. Geographically and historically, the part of Kent in which the resorts are located is known as the Isle of Thanet, because centuries earlier the area was actually separated from the mainland by a channel. The name Thanet was adopted for the name of the new local authority that assumed responsibility for the three resorts as a consequence of the local government reorganisation of 1974. Although residents of the three resorts (and sub-localities such as Cliftonville and Birchington) are attached to the independent character of their communities and, as elsewhere in England, sometimes resent being grouped with other communities for administrative purposes, all are conscious of living in a place called Thanet and will readily use the concept and term in common discourse.

The best available estimates suggested that, in 1990, the area attracted some 750,000 staying visitors spending £55m. (Thanet District Council 1991b, p. 4). Research suggested that of this figure, some £12.5m. could be attributed to spending by overseas students visiting the area for the purpose of learning English (Thanet District Council 1991c, p. 3). Indeed it has been argued that English as a language is a powerful invisible export (Batchelor 1992, Sherwood 1994) whose value is largely unrecognised and whose potential needs to be maintained and developed. This applies in particular to resorts on the south-eastern coast of England, and is just one of a number of growth opportunities for which the resorts of the Isle of Thanet are well positioned. Tourism within the economy of the resorts accounts for roughly 15 per cent of direct employment and 20 per cent of jobs in other service industries (Thanet District Council 1991b, p. 4). The serviced accommodation base of Margate and Cliftonville at *circa* 5,500 beds is slightly larger than that of Bridlington, but it is in the size of the bedstock that the signs of decline in tourism business, widely perceived to have been more acute in the Thanet resorts than in others, is noticeable. In 1984, data produced by the Association of District Councils estimated that Eastbourne and the Thanet resorts had a serviced accommodation base of equal size, at 12,000 beds.

By 1991, Eastbourne's base had shrunk to 10,000, whereas the Thanet figure had reduced to 7,398 bedspaces in 3,632 rooms. However, the good news was that the accommodation base was not only leaner, but fitter: 36 per cent of serviced rooms offered *ensuite* facilities in 1991, compared with 13 per cent in 1987 (Thanet District Council 1991d, Appendix 3). The actual product on offer to the public had been considerably improved, and though this was in part due to the attrition of low quality bedspaces, it also represents considerable efforts by providers of accommodation to upgrade their product.

PRODUCT IMAGE

In many ways the resorts of the Isle of Thanet present an enigma. In comparison with Bridlington, their locational advantages are considerable: situated within two-and-a-half hours' travelling distance of the major population centres of southern England including London, they enjoy easy access to a large market. The railway journey from London to Thanet, although using elderly rolling stock and involving a travelling time comparable with the present InterCity journey from London to York, is at least secure; Bridlington's rail link with the national network has at times been under significant threat of closure. Proximity to the continent of Europe should provide new tourism business opportunities, and the dualling of the road linking the resorts with the M2 motorway, and thus with London and the national motorway network, is due for completion in the mid-1990s. And yet, Thanet's tourism industry has contracted faster than at least one comparable example, as the earlier comparison with Eastbourne demonstrates. What is more, the way the area is perceived by the rest of the south of England is puzzlingly negative. While Bridlington has enjoyed some success at securing the approval of the media, Margate is not always as fortunate. Commenting on an ETB report issued in summer 1993 advocating, amongst other things, the refurbishment of Victorian heritage as a contributor to seaside resort regeneration, *The Guardian* turned its sights on the Isle of Thanet:

Much of the criticism in a study called Turning the Tide by the English Tourist Board is directed at the Kent coast – Margate, Ramsgate and Broadstairs in particular. It highlights garish advertising on buildings as a contributory factor in their demise. It's easy to see what they mean in Margate where boarded up and abandoned guest houses and neon signs proliferate along the beach front. In the almost toy-sized shopping centre, tattooed young men swear loudly at each other while vying to buy posters espousing the virtues of legalised cannabis. (Johnson 1993)

This invective represents a selective view. The decay of the environment as a consequence of the contraction of the domestic holiday industry is not peculiar to Margate. But in terms of cultural values, *ways of seeing*, the journalist is adopting the perspective of a specific class, what has been termed in an earlier chapter the *service class*, and is writing for a similar readership. The angle taken is encapsulated by Urry (1990, p. 94): 'Having good taste would involve looking down on such places [seaside resorts] and only passing through, to view them as a voyeur would ... never to stay.' This way of seeing can be further regarded as part of what Urry in an earlier article (1988, p. 39) described as the *transformed semiotics of everyday life*: 'As Baudrillard argues, what we now consume are not products but signs or images. Identities are constructed through the exchange of sign-values.' In other words, *The Guardian* article creates an identity not so much for Margate, but for the newspaper's readership: their 'good taste' is reinforced by an exchange of sign-values: the alleged unattractiveness of the place in question is documented and their predisposition 'never to stay' in such places is reinforced. However, other articles in the same newspaper, while adopting a similar tone, have made concessions. One journalist described a visit to the resort and admitted its attractions, concluding with a grudging commendation:

For children it's a treat, as my own three would testify. The sandy shore is a key ingredient, and as the sun at last prevailed over the morning's grey cloud cover, a pile of discarded clothes crowned by a pair of Donald Duck underpants and a Pampers maxi-plus symbolised the brood's innocent abandon ...

'Crummy and Cockneyfied?' Depends what you're looking for. In the name of fascinations both sincere and morbid, I shall make it back. The English can be weird like that. (Hill 1993)

And on another occasion, *The Guardian* issues a call to action:

It's tempting to write off a town like Margate as just another candidate for heritage status; a place where in a few years' time actors will dress up as mods and rockers to re-enact the beach battles of the 1960s. Tempting, but premature. Like other seaside resorts, the railway brought prosperity to Margate and the wide-bodied jet took it away. The challenge now is to bring it back again. (Elliot 1991)

This is an image problem which is rooted not just in the particular image of a particular resort, but in the 'transformed semiotics' of a society whose cultural values are dominated by class attitudes which have determined that domestic seaside resorts are unfashionable. And yet, the experience of Bridlington proves that the consistent implementation of bold and well-reasoned policies acquires respect and credibility. It will be argued in the case of the Thanet resorts that inconsistency in political leadership prevented the establishment of such credibility, and thus contributed to accelerated decline. The effect of economic change, public policy and local politics on the well-being of the Isle of Thanet attracted the attention of academics from the University of Kent based at nearby Canterbury, whose studies and analyses were published in two sources (Harloe *et al.* (eds.) 1990; Cooke (ed.) 1989) and which contribute to the evaluation which follows.

PRODUCT AND PERFORMANCE

Margate, like other English seaside resorts, possesses an infrastructure of tourist attractions which dates from earlier decades. The Dreamland amusement park, located close to the railway station behind the seafront buildings of Margate Bay, was established before the Second World War. It is a significant day-out destination in its own right and although visitor numbers are not published, anecdotal evidence suggests two million admissions per year, which would place the park in the league of the top 10 most-visited attractions in Britain. The largest municipally operated facility is the Margate Winter Gardens, a large 1,500-capacity seafront venue built in 1911, with a smaller 400-capacity venue – the Queen's Hall – added during the 1960s. This like its peers elsewhere is a subsidised operation, representing the use of communal funds to maintain the attractiveness of the resort with the object of attracting tourists whose expenditure will trickle down through the local economy, producing economic benefits for private businesses and their employees, and indeed directly back to the council in the form of business rates paid on hotels, restaurants and other facilities which without the tourists would not exist.

Such interventionism is not dissimilar from the style of politics known as 'municipal socialism', except that resort councils with few exceptions tend to be Conservative in character. Buck *et al.* (in Cooke (ed.) 1989, p. 175) noted this similarity and coined the phrase 'municipal conservatism' to describe it. The essential difference is that the objectives of municipal socialism may be primarily social and educational, whereas the objectives of municipal conservatism as practised in resorts are primarily economic: interventionism to support tourism businesses. This of course is one of its weaknesses, in that individuals and groups who perceive themselves to be detached from tourism either economically or socially, or whose direct personal interests are not served by a healthy tourism industry, may choose to oppose such expenditure on an ongoing basis. The resort of Eastbourne, for example, undertook very detailed research to demonstrate that of a visitor spend of £87m. in the town in 1990, after disbursements were subtracted, £23m. remained in the hands of local residents in the form of wages, salaries, rents and profits (Eastbourne Borough Council 1991, p. 40), thereby supporting arguments for the continued marketing and development of the town, by the council, as a tourist destination.

In the late 1980s Thanet Council, faced with the requirement of government legislation to compulsorily seek competitive tenders for its catering operations at the Winter Gardens, decided to contract out catering and the entertainment side of the business as a complete package. The contract was won by the council's in-house team and though the operating costs of the building are now subject to commercial confidentiality, it is thought that significant reductions in operating costs have been achieved, comparing favourably with other similar venues on the south coast. It is a shame that the need for the commercial confidentiality of tendered public services prevents such success stories being told. After all, the venues are still being operated with public subsidy. But in terms of policy, the question remains as to the purpose of maintaining and operating such a building. Margate had been one of the first resorts to respond in the early 1980s to the need for increased flexibility in summer season entertainment, creating a 'Season of the Stars' which featured a change of programme and change of star two or three times per week, in an attempt to increase the audience by diversifying the product. This policy was adopted by a number of resorts and worked successfully for a few years, but the accompanying generic decline of variety, mentioned earlier in the chapter, hit Margate in 1985 when losses on the summer season exceeded budget. This, though arguably a part-consequence of a national trend which was affecting the resort world in general, was treated as an internal failure. It resulted in staff departures and a change in policy which restrained future losses (Buck *et al.* in Cooke (ed.) 1989, pp. 189–90), and also reduced the quality and scale of the entertainment programme.

The other prime function of the Winter Gardens was as a conference venue. The target market for conferences is almost identical to that of Bridlington: trade unions and voluntary associations who require a large venue plus a supply of budget accommodation. One voluntary association conference, the Dunkirk Veterans Association, moves regularly between the two resorts on a north/south alternating strategy. The loss of three-quarters of Margate's large conference business during the 1980s (Thanet District Council 1991d, para. 3.8) was a major failure, and arguably one which could to some extent have been avoided. A detailed study of the number of delegate nights achieved from large conferences using the Winter Gardens as a venue

between 1980 and 1990 provides an illustration, in Table 12.2, of the contraction of this sector of the tourism business.

Table 12.2 Usage of Margate Winter Gardens by large conferences

Year	Conferences	Delegate nights
1980	14	14,470
1981	13	17,405
1982	13	17,835
1983	8	30,195
1984	10	33,850
1985	4	4,370
1986	4	5,500
1987	4	3,220
1988	5	5,100
1989	2	1,550
1990	4	3,840

(*Source*: **Voase 1992**)

Translated into expenditure figures, the data makes similarly alarming reading. In 1988 the ETB estimated an average daily spend of £40 per delegate for conferences at coastal resorts. If that figure is adjusted by the retail price index for each year of the decade and used to calculate total annual delegate expenditure, the total 'lost' when comparing the second half of the 1980s with the average of the first five years, approaches £5m. That sum, if divided by the 157 hotels and guest houses known to have been trading in Margate and Cliftonville at the time of the 1991 bedstock survey (Thanet District Council 1991d, Appendix 3), would have meant an income of nearly £6,000 per establishment for each of the five years.

Such an exercise is hypothetical in that conference business would not be distributed equally amongst all establishments and the serviced accommodation base, as indicated earlier, was more than 40 per cent larger during the mid-1980s. This would have reduced the hypothetical apportionment per establishment to between £3,000 and £4,000 per annum. But what is certain is that the second half of the 1980s saw a dramatic fall in Margate's large conference business and this can reasonably be assumed to have been a major contributor to the accelerated contraction of the accommodation base during the same period. To a small business £4,000 is a lot of money, and it can mean the difference between profitability and loss for a small hotel operating on narrow margins. That the crisis of the Winter Gardens summer show of 1985 also occurred during the mid-1980s may be of significance, if it is indicative of a reduction of available audience because of a drop in tourist numbers. An examination of the municipal environment of the mid-1980s goes some way to offering an explanation, and it is to this that we now turn.

ECONOMIC CHANGE AND LOCAL POLITICS

Since the local government reorganisation of 1974, Thanet District Council had been Conservative controlled. However, Pickvance (in Harloe et al. (eds.) 1990, p. 180) describes events in 1984 when, owing to disagreements which Pickvance attributes to differing views on economic development, the controlling Conservative group split into two and as a consequence left the council in a state of no overall control. One group is described as 'interventionist' and the other as 'anti-interventionist and pro-privatisation', although Pickvance suggests that 'it is not clear to what extent this was linked to their immediate economic interests, or to a national level trend'. Buck et al. evaluate the problem more explicitly:

There is considerable public support for council economic intervention in the abstract. However, specific efforts arouse controversy among different groups . . . The fact of the split among Conservatives over interventionism symbolizes the political significance of the changes in the local economy since the heyday of tourism and municipal conservatism. (in Cooke (ed.) 1989, p. 194)

In other words, the falling-out can be ascribed to economic change and shifts in economic power which occurred as a consequence of the contraction of the tourism sector of the local economy. In particular, the residential care industry had grown substantially from the early 1970s onwards, using the same infrastructure as

the tourism industry: redundant hotel accommodation is in most cases easily adapted to the needs of private residential care. Buck et al. report that this sector, having already grown significantly between 1971 and 1981, received a fillip in 1980 when the DHSS introduced a policy of subsidising the fees of elderly people who fell within means-test limits, though a test for need of specific residential care was not applied. This is said to have resulted in the numbers in residential homes in the area increasing from 1,654 in 1981 to just over 2,000 in 1985. The new industry had a turnover which was estimated in the mid-1980s at *circa* £20m., of which DHSS contributions were estimated at £7.5m. (Buck et al. in Cooke (ed.) 1989, p. 181).

It is tempting to regard residential care as a vibrant replacement for a tourism industry which was being supported in its terminal decline by misplaced interventionist funding, but the reality is that the local care industry in the mid-1980s appeared to benefit more from state support, albeit indirectly from government rather than from the local authority, than did tourism and economic development. Pickvance quotes data suggesting that total net economic support spending by Thanet District Council in 1985/86 represented £25.80 per head of local population which, when multiplied by an estimated population at the time of 123,600, gives a spend of c. £3.2m.; barely half the £7.5m. estimated to be flowing at that time from the public purse into the growing residential care industry (in Harloe et al. (eds.) 1990, pp. 170–1). What is more, this was not the only new publicly funded use to which redundant accommodation was being put. Surplus hotels were also adapted to provide accommodation for people with special needs, and in particular for the young unemployed who were wooed to the seaside with a promise of DHSS-funded accommodation. The council's chief executive summarised the trend and its implications:

the realisation that a regular and often enhanced rent could be gained because of a person's demand on the DHSS has resulted in some resort proprietors even advertising in large cities to attract the unemployed to their area . . . there has been a considerable change of use of tourist accommodation and . . . the greater the number of unemployed, handicapped and elderly in an area, the less likelihood for an innovative approach to lead the town forward into the current demands of tourism. (Gill 1986, p. 4).

There are three points to be made about the change of use of tourist accommodation to these other uses. First, in behavioural terms elderly people, holiday-makers, DSS tenants and people with special mental and physical needs are not similar. At its most elementary, young DSS tenants may have a liking for loud music late in the evening whereas elderly people, or holiday-makers trying to get children to sleep, may not. Since it is the holiday-makers who are the temporary visitors and choose to visit the resort from a range of other possibilities, it is they and not the other groups who are most likely to retreat from the situation by not booking for the following year. In such a conflict, it is the tourism business that is the most vulnerable. Secondly, council planners responded to the problem by designating in 1976 a 'holiday zone' within which the council's policy would be to refuse applications for change of use to residential care accommodation. However, rigid enforcement of the policy was seen to have the effect of denying hoteliers the opportunity to make a living by alternative means in the face of an acknowledged national decline in seaside tourism. The zone was thus amended (Pickvance in Harloe *et al.* (eds.) 1990, pp. 174–5) but continued to attract controversy. Thirdly, prevailing legislation demanded that planning permission for change of use was required for conversion to residential home, but – remarkably – *not* for change to special needs accommodation or DSS hostel. It was only in 1994, on Sunday 27 March, that the government announced through the mass media that the Prime Minister had decided that legislation was to be amended to require conversions of property to DSS hostel to be subject to the scrutiny of local authority planning committees.

STRATEGY AND INVESTMENT

Against this background of contraction of tourism as the traditional industry, accompanied by and to some extent the cause of internal strife, the council made efforts to secure developments which would bring economic benefits. From 1984 until 1991 no one party on the council enjoyed an overall majority, but from 1987 onwards the largest grouping was of Independents and though by definition not disposed to agreeing and maintaining a strict party line on a range of issues, they succeeded in providing some stability. Efforts to discover strategies for success included a fact-finding visit to Bridlington, in the wake of that resort's success in the Resort 2000 competition. But Thanet had its own successes during the 1980s, including the attraction of a cross-channel ferry service operating out of Ramsgate, and the facilitation of the construction of a new-build hotel on a waterfront site in Ramsgate, although internal critics suggested that the council had been too generous in its dealing with private sector partners (Pickvance in Harloe *et al.* (eds.) 1990, pp. 174–5). These ventures were pursued against a difficult background, as outlined by Buck *et al.*

All these projects have to be set against Thanet's unattractiveness for capital investment in most industries, and especially the advanced ones. This stems partly from geographical circumstances, but is largely due to the responses made to these over the last century. It is thus a self-reinforcing historical process. At national level, the area is unattractive for manufacturing; its accessibility to markets is very poor due to the inadequate road and rail links, and its environment, while attractive to older migrants on relatively low incomes, does not compete with that of Berkshire . . . (in Cooke (ed.) 1989, pp. 179–80)

It is not therefore surprising that attempts to attract new investment should require a generous contribution from the local authority in order to offset locational and environmental disadvantages. To draw a parallel with Bridlington, the achievement of a resort entertainment programme which could challenge the best in the country was made possible by having the courage to equal and if necessary exceed the fees which top entertainers could earn in more established destinations elsewhere, and the investment by Bridlington's local authority in the Leisure World complex further documented that community's understanding of the axiom that it is necessary to spend money in order to make money.

In Thanet, however, the acquisition of a ferry link and a new-build hotel were by nature transport and accommodation rather than attractions, and did little to improve its attractiveness as a destination. Pickvance suggests (in Harloe *et al.* (eds.) 1990, p. 181) that after the political conflicts and subsequent fragmentation of 1984 there seemed to be 'considerable continuities in policy', but it is at the *implementation* level that discontinuity seems to have occurred. The discord caused by the Winter Gardens' budgetary problems of 1985 may be one example. The dramatic loss of conference business during the 1980s is arguably another: the head of department responsible for marketing left the council in 1985 and was not formally replaced until 1988. This departure and other staffing discontinuities coincided with, and arguably became a prime cause of, the sustained drop in conference business; and in 1987, the resorts' membership of the British Association of Conference Towns (BACT), the benefits of which included inclusion in relevant publications and referrals of enquiries, lapsed and was not renewed (Thanet District Council 1991d, para. 3.3). Those conferences which continued to visit Margate were accepted and dealt with on a reactive basis, without significant proactive marketing. It was not until 1990 that membership of BACT was renewed and preparations made to relaunch Margate formally as a conference destination (Thanet District Council 1991d, section 3). But by that time, business had declined to the level detailed in Table 12.2, resulting in the loss of income outlined earlier.

The rate of decline of holiday-maker business is more difficult to measure, the best indication being the accelerated contraction of the bedstock as discussed earlier. To compare marketing activity with other resorts, in 1983/84 the council's budget for advertising the resorts was just in excess of £50,000, at a time when other resorts, including Bridlington, were spending twice that amount (Voase 1992, p. 9). This relative under-resourcing appears to have continued under the hung council until 1988, when a head of department for resort marketing was once again appointed and a special fund for tourism development initiatives established, raising the budgets to levels which were comparable with other resorts of similar size. But this came rather late: it was during the years of the mid-1980s rather than the late 1980s that, with the domestic economy having emerged from recession and into a period of prosperity, vigorous marketing was a crucial requirement in order to retain a position in the market-place alongside other higher-spending resorts, most of which had also invested in new tourist attractions. It was unfortunate that the need to act during this crucial period of the mid-1980s coincided in Thanet with political instability and consequent inaction, resulting in damage to the base of the tourism industry which was worse than it needed to be.

During the latter half of the 1980s there was also one very ambitious decision taken which, unfortunately, turned sour. The council was approached with a proposal to adopt a special event, an International Cartoon Festival which hitherto had run at a resort on the Belgian coast. At a time when the council employed no professional marketing adviser of senior rank, the Leisure Committee decided to invest £50,000, plus a guarantee against loss of £100,000, in this event. The event consisted of an exhibition of art cartoons displayed in a marquee on a seafront site in Margate, adjacent to the beach and amusement park. The event attracted *circa* 3,000 attendances, considerably fewer than the 100,000 projected. As with the budgetary problem at the Winter Gardens some years earlier, internal discord and recrimination were the result, providing a spectacle for the media. Had a marketing professional been employed at the time of the decision to accept the event, the wisdom of placing an indoor exhibition of art cartoons next to the beach and funfair of an essentially working-class resort, and expecting it to get an audience, might have been questioned. Thanet of course is not the only destination to have had unrealistic expectations of a special event: the ongoing cost of the 1992 World Student Games to the city of Sheffield has been far more serious. The object-lesson is to recognise the importance of clear conceptual thinking when planning special events, as discussed in Chapter 4.

Notwithstanding this setback, progress was made from 1988 onwards: a *Holiday Guide* embracing all three resorts was produced, superseding three separate guides for each resort; a logo and corporate identity using the term Kent's Leisure Coast was introduced and gained acceptance with the holiday-making public; remarketing as a conference destination was achieved; a large volume of research was undertaken in order to prove to a demoralised industry, doubting public and ambivalent council the value of tourism within the local economy; an enquirer database was established, in preparation for database marketing; and a short-break product was introduced, directly bookable through the resorts' marketing office, and whose success, like the large conference business, would be measurable.

At political level, the split in the Conservative party continued and in 1991, in the run-up to district council elections, municipal intervention in support of tourism became, once again, a political target. Whether this was motivated by ideology, or election opportunism, or was a reaction against a resurgent tourism marketing function is uncertain. But the consequence was a return to discontinuity and some months of uncertainty as to whether the council was serious in discharging its responsibilities toward tourism. The council's policy committee had received a marketing plan at its November 1990 meeting, approving specific projects and allocating monies to realise those projects. At the February 1991 meeting of the same committee, a move initiated from one of the two Conservative groups succeeded in removing almost 50 per cent of the budgets for resort marketing including the funds which it had earmarked three months earlier. In the autumn of the same year, following local elections in May 1991, the budgets were reinstated. Ironically, the about-turn was approved by the same Conservative group, now enjoying an overall majority, which had earlier initiated the budgets' withdrawal. U-turns as a feature of the landscape will be familiar to anyone who has worked for a political body but nevertheless, for an area such as the Isle of Thanet whose options for economic development are limited, six months' uncertainty adds to the accelerated attrition of the industry and its concomitant implications for business and jobs.

More recently, prospects for attracting new inward investment were significantly enhanced when the government announced changes in the areas of Britain designated for special economic assistance, Thanet achieving Development Area Status (Halsall 1993), and thus qualifying for government financial incentives for businesses to locate in the area, and enhanced access to EU structural funds. Thanet was also included in the list of successful bids for funds from the government's Single Regeneration Budget in an announcement made on 6 December 1994. It is to be hoped that these opportunities will facilitate the development which is so urgently needed, whether to secure the remaining base of the tourism industry or to support attempts to create a new economic base.

Analysis: competition and conflict

The dilemma of these resorts, and the contrasts in their struggles to understand and cope with the change enforced upon them, is in principle no different from that faced by a coal-mining community in the north of England, or an iron and steel town in Pennsylvania. What is at stake is the economic well-being of that community. In such a context, tourism is most definitely an *industry*: the right decisions can lead to regeneration and a new lease of life. The wrong decisions, or indecision, permit decline to continue and, in some cases, positively accelerate the process. Unlike declining heavy industries such as steel and coal, tourism globally is a thriving industry which offers segmented potential for growth. In the UK, the markets offering growth potential in recent years have been the shorter second and third holiday. But what bedevils resorts' attempts to take effective turning-point decisions is that other perspective of tourism, that it is an *activity* rather than an industry. The discussion in this chapter has demonstrated how the opinions of residents, and the growth of new service industries such as residential care which take root in the decaying infrastructure of tourism, feed into the economic and political life of a resort community and influence the decision-making process. Just when a resort needs to be at its most businesslike in order to ensure its survival, its decision-making risks becoming unbusinesslike.

The dilemma can be summed up as a conflicting interest in the common environment. To a resident, a beach may be a place to walk a dog in the morning; to the holiday-maker, it is the place where children play. To an entrepreneur whose business is to provide services to clients of the public welfare system, a failing hotel is a bargain purchase for conversion to residential care or DSS hostel accommodation; to the neighbouring hotel, survival as a business may mean *not* having such uses next door.

Inevitably, some resorts become casualties of their own internal conflict. However, in a resort where tourism is relatively strong and there exists significant access to capital for investment, there is more chance of maintaining effective economic and political influence. Middleton's (1989) conclusion was that UK domestic tourism would concentrate in around a dozen large resort areas, where such conditions are more likely to exist; tourism is also more likely to thrive in circumstances where the industry sectors are able to speak with a common voice. Turning-point decisions, though principally taken by public bodies, are the common responsibility of leaders and managers in all the industry sectors which put together the tourism product in a particular destination. Those responsible for the destination-marketing function, usually public employees, have a significant opportunity to influence, but are ultimately subject to political will. Leaders in the private sector can exert a powerful influence and are likely to be listened to, particularly in the socio-political climate of the present day in which communal authority is increasingly seen to be the prerogative of the body of entrepreneurs rather than communally elected bodies.

The difficulty of formulating a strategy for achieving effective turning-point decisions is not to be underestimated, but could be usefully founded on two propositions:

1 *The vigorous marketing of existing products* This was the approach advocated by Middleton (1991) in the summary of his report on the future of England's smaller seaside resorts. Self-evidently, if a resort continues to attract visitors there is still life in the product, and vigorous marketing may increase visitor

numbers, thus providing evidence to potential investors of future potential.

2 *Research the facts of tourism and make them known* This was the advice offered to Thanet District Council by Bishop Associates, consultants engaged to prepare a tourism strategy, in 1987. The view of tourism as an *activity* which is prejudicial to the well-being of the community can be countered by researching the true importance of tourism *as an industry*: how much the industry is worth, how the earnings benefit the whole community, and making the facts known publicly.

Conclusion

In concluding this chapter it is perhaps useful to return to the three theses advanced in Chapter 1. It was argued that tourism is 'largely psychological in its attractions', that this psychology is determined by the evolving culture and mores of society and that competitive advantage can be gained through the nurturing of an instinctive passion for service. The material in the case studies arguably broadens the understanding of these theses in three ways.

First, both the resorts, while being similar in many respects, differed from one another substantially in their communal psychology. Bridlington had its 'convinced' tourism committee and staff of officers and was equal to playing games with the culture and mores of society: although fashionable trends did not in principle favour Bridlington, the resort successfully turned the preoccupation with countryside and heritage to its own advantage in its successful submission for the Resort 2000 competition. By contrast, Margate, Broadstairs and Ramsgate endured what appear to have been severe discontinuities in both the political support for their tourism industry and the provision of staffing and budgets.

Secondly, to not play the game in accordance with fashionable rules is to invite problems. When the psychology of a community as reflected in its popularly elected local authority does not embody the instinctive passion for service by which competitive advantage is gained, then that competitive advantage is lost. It was noted that accommodation owners in Margate, Broadstairs and Ramsgate had made significant progress in upgrading the bedstock with *ensuite* facilities, but this is arguably of limited usefulness when the activity of the popularity elected local authority is ambivalent or unsupportive. The rapid contraction of the bedstock in the three resorts has to be seen as a consequence of this, as well as of the failure to match the promotional spend of competing resorts and the failure to promote as a conference destination.

Thirdly, there is the consequence of a changing population profile as tourist accommodation changes to use as residential home or DSS hostel. The innate aspects of these changes in mature resorts have not been discussed in detail in this chapter but it is interesting to ponder on how the transformation of a resort from a destination for 'tourism-as-escape', to a destination for 'residency-as-escape', may affect the psychology of the resort and the people in it. The next chapter includes consideration of two fictitious examples of resort drama which may offer some illumination on the subject of residency-as-escape. It also compares two other pairs of real destinations from a perspective of role and communal identity.

Chapter **13**

The psychology of the host

This chapter seeks to broaden the insights into the attitude of host populations to tourism in mature destinations. The two resorts considered in the previous chapter appeared to differ in character in this respect: what was termed their 'communal psychology' was one of confidence in the first example, and apparent self-doubt in the second which was rooted, it was suggested, in competition and conflict caused by economic change. The communal psychology of the host community in a destination is arguably shaped by three factors: first, the stage in the resort life cycle; secondly, individual circumstances relating to geographical location and local culture; and thirdly, the capacity of the resort to *reinvent* itself. Examples will be a pair of neighbouring cities in the north of England, namely Hull and York; a pair of mature coastal resorts as depicted in fiction; and a trilogy of resorts which appear to have achieved a degree of reinvention.

A tale of two cities

The last chapter identified the product image of a resort with the way in which it was portrayed in select examples of journalism. A look into the pages of the local newspapers for the neighbouring cities of Hull and York offers an insight into the reaction of local communities to the perceived value of their environment, and the prospect of sharing that environment with visitors.

HULL

Hull is a port which was founded during the Middle Ages, and though its city walls and many of its historic buildings have been lost through commercial development and wartime bombing, a surviving medieval core, known as the Old Town, plus the conversion of former town-centre docks for a variety of leisure uses has enabled Hull to join that band of post-industrial cities which have been able to sell themselves as credible short-break tourist destinations. Hull's development of a tourist 'product' owed much to the institution of the government's Urban Programme in the mid-1970s. In 1978 a government allocation of £2m. per year for the following three years was made for a variety of economic, social and environmental uses (Williamson 1978) and in the same year the city council introduced a 'town scheme' by which £140,000 was to be made available over a five-year period to support structural repairs to historic buildings within the Old Town Conservation Area (Hull Daily Mail 1978a). Another article in the same edition of the newspaper reported the intended conversion of former eighteenth-century warehouses into residential accommodation.

In the same year, councillors agreed to long-term proposals for the expansion of museums provision within the Old Town (Hull Daily Mail 1978b) and the opening of a nightclub in yet another former warehouse was celebrated (Hull Daily Mail 1978c). The following year, the various programmes were acquiring a momentum to the extent that the local newspaper felt able to talk about 'Boom Time in Old Town' on its front page, reporting that schemes in hand totalled £5m., to which new starts totalling £4.5m. were to be added during the following 12 months (Hull Daily Mail 1979). The next year, the newspaper devoted a four-page feature to the redevelopment of the Old Town. Writing under the headline, 'The years of neglect roll away', the newspaper's municipal correspondent celebrates a battle won by conservation over redevelopment:

Like the mythical phoenix, Hull's Old Town is slowly rising from its own crumbling remains. There is now no doubt that it has survived the triple ravages of Hitler, politics and the worst excesses of grandiose and highly impractical redevelopment plans. (Hansford 1980)

Interestingly, in all of the reports cited, none made any mention of tourism, although what was being created undoubtedly now forms the basis of Hull's tourist product. The growth of short-break tourism is a phenomenon principally associated with the 1980s and it was the 1980s conversion of the Old Town dock areas to retailing and marina usage, levering an influx of private capital including a new-build Forte Crest Hotel, which established Hull's credentials as a tourist city.

A report by the city planning officer (Taylor 1975) which antedates the Urban Programme, established the basis of the conservation policy for the Old Town and mentions the potential for tourism generation but, significantly, does not seem to have entirely abandoned the kind of redevelopment plans which attracted such retrospective disapproval from the local newspaper five years later. For example, it was anticipated at the time that the lesser of the city's two medieval churches was to close, and the report hints that the removal of its tower might improve traffic flows on an adjacent road (Taylor 1975, p. 25). To suggest in the present day the removal of a landmark of medieval origin for traffic purposes would beggar belief. The report, in effect, is an insight into the transitional phase between the modernist view for development of the city (Hansford's 'worst excesses') and the cultural shift by which progress was defined in terms of conserving the heritage of the past, rather than pursuing new-build projects for the future.

In terms of Butler's (1980) resort life cycle (see Chapter 4), Hull was arguably in the 'involvement' stage in the 1970s, moving to the 'development' stage in the 1980s. Hull's fascination with its own past, and with its present-day visitor potential, is today apparently unabated. In 1994, the addition of some 200 buildings to those within the city listed by the government's Department of National Heritage as being of historic interest, attracted front-page news in the *Hull Daily Mail*. This time,

there was no doubt of the link between the city's heritage and its tourist potential:

Delighted city council chiefs say the boost should help their drive to promote Hull as a place worth visiting . . . A National Heritage spokesman said: 'This survey has shown that there are another 226 good reasons why Hull is a nice place to live and visit.' (Manning 1994)

YORK

The contrast with the city of York, barely 40 miles away inland, could hardly be greater. York is what can be described as a 'tourist-historic city', retaining city walls, much of its medieval street pattern and buildings, and Europe's second-largest gothic cathedral as a focal point.

At the end of the 1970s, at the time of Hull's waxing enthusiasm about the rediscovery of its historic past, York's citizens were becoming jaded if not resentful at the attention their well-maintained historic city was receiving from tourists. The late 1970s were a time of very considerable weakness in the British economy, one of the consequences of which was a weak pound on the foreign exchange markets. This meant that the country was something of a bargain basement for overseas tourists, who flocked to the capital and other established tourist-historic honeypots, such as York. In the summer of 1978, the *Yorkshire Post* reported that 'the summer of '78 could go down in York's long history as the year when its honeymoon with tourism turned sour' (Scott 1978). A city apparently 'bursting at the seams' with overseas visitors was said to have given rise to a litany of problems: abuse of tourists by frustrated residents, tourists ignoring parking regulations, locals crowded out of car parks, litter, crowded streets, traffic queues, rising prices in the shops, and a wave of shoplifting which demanded the presence of additional police patrols in the retail centre of the city.

In terms of the Butler resort life cycle, York was perhaps in the 'development' phase but was very quickly discovering the urgency of 'consolidation' measures. York's tourist product was already well established by the mid-1970s and had benefited from recent additions such as the National Railway Museum, and was to gain further in the

1980s by such additions as the Jorvik Viking Centre. But in the late 1970s, visitor-management measures such as restricted parking in historic cores and park-and-ride schemes were either unheard-of or in their infancy. Since then, such schemes, as introduced in cities such as York, Lincoln and Cambridge, have helped to mitigate the negative impact of large visitor numbers on historic centres.

Significantly, the *Yorkshire Post* reports that one of the political groups on the York City Council wanted a detailed report to be produced on exactly who was benefiting from the inflow of tourist funds. This would seem to endorse the suggestion advanced in the concluding paragraphs of the last chapter, to 'research the facts and make them known', for coping with internecine conflicts in resort areas. The article concluded with this proposition: 'A debate is inevitable on how high a price the citizens should pay for a new industry and also how widely shared are its profits' (Scott 1978). An editorial in the same edition of the newspaper endorsed the call for research to be undertaken, but counselled the citizens against any hasty decision to discourage tourism. Mention was made of the value of inbound overseas tourism to the national exchequer, and its beneficial influence on what was at that time a very weak economy; of the way in which Spain, and such cities as Florence and Venice, do not waste time moaning about tourists because they recognise the economic benefits which visitors bring; and of the way in which tourist incomes trickle down through the local economy, benefiting the whole community; and concluding with a warning not to bite the hand that feeds:

It should not take the investigators long to discover that the direct beneficiaries are the retail and service trades and the indirect ones are those who are employed by or sell to those trades and so on, ad infinitum. The suspicion arises that what some people in York really want is the tourists' money without the tourists. *(Yorkshire Post 1978, author's emphasis)*

The city continued to develop as a tourist destination, although the attitude of its local government was on occasions ambivalent. The withdrawal of funding from the quadrennial York

Festival and Mystery Plays, although partly the consequence of a variety of messy organisational disputes, was arguably not the action of a municipal government wholeheartedly supporting an established and valued element in the city's tourist product (Anderson 1993).

In 1994, at the same time that Hull was celebrating its continued emergence as a tourist destination, York was almost showing signs of Butler's 'stagnation' phase. In August 1994, the chief executive of the privately operated York Visitor and Conference Bureau, which acts as an umbrella marketing, promotion and booking facility for member businesses in the city, estimated that visitor spending was down by around 20 per cent, and announced the launch of a six-figure promotional campaign in an attempt to recover lost ground. In addition, a joint campaign with the city council and the chamber of commerce was to spend £20,000 to promote Sunday shopping in the city to coincide with the enactment of the Sunday Trading Act at the end of the summer of 1994 (*Yorkshire Post* 1994b). This strategy would seem to endorse the other proposition advanced toward the end of the last chapter, that the route to recovery is the vigorous marketing of existing products.

Realism and reverie

One of the advantages enjoyed by cities as tourist destinations, as noted in Chapter 7, is that they have a life which exists, thrives and progresses, with or without the presence of tourists. Consequently, a realistic and well-thought-out response to a downturn in business, as in the example of York quoted above, comes comparatively easily. But where the destination owes its very existence to tourism, the decline of that industry does more than cause economic problems. It is as if the very identity of the destination is at stake; if the place loses its meaning to visitors, it loses its meaning to itself. The psychology of the community and individuals within it is affected, so that their perspective on the problems, and the remedies proposed to address them, depart to some extent from reality. Hints of this appear in the comments of Buck *et al.* on the attempts of the Isle of Thanet resorts to regenerate themselves, where it is suggested that various large-scale development proposals were characterised by 'excessive aspirations' (in Cooke (ed.) 1989, p. 179). This detachment from reality has perhaps been best expressed through fictional dramas set in coastal resorts, as the following examples demonstrate.

'WESTBEACH'

Westbeach was a television drama based on a mythical coastal town, produced by WitzEnd productions and serialised by the BBC in 1992. The actual location of the filming was Eastbourne on the southern coast of England. The series featured two rival families whose business interests were based in different sectors of the tourism industry. One family was of traditional middle-class origins, long established in the resort, owning the resort's principal hotel which struggled to maintain its star rating while being dogged by, as it appeared, marginal profits which left limited scope for continued investment. The rival family was of more ordinary origins; their wealth was based on revenues from amusement arcades.

These families were linked by personal relationships past and present, but divided by differing commercial interests, which led from time to time to conflict. They were also divided by their conflicting interest in the common environment. The main conflict was over a piece of available land within the resort. The leader of the hotel-owning family sought to establish an indoor resort on this site, offering Westbeach the opportunity to compete, so it was said, with the more attractive climatic conditions found in overseas resorts. Her tactics included the attempted persuasion of what she regarded as a key councillor to endorse her plan. The leader of the rival clan hatched his own plan, based on a conversation with his environmentally aware son, to construct a recycling plant for which, so it was thought, EU financial support, not to mention the commendation of the local environmentally concerned citizens, would accrue.

Although the first of the two schemes appears to be more germane to tourist regeneration than the second, the unanswered question was where the capital would come from. Like the Paradise Island scheme mooted for Bridlington in the early 1980s (see Chapter 12), whether or not private capital could be attracted in sufficient quantities was a debatable point. The second scheme, the recycling plant, appeared to be little more than a fickle idea from an entrepreneur whose personal business interests were secure, and whose boredom led him to tinker with fashionable ideas which he just happened to encounter in his daily round. The implementation of his idea was dependent upon subsidy from an outside source, the EU, and the impression was that its sole attractiveness lay in its capacity to attract largesse from elsewhere. In a declining resort situation where the best days are perceived to have been in the past, the dividing line between realism and reverie can be a fine one. Once the clear focus offered by an annual influx of visitors dissipates, there is some notion of a need to diversify, but uncertainty as to what is appropriate. The resort, unlike the city, does not have a set of economic imperatives which are separate from tourism.

'ATLANTIC CITY'

A vivid and very individual insight into the impact of resort decline on resident hosts was portrayed in the film *Atlantic City* (1980), filmed in the real-life resort of the same name, located in New Jersey on the eastern seaboard of the United States. Directed by Louis Malle, who brought to the production his combined skills as film-maker and documentarist (Hare 1995), the film was described by the *The Guardian* as a 'heartfelt study of little people and their big dreams' (Howlett 1994). The film starred the late Burt Lancaster and is set in the late 1970s. Atlantic City had been at that time, in real life, the object of an apparently successful turning-point decision. In 1978, casino gambling had been introduced as a regeneration strategy and this was held to have had a positive impact on jobs, resort income and property values, although it had also attracted an increased level of crime (Buck *et al.* 1991). This transformation from declining resort to gaming Mecca is one of the main background features of the film, the action of which is interspersed with scenes of demolition and redevelopment.

The protagonists fall roughly into two types: first, those who arrived in the resort during its heyday and who have never left. In the case of Burt Lancaster's character, this is confirmed in an admission that a journey southwards is 'the first time in 20 years I've been out of Atlantic City'. He is a former small-time criminal who is taunted as 'Mr Top-Ten-Wanted' by his ageing female companion because of his failed ambition to make an impact in the world of crime. His companion also looks backwards for her identity, reminding herself that she was once married to a gentleman of some notoriety, albeit within the restricted world of the resort. She admits that she arrived in the resort in 1945 to participate in a Betty Grable lookalike contest, even as a young woman defining her own identity through a person other than herself. The second group of protagonists, which includes a waitress-cum-aspiring-croupier played by Susan Sarandon, is a set of younger characters for whom the resort is also a means of escape. In Susan Sarandon's case, the escape is from the rural confines of Saskatchewan. Her ambitions include learning French, although she has little idea of how to go about it, and an aspiration to work in the casino in Monte Carlo.

Appearances are important in this resort: in fact, excess touching vulgarity is *de rigeur*. Sarandon's estranged husband, also escaping to Atlantic City and accompanied by stolen drugs, is advised to acquire a 'blue leisure suit' if he is to deal effectively in this town. Lancaster enters a florist's and orders the entire stock of red roses, six dozen in total, to be sent on Sarandon's behalf to her husband's family in Saskatchewan following his death at the hand of gangsters. The card accompanying them explains that 'Business prevents me from being with you.' Lancaster himself, on acquiring the ill-gotten proceeds of Sarandon's deceased husband, acquires a light-coloured suit redolent of a swell of the 1920s. There are two external points of reference to the future and the past. America's best-known gambling resort is the oft-mentioned role model for the future: a new casino employs dealers and croupiers, it is mentioned, 'from Vegas'. Due respect is also paid to that community to which Atlantic City owed its past existence, namely Philadelphia. When the name of that city comes up in conversation, Lancaster's companion comments reverently, and irrelevantly: 'Philadelphia is a nice place'. Just as Blackpool has the Lancashire mill-towns and Margate has east London, Atlantic City enjoyed a symbiotic relationship with its industrial donor-town. The older characters identify this relationship with their own pasts, and as something that has changed. As Lancaster reminisces, even the timelessness of the sea appears, in his reverie, to have changed: 'The Atlantic Ocean was something then . . . yes, you should have seen the Atlantic Ocean in those days . . . they used to call Atlantic City "the lungs of Philadelphia".' Lancaster's existential joy at successfully defending Sarandon by shooting two gangsters dead, and his cheerfully self-destructive remark to a hotel porter that 'I did that', pointing to the pictures of the killing on the front page of newspapers on a reception desk, fulfils at one and the same time a lifelong search for identity, and the totality of his isolation from conventional reality. In *Atlantic City*, the fulfilment of the dream proves to be as illusory as the dream itself.[5]

Invention and reinvention

Atlantic City as a *real* place could be viewed as an example of a bold principle in action. If a strategy for tackling the turning-point involves re-marketing to deliver results which form a basis for reinvestment leading to regeneration, all well and good, and traditionally fashionable destinations such as Bournemouth, Torquay and Brighton go some way toward demonstrating the principal at work. But for less 'fashionable' resorts, such as Atlantic City, a more radical option was needed, and that is *reinvention*. As a product relaunch strategy in the world of consumer goods, this is not uncommon. The health drink known to decades of post-war consumers as Lucozade is a very different product from what is now known and marketed as Lucozade Sport. Everything, from brand image to target market, has changed; the actual drink bears little resemblance to the original product. Its sole connection appears to be a shared name, and a notion that this drink is

[5] *This also appeared to be the underlying theme of the short-lived BBC soap opera Eldorado, set in a British expatriate community in Spain. All the characters, it was said, were running away from something. What they were seeking was as mythical as the city after which their community was named.*

supposed to have some healthy effects.[6] Atlantic City pursued a strategy of reinvention through gaming, and it is useful in this context to take a closer look at that better known of American gambling towns, Las Vegas.

LAS VEGAS

The *Economist* (1994b) reported on Las Vegas's multitudinous changes of image through the decades of the twentieth century, commenting on its capacity to 'reinvent' itself. The resort was described as having been an 'ersatz old West' during the 1930s and 1940s; a 'mafia and Hollywood fleshpot' in the 1950s; a blue-collar attraction in the 1970s and 1980s; and now a 'theme park for adults'. The number of new beds created since the late 1980s had totalled 20,000, and bed occupancy ran at 87 per cent, compared with a national average for the USA of 67 per cent. Las Vegas, like York, Margate and Bridlington, is not free from conflicting interests in the common environment. Although two-thirds of the work-force were said to be employed in the gaming industry (which also, incidentally, pays half of local taxes), this did not prevent Nimbyism making an appearance. Neighbourhood groups lobbied for zoning protection against the intrusion of casinos into their areas; and there were calls for additional policing and parks for local residents' use. Voters, however, rejected these when they were asked to pay for them in the form of a bond issue.

Nevertheless, in spite of the ambivalence of the city's residents, Las Vegas seems to have the knack of re-creating itself and its image. The recent transformation from 'blue-collar attraction' to 'theme park for adults' was a crucial one, since with the contraction of traditional blue-collar industries in the USA as elsewhere, the market, and its associated culture, was disappearing. The danger of becoming trapped in a 1970s time-warp of flared trousers, medallions and sideboards must have been considerable. That type of cabaret attraction is still of course associated with Las Vegas, but is made possible by the kind of self-parody that becomes possible when a place

[6]*This illustration was used by Mike Richardson, former Marketing Director of the English Tourist Board, in a presentation to the annual conference of the British Resorts Association in June 1991.*

portrays itself as fictional, rather than real. That, after all, is what theme parks are about.

BLACKPOOL

A comparable UK example may be the resort of Blackpool. Claiming to be Europe's largest resort, with 120,000 beds, Blackpool has not quite reinvented itself but has turned around its image and visitor markets so successfully that it has come quite close to having done so. Research (NOP research 1989) has shown that total visitor nights increased from 12.2 million in 1987 to 15 million in 1989, recovering the level of bednights recorded by earlier research in 1972. The number of actual visits had increased rather dramatically, but was offset by a considerable shortening of the average length of stay. The other significant change was the age profile of visitors: this was found in 1989 to be considerably younger, with the 15–34 age group accounting for 43 per cent of all visits.

This success story could be explained as a combination of social trends and appropriate action by Blackpool's resort authority. For one thing, there was a documented national recovery in domestic holiday-taking which began in 1988 (Middleton 1989) and of which Blackpool appears to have been a conspicuous beneficiary. Also, as variety entertainment declined nationally during the 1980s, leading to Bridlington's decision to reposition itself with environment rather than entertainment as its main product attribute, the vestiges of the business tended to cluster in those few resorts with a critical mass to deliver audiences. Of these, Blackpool was the largest: Blackpool's image as a summer show playground, already powerful, became stronger. Considerable investment in resort facilities by national operators such as First Leisure and, locally, the Blackpool Pleasure Beach, created a constant updating of the product and a continued novelty for a mass-consumption holiday market.

As a means of tackling the problem of bathing waters which did not consistently meet the standards laid down in EC directives (Magrath 1993), Blackpool effectively ceased to promote itself as a beach resort, concentrating on the entertainment and nightlife by which it was increasingly defined. And finally, the active promotion of the resort as a short-break destination, in acknowledgement of the fact that Mediterranean destinations would become the preferred destination for long holidays, took advantage of a known growth market in domestic tourism and at the same time built on the strengths of existing out-of-season promotions such as the acclaimed Blackpool Illuminations.

Undoubtedly reinvention is an attractive proposition, but a prerequisite may be that it is acceptable to wipe the canvas clean, and start again. One shared feature of Blackpool, Las Vegas and Atlantic City is that the built and natural environments are very ordinary. Historic buildings and natural beauty are powerful assets to a tourist destination, but they place limitations on the amount of alteration that can be made, or tolerated. What is more, destinations with very attractive environments that are in their 'consolidation' or 'stagnation' stages are likely to attract retired persons who value their attractive qualities, thereby creating an especially vigorous residents' lobby against change, as was the case in Bridlington when the 'Paradise Island' proposal ran into opposition.

Residency-as-escape

A notable feature of some resort destinations is this capacity to convert tourists into residents. Traditionally the model is one of industrial tourists, living and working in a conurbation, whose dream and intention is to retire to their favoured holiday destination. During the post-war years, the drift of retired people to the coast had the effect of creating significant elderly populations in coastal resorts, whose conservative views on future development feed into the political processes of the resort community and give rise to some of the complications associated with turning-point decisions. Since the popularisation of international tourism, destinations such as Spain have received a similar drift of retired persons from donor conurbations of northern Europe. More recent social and economic trends have given rise to another sort of population drift which could, conceivably, have an impact of no less significance in coming years. Its origins lie in the economic structures of post-industrial society, which through advances in communications technology have freed certain types of business and certain types of work to locate where they choose, perhaps in a location which is geographically remote from their markets. It can be hypothesised that places which have emerged as acceptable places to visit will also emerge as acceptable places to which to relocate if possible.

In a sense this is not news. Attractive towns, attractively located, have traditionally been attractive places to work for people whose job choice enables them to determine where they work. Local government officers and certain other kinds of public sector professional, whose presence is demanded as part and parcel of the organisational structure of communities of all sizes, can in principle exercise a great deal of discretion as to where they live and work. Once they are established in an attractive spot, the attraction of staying there competes powerfully with other ambitions. For example, Cowen *et al.* in a socio-economic study of Cheltenham, Gloucestershire, identified the hold that an attractive Regency town and its surrounding Cotswold countryside exerts over members of the teaching profession:

The environment has not only affected decisions based on capital's demand for land and built resources. It has also been held in high regard by labour, especially among those with more marketable skills. Our research into the impact of environment has in fact produced pointed examples of careerism being traded for housing or the less tangible ambience. (in Cooke (ed.) 1989, p. 113)

Cowen *et al.* describe certain problems in the town's public-sector schools and consequent low morale amongst teachers, but point out that paradoxically these had not resulted in high turnover of staff. What was more important to the teachers was 'the relatively more comfortable existence in a place "as nice as anywhere"' (p. 114). What *is* new is that communities, recognising as Ashworth and Voogd put it, the 'increasing freedom of activities to locate without restraints' (1990, p. 2), have realised that there is everything to play for and actively market themselves, not just to attract tourists, but to attract businesses and *residents*. The real agenda of much of the cultural regeneration of cities, which was discussed in Chapter 7, was pursued with three intentions in mind: to provide a superior environment for residents, to create a product attractive to tourism as a growth service industry to compensate for manufacturing decline, and to attract business relocations and employees with 'marketable skills'. Looking again at the earlier-quoted extracts from the city of Hull's local newspaper, the 1994 quotation is different from the 1970s extracts in two respects: first, it implies that *bona fide* heritage means that Hull is a 'place worth visiting', undoubtedly with tourism in mind. But also, it is a place '*to live in and to visit*' (author's italics). There is a sense that the value of this city as a place to live is not solely a message for local residents: it is something which is to be broadcast to the wider world.

Myerscough set out to study the wider significance of 'cultural industries' in his seminal volume *The Economic Importance of the Arts in Britain* and noted that:

There is growing belief that the arts can bring a competitive edge to a city, a region and a country as a source of creativity, a magnet for footloose executives and their businesses, and as a means of asserting civic, regional or national identity through the quality of their cultural life. (Myerscough 1988, p. 3)

His various researches included seeking the views of middle managers as to the features they valued about the place where they currently lived, and what they would look for in a new place of residence. For a prospective move, cultural facilities appeared to be less important than proximity to pleasant countryside, good transport links, housing and schools; but in terms of features valued in their present place of residence, cultural life came second only to pleasant countryside (Myerscough 1988, ch. 9). It has been argued elsewhere by this author (Voase 1994) that the 1980s were a transitional decade in which the growth of short-break tourism, service industries and an attendant *service class*, and the availability of funds from sources such as the UK government's Urban Programme and the European Regional Development Fund (ERDF), coincided to place cultural and environmental regeneration, with its derived image benefits, at the top of many municipal agendas.

But the competition was not solely between cities. The freedom to relocate included greenfield, rural sites for the newer kinds of manufacturing based on high technology, and rural fringe sites for the retail shopping parks which posed a threat to so many traditional city centres. Cooke (in Cooke (ed.) 1989, figs. 1.2 and 1.3) graphically shows that while manufacturing industry contracted during the decade 1971–81 in the expected conurbations of London, Yorkshire/Lancashire and the West Midlands, manufacturing growth occurred in peripheral areas such as the south-west and South Wales. The most rapid growth of new service industries occurred, not in the metropolitan centres, but in a variety of traditionally rural regions such as East Anglia. Vigorous place-marketing by cities, and the acquisition of a cultural profile, is not just a race between metropolitan rivals. Myerscough's 'pleasant countryside' is the ever-present alternative for the increasing number of 'footloose' professionals.

So, Hull's *visitors* may be short-break tourists, or business tourists, opinion-formers such as visiting journalists, or footloose professionals actively considering relocation. The footloose may also consider Cheltenham, Cambridge, Wiltshire, mid-Wales, or just about any other place that comes to mind. The idea of retirement to the Cotswolds may have a long pedigree, but a footloose work-force is something comparatively new to be reckoned with. Increasingly for some, the dream of living in a favoured location does not have to wait until work ceases. The prospect of surrounding oneself with the kind of environment that suits one's personal preference is opening up to more and more people.

What stands out from this study is that attractive urban and rural environments such as the one offered by Cheltenham can become destinations for residency-as-escape based on *choice*, whereas the resort in decline becomes, for some, a destination for residency-as-escape based on *compulsion*. The compulsion can be material or psychological in nature. An elderly person seeking a place in a residential home, or a young person who is dependent on state benefits and who removes to the resort in order to find accommodation, is limited by available finance and may regard himself or herself as having few alternative options. For Burt Lancaster and Susan Sarandon in the fictional Atlantic City, their residency is enforced by what appears to be a lack of confidence in tackling the wider world. This question of residency, as complement and competitor to tourism, is a theme that reappears in the next, and final, chapter.

Chapter 14
Expectations

Forecasting the future

There are a number of ways of trying to predict what is going to happen in the future, some of which, improbable though it may seem, are ably illustrated by analogies drawn from the world of accountancy. An organisation which is planning its budgets for the coming financial year has three possible starting points. First, it can take its existing budgets and add money for inflation, and make adjustments to each expenditure and income head in accordance with whatever changes in strategy and planning have been agreed since last year's budget was set. Such an exercise is based on the historical accounts of the organisation, which are prepared and maintained on a yearly basis by a financial accountant. The underlying assumption of the exercise is that what happened last year will happen next year, and that some adjustments need to be made to accommodate changes of policy and other factors. The limitation of this approach is that what happened last year will not necessarily happen next year. There was a time when some organisations, particularly public service bodies, could predict with some certainty that their next year's intentions would resemble their previous year's, and so this 'historical' approach worked for them, after a fashion.

A second approach might be to take a closer look at the present – *this* year – as a means of determining the future. In this case, it is the *management accounts* of the organisation that form the basis of the exercise. Management accounts provide the organisation with information on a week-by-week, month-by-month basis. They reflect what is actually happening during the present. Management accounts, unlike financial accounts, do not have the kudos of being presented at the board's annual general meeting or being filed at Companies House, but are arguably a better indicator of what the future will be like.

A third approach might be to acknowledge that both the first and second models are limited in what they can offer, and opt for what might be termed *zero-based budgeting*. An organisation adopting such an approach acknowledges that the financial targets of the future need to be set, not in accordance with what is happening now, or last year, but through an appraisal of the economic, business and consumer trends that can be anticipated during the coming years. That is, there is a need to look elsewhere, outside the world of accounting, in an attempt to forecast what the world can be expected to be like. Forecasting some events, such as some kinds of demographic change, is comparatively easy. For example, the young singles of the 1980s will inexorably become the young parents of the 1990s. But anticipating an event such as the fall of communism in eastern Europe at the end of the 1980s is a greater challenge. The liberalisation of the Soviet Union during the presidency of Mikhail Gorbachev from the mid-1980s onwards gave some indication that change could be expected, but the collapse of a whole succession of communist governments during the latter part of 1989 was as rapid as it was dramatic.

The reality confronting any organisation facing a budgeting exercise is that accuracy must be traded off against time. Zero-based budgeting is a time-consuming business, and so the actual method of budgeting adopted is likely to draw on all of the three models outlined above. Very often it will be quite safe to make certain assumptions about consistency from one year to the next. The art of management is to know when a change in strategy, and its attendant financial implications, is required. In this respect the art of management has need of the techniques of social science. For example, how will the increased incidence of skin cancer, the product of 30 years' excessive exposure to the sun by north Europeans, affect the massive German outbound holiday market? Germans are noted for their considerable sensitivity to health issues; this was demonstrated during 1994 in the German government's prohibition of imports of British beef because of fear of bovine spungiform disease, even though the UK and other European governments could identify a negligible risk to human health. How will this health sensitivity affect German outbound holiday-taking habits as concern grows over skin cancer? Given that Germany accounts for one in three of all European outbound tourist trips, even a small change in consumer behaviour could have significant effects on receiving destinations.

The purpose of this final chapter is to undertake a brief examination of the future for tourism. In keeping with the theses of this book outlined in Chapter 1, it is suggested that it is people's diverse expectations translated into consumer behaviour that determine future trends; that is, first, that the tourist product is psychological in its attractions; and secondly, that the attractiveness is determined by the evolution of the culture and mores of tourism-generating societies. The third thesis suggested that the demands of serving the tourist of the future will be determined by an empathy with the tourist based on an insight into the psycho-cultural nature of the tourist experience. It was suggested that this demand was to be met by a passion for service which was described as the *hospitality instinct*. This concluding chapter brings together an eclectic assemblage of observations which together, it is argued, suggest an endorsement of these theses.

The future for travel and tourism

Euromonitor identifies five strands of social change which emerged during the 1970s and 1980s and which it considers likely to continue. Quoted directly, they are:

- *A move toward healthier living*
- *A shift toward more active rather than less active recreational pursuits*
- *The growing importance of the 'quality of life' factor*
- *An interest in the natural environment, its flora and fauna*
- *A growing interest in exploring other cultures (1992a, p. 3)*

Euromonitor notes that the industry response to these trends has been increased segmentation of products and a reduction of sun-and-beach holiday provision in favour of a more diverse product base, but underlines that the sun-and-beach holiday still remains the major feature of tourism, and will continue to do so. There was an identifiable trend toward independent travel and tailor-made packages but on the other hand, it is noted that all-inclusive resorts on the model of Club Méditerranée have been successful too (Euromonitor 1992a, pp. 2–3). Examples of these are Sandals in the Caribbean, and Center Parcs in England whose holiday centres have maintained occupancy levels at well over 90 cent. Other trends such as the growth of the short break, and the growth of city and rural tourism, have been discussed in Chapter 7 and look set to continue. As noted in Chapter 7 and in Chapter 13, one very compelling reason for the continued attractiveness of the city is that, unlike a purpose-built destination, it is not a 'product' in the same way and may be insulated to some considerable extent from the inexorability of the resort life cycle. The whole point of being, to use Urry's term, a *post-tourist* in a post-industrial city is that it is not a resort at all, but rather an opportunity to play at other lifestyles, past and present.

It is in the short-break market that, on a European scale, significant developments can be expected. These will be facilitated by improvements in transport infrastructure, although it is strongly argued that the infrastructure improvements themselves will not cause the change; they will merely make possible the continued development of a fast-growing market sector whose growth is due to increased leave entitlements, higher discretionary incomes and the 'discovery' of the city and countryside as destinations. On a European scale this facilitation will be provided, principally, by technological advances in rail travel. Euromonitor lists a couple of dozen projected high-speed rail links which will cut the journey time from Paris to Amsterdam, for example, from 5 hrs. 7 mins. to 2 hrs. 48 mins. in the year 2000. Similarly, by using the Channel Tunnel, the journey time from London to Paris will be reduced from 5 hrs. 12 mins. to 2 hrs. 30 mins. (1992b, pp. 250–1). The implications for tourism are that business travellers will find the rail links between some cities faster than air travel, and that holiday-makers will be able to reach the Mediterranean from northern Europe in one night, but they still suggest that because of the overall expansion of tourism, air travel will continue to grow even if some traffic is lost to the railways (Euromonitor, 1992b, p. 46). Quoting the French State Railway company SNCF, Euromonitor suggests that for journeys of up to three hours, trains will hold the dominant share of the market; for those of from three to five hours, it will be shared 50/50 with the airlines; and that for those of over five hours, the airlines will dominate (1992a, p. 11).

Within the UK, Mintel has suggested that the domestic holiday industry is likely to show some small growth, although spending should grow more rapidly than the numbers of trips owing to the growth of short breaks as a proportion of the whole, and because short-break tourists tend to be pro-rata higher spenders (1992, p. 30). Globally, world tourism receipts are expected to increase by 5 per cent per annum up to 1997 (Euromonitor 1992b, p. 253). Within this picture, some of the more mature outbound markets, such as Germany and Sweden, are expected to show comparatively modest growth in numbers of trips between 1989 and 2000 of 21 per cent and 25 per cent respectively. Countries with latent outbound potential could produce more dramatic results. Japan, for example, with lengthening holiday entitlements, is projected to produce an 80 per cent increase in outbound tourist trips. Italy, whose economy like others in southern Europe is closing the gap with northern Europe, is projected to produce a 70 per cent increase (Euromonitor 1992b, p. 254).

The new consumers

The underlying purpose of this book has been to paint a picture of the tourist as a consumer: his or her needs, motivations, interests, preferences. Chapter 7 in particular addressed the question of fashion and fashionability. This picture can be summarised by drawing perspectives from Martin and Mason (1993), who, though writing about the future for visitor attractions, assembled a body of comment which they rightly observed to be of 'wider relevance'. Of direct importance was the increase in paid holidays which has been referred to in earlier chapters, giving rise to more opportunities for taking holidays.

There is also the related but nevertheless different issue of the shortening of working hours, and herein lies a paradox: when earning potential is at its highest, working hours are at their longest. The *Economist* has reported that in spite of reductions in working hours, managerial and professional people actually seem to be working longer hours. Quoted research suggested that the working hours of business executives in OECD countries rose by 20 per cent in the 1980s, and that out of 1,300 businesspeople, 40 per cent took only two or fewer weeks of their holiday entitlement. It was suggested that these people have high expectations of such leisure time as they allow themselves: the term 'playaholic' was used (1991). These people are quite literally work-hard, play-hard consumers.

Martin and Mason consider that concern for the environment, regarding time as well as money as a valuable resource and using it carefully, an active lifestyle and 'consuming with a mission', further defined as 'positive use of purchasing power for social ends' will translate into a shift from 'passive fun to active learning' (1993, p. 37). This, combined with the demographically growing importance of the affluent middle-aged, could mean a greater interest in traditional museums, country houses and gardens which arguably issue more of a challenge to the imagination than the 'heritage centres' of the 1980s, whose characteristics are, in the view of some, an excess of interpretation.

The spending power of the affluent middle-aged should not be underestimated. The vision of the British prime minister, John Major, of wealth 'cascading down the generations' was shown to be very accurate when a firm of probate specialists produced a report showing the increases in inheritances within England and Wales. The average inheritance was £68,000 in 1992, representing a 5 per cent increase over the previous two years. One in six estates was worth more than £100,000. It was predicted that property worth £24.3bn., similar to the total sum that would be spent on all tourism by UK residents in that year, would be passed on between 1992 and the year 2000 (Davison and Bradberry 1992). An industry analyst suggested that the volume of heritable property wealth 'illustrated a remarkable transformation in society' and was quoted as saying:

The typical age when people receive this inheritance money is 50, meaning a massive transfer of funds at a time when they don't need it. The kids have left home, the mortgage is paid off and the beneficiaries are still working. This ultimately means more people enjoying wealthier retirement than ever before. (quoted in Davison and Bradberry 1992)

The other demographic change of significance, as outlined in earlier chapters, is that of the family formation group. These people still have some time to wait until inheriting wealth from their parents, but are burdened with a range of financial responsibilities. It has been suggested that these people are perhaps suitable targets for domestic holidays and indeed have been targeted by such initiatives as the English Seaside campaign. In other respects, it is likely that they share with the middle-aged some of the newer values of the 1990s which differ from the conspicuous consumption of the 1980s. Present evidence of this in producer terms could well be the new emphasis on interactive displays in visitor attractions, such as Eureka! in Halifax, West Yorkshire. Further, an examination of attendances between 1987 and 1992 at the top 17 visitor attractions that charge for admission shows that the only attractions which enjoyed uninterrupted growth were two traditional museums, the Natural History Museum in South Kensington, London, and the Science Museum, London. Perhaps this was in part due to more vigorous marketing by the museums themselves, but it could represent a tentative indication of a trend away from packaged amusement and toward leisure activities which place greater demands on the imagination. How, exactly, does the relative attractiveness of various pursuits wax and wane? What mechanisms are at work? An examination of the phenomena of fashion and fad may offer some clues.

Fashions and fads

Fashion and fashionability are concepts that are distinct from the normal course of cultural evolution. There is an ephemeral quality about both, especially about fads whose duration may be limited to months or weeks. Nonetheless, fashionability can give rise to enduring outcomes which have powerful implications for holiday-taking patterns. The suntan, discussed earlier, may be such an example, its fashionability having part-guaranteed the value of the sun-and-beach holiday for some decades. Its demise as a fashion accessory could have serious consequences for such types of holidays. Fads are particularly intriguing: the general manager of a suburban hotel and restaurant complex was asked about the competitive threat posed by a new themed restaurant which had opened in close proximity to his establishment. He was confident that after an initial fascination with the idiosyncratic interior, interest would wear off and his customers would return to the less flashy but more durable attractions of his own restaurant. And yet he posed the question quite seriously: how can it be known what will work, how, and for how long? In short, how do fashions and fads arise? For example, the Mediterranean island of Ibiza gained a reputation during the 1980s as the island in the Balearics where young people could have the liveliest time. As the destination became associated with them and almost synonymous with their lifestyles, an over-dependency and an excess of association with the youth market was the result. As a consequence, other markets avoided the island. The young singles of the 1980s then grew up to become the young parents of the 1990s, leaving Ibiza in a fashion trap.

By what mechanism do fads arise? The *Economist* (1994e) attempted some answers to this question by addressing what it termed 'instances of mass conformity' by discussing an economic theory described as 'informational cascades', based on work undertaken at the University of California at Los Angeles (UCLA). Existing theories were said to include 'pay-off interactions'; so, for example, one could hypothesise that the extraordinary 1994 box-office success of the film *Four Weddings and a Funeral* in both the UK and the US was in part due to the need to be able to discuss the film with other people who had seen it. That is to say, initially some people saw it and thought it was good in a very individual sort of way, which meant that in order for others to participate in these conversations, it was necessary for them to see it. This however does not explain why, to use the examples quoted by the *Economist, Jurassic Park* was an enormous box-office success, while *Last Action Hero* was a flop. Another theory cited is 'conformity preference'; that is, people conform to what other people do, or do not do, because of the need to 'belong' to a set or peer group. This is suggested as the reason why some fads only affect some sectors of society; the aversion of the *service class* to the domestic seaside may be an example of conformity preference. 'Informational cascades' do not fully explain how fads and crazes catch on, but go some way toward illuminating the mechanism. The theory, based on the *Economist*'s (1994e) summary, goes like this:

1 No one person knows everything. Consumers watch each other's behaviour and use the information to influence their own decisions.
2 Very often, it is sensible and convenient to imitate others rather than make an individual decision.
3 A second consumer decides to purchase, based on information gained from observing an original (first) consumer.
4 A third consumer sees both first and second consumers acting on first-hand and second-hand information.
5 The third consumer observes that the second-hand information is perceived as valid by the second consumer.
6 Even if the third consumer's personal information is negative, this is outweighed by what he or she has observed.
7 The third consumer decides to purchase.

In this way, a 'cascade' of information results. The *Economist* points out that information cascades can act negatively as well; if the first and second consumers had decided not to purchase, then it is very likely that the third would also so decide.

Three conclusions reached by the UCLA researchers were as follows: that the fate of a product can be determined by the initial consumers; that a large number of consumers can make choices which are, rationally speaking, bad; and that large variations in demand can be caused by minor nuances in the information available to the initial consumers. As an example, the extraordinary success of the Center Parcs concept in the UK could well be the product of just such an information cascade. Anecdotal information includes mention of significant extra costs incurred in paying for the various activities once there and of allegedly unatmospheric restaurants; yet occupancy levels remain above 90 per cent all year round. The 'third consumer', while hearing all of this, bases the decision to purchase on an apparent general level of satisfaction. As a second example, stories of illness and heat exhaustion suffered by north Europeans when visiting resorts on the north African coast during the height of summer do little to discourage tourism to those destinations. Perhaps 'conformity preference' compels repeat visits, or maybe even 'pay-off interactions' in which post-visit discussion involves comparing notes on how hot it was, and how much time was spent in bed with stomach upsets. Exchanging holiday horror stories is known to be a feature of *post hoc* tourist discussions, and the pressure to participate in these grisly games of one-upmanship makes the initial experience perversely worthwhile.

No less significant in their power to influence tourism and leisure trends, and arguably explainable in terms of the theory of information cascade, are the proliferation of pressure groups in the UK. They are the active vehicles of the countryside and heritage obsession, the product of 'a thirty-year wave of middle-class energy, money and talent that has poured into single-issue causes . . . Being "concerned" now seems to be a national pastime' (*Economist* 1994a). Some of the 'concerned' emerge and become active only when their own backyard is threatened, the so-called NIMBYS. Others are active over a much wider field and have been termed NOTES (see Chapter 4). One major battleground, during the year 1994, was over road building. Considerable furore had already surrounded the construction of bypass roads around the cities of Winchester and Bath. The *Economist* (1994d) pointed to recent successes of the anti-road-building lobby, including the dropping of plans for a new Thames crossing because it threatened Oxleas Wood, a historic stand of trees; the deferral of a proposed rural bypass around the city of Hereford; and the shelving of two link roads to the M62. Discussing the make-up of the anti-road-building lobby, the *Economist* identified 'Shire Tories', 'Nimby protestors' and 'Radical greens' as its major constituent parts. The paradox is clear: if swathes of rural countryside and historic town centres are equally unacceptable locations for new road buildings, how can the burgeoning presence of the motor car, owned and operated by middle-class households in single if not multiple numbers, and of whom the Shire Tories and the Nimby protestors are representative, be accommodated? The proliferation of the private car has been particularly dramatic: between 1981 and 1990, the number of households operating two or more vehicles increased from 15 per cent to 23 per cent of the UK total; and between 1969 and 1990, the number of households operating at least one vehicle increased from half of the total, to two-thirds (Central Statistical Office 1993, pp. 182–3).

Since the early 1980s, government policy has been generally favourable to investment in road transport rather than rail. Yet it is quite obvious that to continue to encourage growth in car ownership while the car owners object to new roads is not a policy which can be sustained into the future. In 1994 controversy erupted over plans for a second runway at Manchester Airport (Halsall 1994). Only a dozen properties were to be sacrificed for this project, but it involved the felling of ancient woodland and though there was agreement by regional businesses that the second runway would improve employment in the region, the proposal flushed out NIMBY protestors whose angle of protest, which included the expansion of a smaller airport on Merseyside as an alternative, took the familiar environmental position:

'Is ripping up precious resources the only way to solve a problem? I'm not a hair-shirt donger, but the strain this kind of development puts on finite resources is making people throughout the world stop and think.' (quoted in Ward 1994)

In July 1994, plans to turn London's orbital motorway, the M25, into a 14-lane superhighway were deferred as objections from the National Trust, English Nature, Surrey County Council and the Council for the Protection of Rural England were included amongst 10,000 others received by the Department of Transport. The knock-on effect of not proceeding with this proposal would put into doubt a scheme for an additional, fifth terminal at Heathrow Airport (Barr and Brown 1994). As the year progressed, the government appeared to be reconsidering its commitment to road-building; under the headline, 'Tories plan U-burn on car culture', the *Observer* reported indications from the Secretary of State for Transport which it interpreted as an impending reversal of policies that had supported, in the words of the previous Prime Minister, Margaret Thatcher, the 'great car economy' (Ghazi 1994). A leader in the same edition of the newspaper called for the regeneration of public transport networks, arguing that the use of the motor car could not be reduced without a commitment to an effective alternative (*Observer* 1994). This at the time of writing presents an intriguing picture of change, and it will be interesting to see if significant cutbacks in the UK's £19bn. road-building programme are matched by renewed investment in public people-movers such as railways.

Accessibility

Much is made of the role of accessibility in facilitating tourist flows, and the underpinning element in accessibility is transport infra-structure. Therefore, for example, cheap air travel was one element in opening up Spain to a mass northern European tourism market in the 1960s and 1970s, but space in the skies above Europe plus suitable airports are the supporting infrastructure that makes this possible. Congestion in the skies, or resistance to expansion of airports, can limit accessibility even if the technology to travel exists. The notion of 'accessibility' is not limited to physical access: culture, motivation and lifestyle also encourage or inhibit access, as one would expect of a product which is 'largely psychological in its attractions'. This was ably demonstrated by the advertising campaign used to launch the Channel Tunnel in 1994: a very different approach was used on the two sides of the Channel. Eurotunnel estimated in 1989 that 15.3 million passengers would pass through the Channel Tunnel in its first full year of operation, of whom 2.2 million would be new customers (Euromonitor 1992a, p. 11). However, the appeal through advertising for this 'new business' does not use the 'because it is now possible' angle to woo customers. The images used differed in the UK and France:

British newspaper advertisements for the Channel Tunnel show cartoon-like figures snoozing their way through the tunnel or driving down tree-lined French roads. The French press advertising campaign, by contrast, features Napoleon, Churchill and Queen Victoria giving their blessing to the venture. (Batchelor 1994)

The different approach is representative of the supposed differences in cultural attitudes to the venture which may be encountered in France and Britain. The appeal of the advertising is to *motivation* and has nothing to do with technical accessibility. The UK advertising's depiction of cartoon figures driving along a French lane signify and connect with the kind of countryside lifestyle associations which were discussed in Chapter 7 and associated with the *service class*. The French advertising's portrayal of persons of monarchical stature endorsing the tunnel presents a comfortable spectacle of autocratic achievement in the French tradition, much in the same way as the diverse *grands projets* such as the Opéra de la Bastille and the Grande Arche de la Défense, completed in Paris during the 1980s, were the result of the personal initiative of the French president.

It can be argued that mass tourism to the Mediterranean from northern Europe has little to do with the fact that it became technically possible because of the cheapening of air travel,

and everything to do with the need to consummate a love affair with the sun. The means to travel do not of themselves create the will to travel. It is the motivation to drive down gallic country lanes, take part in history-in-the-making or bask in the sun which provides the impetus. By implication, means to travel when not associated with a motive to travel will not be taken up.

An illustration of this point is to be found in a particular development of transport infrastructure which has not had the benefit of strong motivation to facilitate its use. The Humber Bridge, opened by the Queen in 1981 and spanning the two banks of a major estuary, owes its origins to a promise in 1966 by an incumbent government with a wafer-thin majority, whose need to win a key by-election in the city of Hull led them to make the dramatic promise to provide a bridge. The bridge does not link significantly large centres of population, the city of Hull on its north side being the sole major centre in the Humberside region, and its meagre toll revenues have led to an escalating debt and subsidy from the Treasury (Hencke 1994). In itself, it has been described as a 'genuine world wonder . . . grander than the Golden Gate . . . the longest single-span suspension bridge in the world' (Wainwright 1994), but also as 'one of Britain's most notorious white elephants' (Hencke 1994). Accessibility, without incentive, does not work. In the absence of a clear purpose, the rationale for a project such as the Humber Bridge has to be innate self-worth; in the words of the Bridge-master, 'imposing proof of British engineering skill' and, inevitably, 'an important tourist attraction' (quoted in Wainwright 1994).

These examples point to the conclusion that technological or physical accessibility is not the root cause of tourist flows. The appeal to the people of France and Britain to use the Channel Tunnel is based on culture rather than physical possibility; the presence of a fixed link across the River Humber does not of itself facilitate a flow of traffic; and the facility to fly vast numbers of northern Europeans south to the Mediterranean each summer would be of little importance if the sun was not there to attract them. To acquire the *hospitality instinct* is to remember that people do not travel simply because it is possible, except perhaps when, as with the moon programme discussed in Chapter 5, the venture is linked with endeavour and the prestige of doing so becomes the end as well as the means.

Global warming

Although the precise implications of the warming up of the earth's atmosphere are as yet unknown, there is sufficient concern, and sufficient implication for holiday-making patterns, for it to be included in an appraisal of the future. The essence of the situation is that 'global warming', occurring naturally as part of a general and well-documented heating up of the earth's atmosphere, will accelerate as carbon dioxide gases from motor vehicle engines and industrial processes create a shield which limits the escape of warmth from the earth. This would result in some melting of the polar ice-caps and is of particular concern to countries like the Netherlands, for which a modest rise in sea level of (say) one half of one metre would result in serious indundation (Kemp 1990, p. 158). A second consequence would be the change in climate for areas which are located on the edges of existing climatic zones. A working group of scientists on the Intergovernmental Panel on Climate Change (IPCC) concluded that vulnerable regions were those which were 'arid and marginal', including the north coast of Africa and the Mediterranean (Leggett (ed.) 1990, p. 127). What this could mean is that countries currently enjoying a Mediterranean climate, and currently Europe's premier holiday playground, could see a significant deterioration in the natural environment as the north African desert 'moves' northwards. Anthony's article about Broadstairs, quoted in Chapter 12, includes some wistful words:

I have a recurring dream. In this dream somehow – the details have yet to be revealed to me – Britain loosens itself from its present latitudinal moorings and drifts southwards towards warmer, sub-tropical climes. (1994)

To 'reveal' those details, global warming offers the possibility, not of Britain drifting southward, but of sub-tropical climes drifting northward. Owing to the uncertain nature of the likely effects, it is inappropriate to speculate further and con-sequently difficult to evaluate Kemp's reference to 'the development of entirely new patterns of recreational activity' as one of the possible outcomes of global warming (1990, p. 158). However, a total change in current European holiday-making patterns would be a certain outcome if some of the more extreme predictions were to prove accurate.

Rediscovering a sense of place

The ways in which people form attachments to their home environments have already been touched upon in Chapter 3, in the context of the elements of home which they seek to 'accompany' them on holiday. In that chapter, various types of *place attachment* were discussed; the ways in which individual human beings form relationships with specific places, and specific kinds of places. Social scientists also have a terminology for types of society which are held together by different kinds of bond, summarised in Walmsley and Lewis (1993, p. 222): a *Gemeinschaft* society – the German word meaning 'community' – can be related to a specific geographical area and characterised by a network of 'primary relationships', such as kinship. A *Gesellschaft* society, by contrast – the German word means 'society' – is characterised by more impersonal interpersonal patterns defined by role rather than relationship. A city is an example of *Gesellschaft*, and the countryside of *Gemeinschaft*, although as the authors point out, the model should be viewed as a 'continuum' rather than an either/or. In contemporary society, most communities will be mixtures of the two.

We have already discussed, in earlier chapters, the diverse psychological attractions of each type of society to the mind-set of the tourist. A visit to the countryside, staying in a farmhouse bed-and-breakfast and enjoying family-style hospitality, is a form of tourist game which is psychologically the opposite of the city break, where the tourist cherishes the anonymity of the city and the option to opt in and out of the diverse lifestyles represented in a metropolitan environment. Both types of trip are tourist experiences of the post-industrial variety, in that both destinations are regarded as visitable simply because they are *not* purpose-built resorts. But there remains a dichotomy between the two. Short considers that it is the countryside that defines the sense of place and patrimony:

In most countries the countryside has become the embodiment of the nation, idealised as the ideal middle landscape between the rough wilderness of nature and the smooth artificiality of the town, a combination of nature and culture which represents the nation-state. (1991, p. 35)

This 'combination of nature and culture' has of course been the cause of much human distress when different cultures struggle for dominance over territory. Short points to the way in which the Nazi party fostered an image of rural Germany charged with a 'Nordic' ideal as a counterpoint to the cities, which were regarded as a 'melting pot of all evil' because of their polyglot populations and cultures (1991, p. 57). To some extent, alongside economic and political motives, it fuelled the doctrine of separate development designed in South Africa at the end of the 1940s, known as *apartheid*. More recently, its continued strength can be seen in the regionalisation tendencies which can be observed in many European states, and the hostilities in such areas as the Balkans where, for many years, the self-definition of culture by patrimony was suppressed under authoritarian regimes. Within the United Kingdom, Johnston argued that the so-called north–south divide between the manufacturing, urbanised north and the rural south became more noticeable during the 1980s through, as it seems, a heightened sense of place-awareness which was reflected in voting patterns:

the relative preponderance of Labour supporters in the North provides milieux within which new voters, whatever their 'objective' class position, are more likely to be socialised into pro-Labour attitudes than is the case in the South . . . the result has been a country which is spatially polarised electorally – both North–South and urban–rural. (1991, p. 223)

Johnston observes that this divide is also seen in the role of local governments, local authorities traditionally being higher spending when under Labour control than under Conservative, although in the 1990s the pattern has become more complex. One noteworthy development in the south has been the proliferation of cultural facilities provided by local governments in the south-east of England. In what could be interpreted as a drive to create for themselves an identity independent of the London metropolis, for which many south-eastern towns are dormitory suburbs, some of these communities have begun to equip themselves with the trappings of civic life. For example, Basingstoke has recently opened a new concert hall, the Anvil, and refurbished a theatre; High Wycombe has opened a new theatre, the Swan; and as an earlier example, Reading opened the Hexagon theatre during the 1970s. These can be viewed as examples of municipal self-definition in the same tradition that influenced the building of the municipal palaces and concert halls of the industrial North one hundred years earlier, and arguably afford themselves the elements of *Gesellschaft* and *Gemeinschaft* which were hitherto lacking.

It is startling to think that the emergence of the countryside and the post-industrial city as tourist destinations, with the attendant self-esteem and self-definition which ensue, could potentially in the long term threaten tourism as the very phenomenon which created it. If non-resorts become places to visit and thus become developed as tourist products in their own right, they are attractive places to visit *and* to live. If both recreational opportunities and a 'sense of belongingness' as a satisfaction can be found increasingly in the place of domicile, will the 'need' for a holiday, in particular, tourism-as-escape, continue unabated? In Chapter 7, it was argued that the near-obsession with rural environments is a consequence of service-class tastes and the attachment to the countryside and heritage traditions. This chapter has considered the paradoxical conflict between middle-class car use and middle-class single-issue pressure group activity. Another observation, drawn from the concept of the 'sense of place', may lead us to argue that the obsession with the countryside is indicative of a search for an attachment to or perhaps a rediscovery of a sense of patrimony, of *place*. As lifestyle replaces relationship in a post-modern world as a means of self-definition, the apparent trappings of both *Gesellschaft **and** Gemeinschaft*, keeping the local post office open, having a theatre in one's town, enjoying rural surroundings free from the spoilings of progress, become lifestyle essentials.

This trend was interestingly summarised by Wright (1994), reviewing a report produced by the Council for the Protection of Rural England concerning the impact of leisure and tourism on the countryside (CPRE 1994). Quoting some of the elementary conflicts such as yachtsmen v. power-boat racers, walkers v. mountain bikers and to which could be added the earlier example of jetskiers v. swimmers, Wright observes that the countryside is a battleground between different, growing activities which roughly divide off into active and contemplative pursuits. Pointing to the way in which new kinds of tourism, increasing holiday entitlements and discretionary income have married with the consequences of the EU set-aside policy as a potent mixture for developing leisure use of the countryside, Wright outlines the main point of the report as being that all the varied and conflicting uses are legitimate, and that the apparent 'empty landscapes' vision of some conservationist bodies is unrealistic. Equally unrealistic, it is suggested, are the opposite attitudes which confuse the nature of tourism as an activity and as an industry and by which 'the needs of the tourists are apparently conceived as the needs of the industry'. His conclusion is that visitor management policies are not of themselves enough.

Rediscovering a sense of people

An article in a UK provincial newspaper during 1994 reported on the growth of numbers of managerial and administrative staff within the local region of the National Health Service from 8,800 in 1990 to 11,720 in 1992. During the same period, the numbers of nursing staff and midwives were reduced from 30,139 to 27,560. When challenged to explain why funds were being channelled into support rather than frontline staff, a spokesperson was quoted as saying that 'It is vitally important everything is costed so we get

value for money' and that 'these people are necessary to make the NHS the success it is'. There had also been significant movement of administrative and clerical staff into the managerial salary grades, 'so they would be on performance-related pay' (Hirst 1994). Almost 30 years earlier, two practitioner-academics used the following illustration to demonstrate how 'task orientation' can depart from true objectives. It relates to a graduate student who was working in hospital administration and aiming to make a career in that field:

In a term paper, he wrote: 'The concept of the patient-centred hospital is all very well, but it should not be allowed to interfere with good administration.' Apparently no-one, either on the job or in graduate school, had ever said to him: 'Why do we have hospitals at all? What are they for? To provide jobs for administrators?' (Dale and Michelon 1966, p. 71).

'Cost disease', the symptoms of which appear when organisations need to save money and end up spending money, is one of the particular risks of the organisational climate of the 1990s. It has been more emotively described by opposition politicians as the 'cost-of-everything, value-of-nothing' culture. The principal victim of cost disease can be the primary purpose of the organisation. Is the purpose of the National Health Service to chase financial objectives and account for every penny no matter what the cost? Or is it expected to pursue social objectives which coincide with its founding principles?

In the tourism and hospitality industries, too, it is important to keep in touch with customers' real expectations. Enquiries into what customers actually want can be revealing. Coyle and Dale conducted research into what customers of hospitality organisations defined as 'good quality' in service, and also into hospitality managers' *perceptions* of what the customers would rate as 'good quality'. Managers' perceptions were coloured very much by their own demands, as providers, for the performance of their staff: they thought that customers' prime requirements were reliability, courtesy and understanding, in that order. Customers, by contrast, rated reliability *third* on their list. Their prime requirements were responsiveness, that is attentiveness and speed, courtesy, and then reliability. What emerges is a picture of customers who value competence in hospitality industry staff, but who are willing to trade a modicum of human error against attentiveness to their needs (1993). In other words, warm humanity and a passion for service, the *hospitality instinct*, is more important than cold, measurable competence.

An increasing sense of 'people' is also discernible in the Henley Centre for Forecasting's model for the development of international holiday-taking (Henley Centre 1992, pp. 25–7). Basing the model on the fact that increased wealth leads to increased tourism, but that it is those who are already tourists who travel more (as opposed, perhaps, to the 40 per cent of UK adults who do not take a main holiday), they postulate four phases of development by which tourist tastes and activities mature: in the first phase tourists are *bubble travellers*. These people are probably new to overseas travel and low in confidence in dealing with alien cultures. They generally seek a short-haul tourist experience within an environmental 'bubble', within which familiar necessities of their own culture such as English food, the English language and English people are available. The Henley Centre defines its second phase as that of the *idealised pleasure seeker*. This is a more mature traveller who can handle some alien cultures on an independent basis, for example booking a *gîte* holiday in France and travelling independently to the destination. But when travelling long haul to non-European cultures, they are still likely to be bubble travellers. Phase three travellers are defined as *wide horizon travellers*. These tourists have yet further confidence and seek to experience a wide range of alien cultures as objectives of their tourist activity. The Henley Centre points to the growing importance of 'off the beaten track' destinations and signs in the particularly mature German outbound market of increasing interest in Latin America, Africa and South-East Asia. A desire for greater 'authenticity' in cultural experience is said to be sought. Phase four – that characterised by *total immersers* – is posed by way of hypothesis rather than observation, although it is claimed that there are signs of its emergence in the German market. 'Total immersers' are said by the Henley Centre to seek to 'reproduce the cultural

experience of a native of that country; to become fully exposed to and fully immersed in its language, culture, heritage and patterns of life' (Henley Centre 1992, p. 27).

This typology was formulated as a way of showing the changing demands to which producers will need to respond as markets grow more mature, but it is also interesting to note that as the tourist matures, there is a change of emphasis from *place* to *people*. Admittedly, tourism by definition always involves relocation to some other place, but the bubble traveller eating English food, drinking English beer and socialising with English people in a mass-market Mediterranean resort might just as well be in England. The relocation is determined by motives of escape, the presence of the sun and possibly cost. The *place* is at one and the same time irrelevant and essential. By contrast, the mature traveller views himself or herself as visiting the *culture*, rather than the *place*. The significance of the *culture* is as a reflection of the *people*. To the mature traveller, the state of the weather may well be irrelevant, and the presence of English food, English beer, even other English people, may be viewed as an unwelcome intrusion.

Of course, access to tourism-as-discovery, the pursuit of people instead of place, is limited by income and lifestage. Mature tourist activity of the kind described above does not come cheap, and is dependent upon a predisposition which will be governed in all likelihood by a high level of education. Students are in a good position to undertake off-the-beaten track travel from the point of view of lifestage and relative absence of personal responsibilities, but at the family formation stage it becomes difficult.

The idea that tourism is a means of fostering international understanding has been advanced in some quarters, but it does not take much thought to realise that such a notion is seriously flawed. North Europeans converging on a mass-market destination will behave in accordance with their group identity, which will serve to reinforce stereotypes rather than dispel them. The same people descending on an exotic but undeveloped destination enjoy a relationship with the host community which is as economically unequal as it is temporary. Interestingly enough, there is an established mechanism whereby people, regardless of lifestage and to some extent regardless of wealth, can build authentic relationships with people from other cultures, and that is the often-derided practice of town twinning. Such links are made between local authorities and are fostered on the basis of hosting, and reciprocation: that is to say that people stay not in hotels, but in each other's homes, and that visits and hospitality must be reciprocated. Municipalities in the UK maintain around 1,600 twinning links, many of these between towns and regions within Europe (Donaldson 1992). The growth areas are in eastern Europe and the developing world, where the UK's Local Government International Bureau (LGIB) is keen to ensure that the inequality and temporariness of tourism-type relationships is avoided:

one-sided twinning, without the traditional cultural and friendship links, is discouraged by the LGIB ... its assistant director says the two aspects – cultural and business – must go hand in hand, in order to avoid the 'snowploughs to Ghana' syndrome, where inappropriate technology and solutions are applied because of lack of knowledge about a particular country. (Donaldson 1992)

If tourism has a contribution to make to the forging of authentic cultural and friendship links it may well be the effect of business tourism, rather than pleasure vacations, that will achieve that objective more effectively. Where people focus efforts on common endeavour, mutual reliance and a degree of mutual understanding are the result. Where business relationships progress beyond business endeavour and lead to social relationships involving spouses, children and friends then the outcomes in terms of mutual understanding are not dissimilar from those achieved through the structures of twinning.

Three propositions

To conclude this commentary it is proposed to advance three propositions which may influence the shape of tourism in the future. This is not to say that these will be trends in themselves, but that they will have some effect on the character of future trends.

'TOURISM AS PEOPLE' REPLACING 'TOURISM AS PLACE'

For tourists are, in the main, a very gloomy-looking tribe. I have seen much brighter faces at a funeral than in the Piazza of St Mark's. Only when they can band together and pretend, for a brief, precarious hour, that they are at home, do the majority of tourists look really happy.
Aldous Huxley in his essay, 'Why Not Stay At Home?' (Venter 1992)

Even the grandeur of Venice is possessed of a two-dimensional blandness when there is no rapport between the place and its beholder. Huxley goes on to acknowledge that there is such a thing as a genuine traveller, but considers that most tourists are travellers for the sake of consumption and convention, doomed to disappointment because the fashionable wonders of tourist destinations ultimately fail to satisfy. His conclusion is that tourists' solution is to seek out fellow travellers to create a 'little oasis of home'. Perhaps the 'tourism as people' proposition may manifest itself in the greater enjoyment of the domicile and the realisation that it, as a place, can provide some of the benefits which have been associated exclusively, perhaps clumsily or perhaps mistakenly, with overseas pleasure vacations. Complementing this may be the emergence in greater numbers of mature travellers whose ability to enjoy a place is rooted in place-as-people rather than place-as-place.

SUSTAINABLE DOMESTICITY

As the industrial city metamorphoses into the leisured city, the countryside becomes the playing field for a diversity of individualist pursuits and work becomes less tethered to particular places, people find their recreational needs provided for within the locality of domicile in ways that could not have been imagined 30 years ago. 'Home' for many people is becoming, increasingly, a hive of lifestyle opportunities for recreational and cultural fulfilment. Within the concept of 'active learning', to use the phrase coined by Martin and Mason (1993), should be included the increasingly flexible access to education offered by post-school educational institutions. 'Sustainable tourism' is the fashionable but furry concept which is offered as a response to the problems of excess visitation. Perhaps the focus of attention is mistaken. 'Sustainable domesticity' may be the more appropriate solution.

TOURISM INTO EQUILIBRIUM

A cynic could view tourism as the developed world's most recent questionable export, a form of economic imperialism. Mass overseas tourism is still a relatively recent phenomenon, the scale of which could well turn out to have some of the characteristics of a fad. Consider, for example, a recreational pursuit such as cinema going: in the early 1950s, every UK adult went to the cinema on average once per week; this reduced to once per year in 1985, and has since increased to twice per year. It is tempting to talk in dramatic terms about the rise and fall of the cinema, but in reality the cinema is still with us: what has happened is that the cinema, after the post-war golden age when other leisure pursuits could not rival it for glamour and availability, has now taken its place alongside other leisure activities. For a brief period, in the artificial climate of post-war austerity, it enjoyed unrivalled dominance as a mass-market leisure pursuit.

Similarly, what is witnessed in contemporary tourism could be a parallel process. A love affair with the sun was made possible by air travel, first short haul, now long haul, at prices affordable to the rising disposable incomes of the northern European mass market. Perhaps the recent growth of the domestic short-break holiday and the proliferation of segmented lifestyle activities and interests are witness to the creation of an equilibrium, where 'home' and 'away' are viable alternatives for spending free vacational time, and where people and activity replace place and climate as the foci of interest.

Viewed in this way, it seems rather odd that the annual 'need for a holiday' should retain such a hold on the western mind; perhaps it is a yet-to-be-exorcised throwback to Fordist lifestyles where an annual escape was necessary for aesthetic as well as recreational reasons. Huxley's 'genuine travellers' will still enjoy a panoply of opportunities for exploring the four corners of the world, but there will be less of a social obligation on the 'gloomy' ones to go along too, except when they really want to. And when they do go, they may be better prepared, like the Henley Centre's 'wide-horizon travellers'. Perhaps it is no coincidence that early planning and booking should be a feature of the German outbound market, commonly regarded as the world's most mature: one-quarter of vacational travel plans are decided before Christmas of the previous year (British Tourist Authority 1993). And when by contrast people indulge themselves in tourism-as-escape, facilities rather than climate may increasingly become determining factors: the overwhelming success of Center Parcs which enjoys occupancy rates of 95 per cent and more, and high levels of repeat business (Lavery 1990; Crabbe and Lynn 1992), is perhaps an early indication of this.

The global resort

The contemporary world has been referred to as a 'global village', in that communications and the globalisation of business are making the world a smaller place. As a global resort, the world may, arguably, expect to pass through some phases of the resort life cycle. Those developments in communications, particularly in the field of multimedia, will surely enhance the vicarious travel opportunities already available through books, television and video; the armchair tourist will have a feast. It is interesting to speculate that as the global resort matures in its global life cycle, the novelty of allocentric personal discovery may wear off and the challenge of psychocentric vicarious discovery may become fashionable; perhaps, even, equally addictive. The mass scramble to actually *visit* places, have oneself photographed at them, buy memorials of them and hack chunks off them to take home, may like mass cinema going subside and eventually find itself in equilibrium with domestic recreation and the enjoyment of vicarious travel. A picture of sustainable domesticity, punctuated with occasional but profound tourist voyages for which preparatory work has taken months if not years, is a tantalising thought.

Bibliography

Adburgham, R and Summers, D (1994) After the dust has settled, *Financial Times*, 28 April, p. 21.

Altman, I and Chemers, M (1980) *Culture and Environment*. Cambridge: Cambridge University Press.

Anderson, B (1993) Plans afoot to secure future of York Festival, *The Stage and Television Today*, 30 September

Anthony, A (1994) The last resort, *Observer Life*, 13 March.

Appleton, E (1991) Value-added culture, *Marketing*, 14 February.

Ashworth, G and Voogd, H (1990) *Selling the City*. London: Belhaven Press.

Atkinson, D *et al.* (1985) *Bridlington: A Seaside Resort*. Beverley: Humberside County Council.

Baker, M J (ed.) (1991) *The Marketing Book*, 2nd edn. Oxford: Butterworth-Heinemann.

Bar-On, R (1989) *Travel and Tourism Data*. London: Euromonitor.

Barr, C and Brown, P (1994) Inquiry delay by minister plus 14-lane plan for M25 into doubt, *Guardian*, 16 July.

Barrett, A (1987) Bridlington Leisure World, *The Leisure Manager*, June, p. 23.

Barthes, R. (1972) *Mythologies*. London: Vintage (Edition published 1993).

Batchelor, R (1992) English Language Teaching Market in the UK, *Insights* B-19. London: English Tourist Board.

Batchelor, C (1994) Softly, softly approach, *Financial Times*, 10 February, p. 18.

Battersby, D (1990) Lifting the barriers: Employment and training in tourism and leisure, *Insights*, D 7–1, 1989/90. London: English Tourist Board.

Bayley, S (1991) *Taste: the Secret Meaning of Things*. London: Faber and Faber.

—— (1994) Stay the night in a laboratory of taste, *The European*, Élan, p. 20. 11–17 March.

BBC Radio 4 (1993) *File on Four*. 2 November.

Beioley, S (1991a) Business Tourism, *Insights*, vol. 3, B-7. London: English Tourist Board.

—— (1991b) The short breaks market, *Insights*, vol. 3, B-29. London: English Tourist Board.

Bennett, R (1993) *The Handbook of European Advertising*. London: Kogan Page.

Bierce, M (1991/92): Baléares: la 'muerte' du modèle? *Espaces*, no. 113, Dec 1991/Jan 1992, pp. 47–50.

Binford, L (1962) Archaeology as anthropology, *American Antiquity*, vol. 28, no. 2, pp. 217–25.

Blackhurst, C (1994) Notes: the rural taste tyrants, *Observer*, 21 August.

Bradshaw, J (1972) The concept of social need, *New Society*, 30 March, pp. 640–3.

Brendon, P (1991) *Thomas Cook; 150 Years of Popular Tourism*. London: Martin Secker & Warburg.

British Tourist Authority (1993) *Market Guide: Germany, Austria & Switzerland*. London: BTA.

Broadbent, G (1980) Architects and their symbols, *Built Environment*, vol. 6, no. 1.

Brown M (1994) Peer attacks 'arrogance' of National Trust, *Yorkshire Post*, 11 August.

Buck, A *et al.* (1991) A Von Thünen model of crime, casinos and property values in New Jersey, *Urban Studies*, vol. 28, no. 5, pp. 673–86.

Bundesminister für Arbeit und Sozialordnung (1976) *Arbeitsförderungsgesetz*. Bonn.

Bunting, M (1990) Costa ditched as Spain loses shine, *Guardian*, 24 May.

Burgess, T (1980) Accountability makes councillors good accountants, *Guardian*, 14 July.

Burkart, A J and Medlik, S (1981) *Tourism: Past, Present and Future*. London: Heinemann.

Burtenshaw, D *et al.* (1991) *The European City: a Western Perspective*. London: David Fulton.

Butler, R W (1980) The concept of a tourist area cycle of evolution: implications for management of resources, *Canadian Geographer* vol. XXIV no. 1, pp. 5–12.

Car magazine (1990) The good, the bad and the ugly, *Car*, September, p. 150.

Central Statistical Office (1993) *Social Trends* 23. London: Her Majesty's Stationery Office.

—— (1994a) *Annual Abstract of Statistics*, no 130. London: Her Majesty's Stationery Office.

—— (1994b) *Social Trends* 24. London: Her Majesty's Stationery Office.

Channel 4 Television (1986) *The Marketing Mix.* Programme 3 of a ten-part series.

Childe, V G (1929) *The Danube in Prehistory.* Oxford.

Chisnall, P M (1992) *Marketing Research*, 4th edn. Maidenhead, England: McGraw-Hill.

Clouston, E (1994) Ffyona, born to be on her own planet, *Guardian*, 15 October.

CNAA (Council for National Academic Awards) (1993) *Review of tourism studies and degree courses.* London: CNAA.

Cooke, P (ed.) (1989) *Localities: the Changing Face of Urban Britain.* London: Unwin Hyman.

Cooper, C P (ed.) (1990) *Progress in Tourism, Recreation and Hospitality Management*, vol. 2. London: Belhaven Press.

—— (ed.) (1991) *Progress in Tourism, Recreation and Hospitality Management*, vol. 3. London: Belhaven Press

—— *et al.* (1993) *Tourism: Principles and Practice.* London: Longman.

Council for the Protection of Rural England (1994) *Leisure Landscapes: leisure, culture and the English countryside.* London: CPRE.

Coyle, M and Dale, B (1993) Quality in the hospitality industry: a study, *International Journal of Hospitality Management*, vol. 12, no. 2, pp. 141–53.

Crabbe, M and Lynn, M (1992) Leisure profits thrive under Center Parcs glass dome, *Sunday Times*, 12 July.

Crompton, J L (1979) Motivation for pleasure vacation, *Annals of Tourism Research*, vol. 6, no. 4, pp. 408–24.

Dale, E and Michelon, L (1966) *Modern Management Methods.* Harmondsworth, Middlesex: Penguin.

Dann, G M S (1977) Anomie, ego-enhancement and tourism. *Annals of Tourism Research* vol. 4 (4) 184–94.

—— (1981) Tourist motivation: an appraisal, *Annals of Tourism Research*, vol. 8, no. 2, pp. 187–219.

Davidson, A (1989) The marketing interview: Robert Heller, *Marketing*, 23 March, p. 27.

Davies, M (1989) A loss of vision, *Leisure Management*, vol. 9, no. 10.

Davison, J and Bradberry, G (1992) Inherited millions release 'cascade of wealth', *Sunday Times*, 3 May, p. 5.

de Bono, E (1994) When is a box not a box? When it's a straitjacket, *Guardian*, 3 September.

Devas, E (1993) *The European Tourist: A Market Profile.* London: TPR Associates.

Donaldson, L (1992) A twinning combination, *Geographical Magazine*, December, pp. 16–19.

Doyal, L and Gough, I (1984) A theory of human needs, *Critical Social Policy*, vol. 10, pp. 6–38.

East Yorkshire Borough Council (1980a) *Survey of Tourism in Bridlington and the North Wolds.* Bridlington: EYBC.

—— (1980b) *Tourism in Bridlington: Key Facts.* Bridlington: EYBC.

—— (1983) *Bridlington Holiday Guide 1983,* Bridlington: EYBC.

—— (1987) *Tourism in Bridlington: Key Facts.* Bridlington: EYBC.

Eastbourne Borough Council (1991) *Eastbourne Tourism Study 1990.* Eastbourne: Eastbourne BC.

Economist (1991) Working hard, playing harder, *Economist*, 22 June, p. 86.

—— (1994a) A nation of groupies, *Economist*, 13–19 August, p. 25.

—— (1994b) Fifty ways to lose your wallet, *Economist*, 26 March, p. 59.

—— (1994c) For richer, for poorer, *Economist*, 5–11 November, pp. 19–21.

—— (1994d) The classless society, *Economist*, 19 February, p. 27.

—— (1994e) Yes, ten million people can be wrong, *Economist*, 19 February, p. 93.

—— (1994f) Author! Author!, *Economist*, 11 June, pp. 113–14.

—— (1994g) All our yesterdays, *Economist*, 11 June, p. 18.

Economist Intelligence Unit (1992a) Plastic Money in Germany, *Marketing in Europe*, no. 353, April.

—— (1992b) *The European Tour Operator Industry*. Special Report 2141.

Editions la Découverte (1992) *L'État de la France*. Paris.

Elliott, L (1991) Dreamland waits for the tide to turn in its favour, *Guardian*, 12 August, p. 10.

Ellison, M (1994) Literary analysis comes to Lear, *Guardian*, 18 June, p. 13.

English Tourist Board (1988) *Visitors in the Countryside: Rural Tourism, a Development Strategy*. London: English Tourist Board.

—— (1990) *The UK Tourist: Statistics 1989*. London: English Tourist Board.

—— (1991) Overseas tourism to the UK, *Insights*, F-5, November. London: English Tourist Board.

—— (1992a) *Shorelines*. London: English Tourist Board.

—— (1992b) *The UK Tourist: Statistics 1991*. London: English Tourist Board.

—— (1993) *Turning the Tide: A Heritage and Environment Strategy for a Seaside Resort*. London: English Tourist Board.

Erlichman, J (1993) Business backs law on global warming, *Guardian*, 8 May.

Esslin, M (1970) *The Peopled Wound: The Plays of Harold Pinter*. London: Methuen.

Euromonitor (1992a) *The European Travel and Tourism Marketing Directory*. London: Euromonitor.

—— (1992b) *The Book of European Forecasts*. London: Euromonitor.

—— (1992c) *The European Compendium of Marketing Information*. London: Euromonitor.

Eurostat, D (1992) *Tourism in Europe: Trends 1989*. Brussels: Eurostat.

Freemantle, D (1992) *Incredible Bosses*. Maidenhead, England: McGraw-Hill.

Foster, D (1985) *Travel and Tourism Management*. London: Macmillan.

Garner, J (1994) Up the hill, on the farm and down the close, *The Stage and Television Today*, 4 August, p. 20.

Getty, J P (1971) *How to be a Successful Executive*. London: Star Books (1976 edn.).

Ghazi, P (1994) Tories plan U-turn on car culture, *Observer*, 16 October.

Gill, I (1986) Tourism and entertainment services in local government, *The Future Role and Organisation of Local Government*, Functional Study no. 4, Leisure. Working Paper 4.6. Birmingham: Institute of Local Government Studies.

Gray, H P (1970) *International travel – International Trade*. Lexington, Maine: Heath Lexington Books.

Griffiths, R (1993) The politics of cultural policy in urban regeneration strategies, *Policy and Politics*, vol. 21, no. 1, pp. 39–46.

Hall, C M (1992) *Hallmark Tourist Events*. London: Belhaven Press.

Halsall, M (1993) Once-rich South moves up the queue for aid hand-out, *Guardian*, 24 July, p. 8.

—— (1994) Manchester runway enquiry ready for take-off, *Guardian*, 18 June, p. 13.

Hamilton-Smith, E (1987) Four Kinds of Tourism?, *Annals of Tourism Research*, vol. 14, pp. 332–44.

Hamnett, C *et al.* (eds.) (1989) *The Changing Social Structure*. London: Sage.

Handy, C (1991) *The Age of Unreason*. London: Arrow Books.

—— (1991a) *Gods of Management*. London: Business Books Ltd.

—— (1993) *Understanding Organisations*. London: Penguin.

Hansford C (1980) The years of neglect roll away, *Hull Daily Mail*, 7 October.

Hare, D (1995) Perfectly simple, *Observer Review*, 1 January, pp. 10–11.

Harloe, C *et al.* (eds.) (1990) *Place, Policy, Politics: Do Localities Matter?* London: Unwin Hyman.

Harvey, D (1989) *The Condition of Postmodernity*. Oxford: Basil Blackwell.

Harvey-Jones, J (1988) *Making It Happen: Reflections on Leadership*. London: HarperCollins (1994 edn.)

Hencke, D (1994) Minister in hot water over Humber debt, *Guardian*, 15 November, p. 2.

Henley Centre for Forecasting (1989) *Leisure Futures*. London: Henley Centre for Forecasting.

—— (1992) *Inbound Tourism: A Packaged Future?* London: Henley Centre/NEDO.

Hepple, P (1992) You've got to be special to survive in summertime, *The Stage and Television Today*, 20 August.

—— (1993) Seasons to be cheerful, *The Stage and Television Today Summer Preview*, 1993.

Heron, P R (1991) The institutionalization of leisure: cultural conflict and hegemony, *Loisir et Société*, vol. 14, no. 1, pp. 171–90.

Herzberg, F (1968) *Work and the Nature of Man.* London: Staples.

Hewison, R (1987) *The Heritage Industry.* London: Methuen.

Hickman, M (1994) Resorts 'ruined' by hostels, *Hull Daily Mail*, 28 March.

Hill, D (1993) Mayday for May Bank Holiday, *Guardian*, 1 May.

Hirst, A (1994) Dramatic slump in number of nurses and midwives, *Huddersfield Daily Examiner*, 25 February, p. 1.

Holloway, J C (1989) *The Business of Tourism*, 3rd edn. London: Pitman.

—— **and Plant, R V** (1992) *Marketing for Tourism*, London: Pitman.

Howlett, P (1994) Preview: Atlantic City, *Guardian*, 'Guide', 12 November, p. 14.

Hull Daily Mail (1978a) £140,000 for Old Hull facelift. 14 June, p. 1.

—— (1978b) Councillors welcome Old Town museum ideas. 20 June, pp. 1 and 7.

—— (1978c) One more aspect of Old Town revival. 3 July.

—— (1979) Boom Time in Old Town Today. 10 October, p. 1.

Humberside County Council (1992) *Tourism Tomorrow: A Five-Year Strategy for Humberside.* Beverley: Humberside County Council.

Hutton, W (1995) Wrench this place apart, *Guardian*, 21/22 February.

Ignatieff, M (1984) *The Needs of Strangers.* London: Chatto & Windus.

InterCity Derby (1993) *InterCity Holidaymaker: Yorkshire Edition.* Leaflet 93/068D.

InterCity East Coast (1993) *Apex from North and West Yorkshire.* Leaflet AS1378/A130/10.93–5.94.

Jackson, P (1989) *Maps of Meaning.* London: Routledge.

Jackson, T (1994) *Virgin King.* London: HarperCollins.

Johnson, A (1993) Victorian values washed up on the seashore, *Guardian*, 9 August, p. 16.

Johnson, P and Thomas, B (eds.) (1992) *Choice and Demand in Tourism.* London: Mansell.

Johnston, R J (1991) *A Question of Place.* Oxford: Blackwell.

Kalimo, R *et al.* (eds.) (1987) *Psychosocial Factors at Work and their Relation to Health.* Geneva: World Health Organisation.

Kemp, D (1990) *Global Environmental Issues: a climatological approach.* London: Routledge.

Kirsch, B (1994) Clampdown on speaking out, *NATFHE Journal*, Summer 1994, p. 15.

Kotler, P (1984) *Marketing Management: Analysis, Planning and Control*, 5th edn. Englewood Cliffs, New Jersey: Prentice-Hall.

—— (1991) *Marketing Management: Analysis, Planning and Control*, 7th edn. Englewood Cliffs, New Jersey: Prentice-Hall.

—— **and Armstrong, G** (1991) *Principles of Marketing*, 5th edn. Englewood Cliffs, New Jersey: Prentice-Hall.

Krippendorf, J (1987) *The Holiday Makers.* London: Butterworth-Heinemann.

Lash, A (1990) *Sociology of Postmodernism.* London: Routledge.

Lavery, P (1990) Center Parcs, *Insights*, 1989/90, C7–1. London: English Tourist Board.

Lazenby, G (1989) Case Study: Polurrian Hotel, *Insights*, C2–1. London: English Tourist Board.

Leggett, J (1990) *Global Warming: the Greenpeace report.* Oxford: Oxford University Press.

Lundberg, D E and Lundberg, C B (1993) *International Travel and Tourism.* New York: John Wiley.

Magrath, P (1993) Beaches fall below EC standard, *Independent*, 24 August.

Mannell, R C (1984) A psychology for leisure research, *Leisure and Society*, vol. 7.

—— **and Iso-Ahola, S E** (1987) The psychological nature of leisure and tourism experience, *Annals of Tourism Research*, vol. 14, pp. 314–31.

Manning, J (1994) Historic Hull – official! *Hull Daily Mail*, 10 February, p. 1.

Marketing Week (1993) Cuts could injure the ETB, *Marketing Week*, 6 August.

Martin, B and Mason, S (1993) The future for attractions: meeting the needs of the new consumers, *Tourism Management*, February 1993, pp. 34–40. London: Butterworth-Heinemann.

Martins, C (1980a) Bold Bridlington and subtle Scarborough, *Municipal Journal*, 10 October, pp. 1188–9.

—— (1980b) The miracle of Bridlington, *Catering Times*, 13 November, pp. 5 and 12.

Maslow, A H (1970) *Motivation and Personality*, 2nd edn. New York: Harper and Row.

Mathieson, A and Wall, G (1982) *Tourism: Economic, Physical and Social Impacts*. Harlow, Essex: Longman.

McAndrew, F T (1993) *Environmental Psychology*. Belmont, California: Brooks/Cole.

McClarence, S (1981) Sickest show on earth, *Sheffield Star*, 11 July, p. 7.

McGregor, D (1960) *The Human Side of Enterprise*. New York: McGraw-Hill.

Mellor, C (1993) Holiday family shocked by 'circumcision party', *Huddersfield Daily Examiner*, 10 September.

Mellor-Stapelberg, A (1994) Where the grass is greener, *Guardian Weekend*, 14 May, p. 17.

MEW Research (1992) Holiday Destination Choice Survey 1991, *Insights*, A-17, July. London: English Tourist Board.

Middleton, V T C (1988) *Marketing in Travel and Tourism*. Oxford: Butterworth-Heinemann.

—— (1989) Seaside resorts, *Insights*, vol. 1, B 5–1. London: English Tourist Board.

—— (1991) *The Future for England's Smaller Seaside Resorts: Summary Report*. London: English Tourist Board.

Mill, R C and Morrison, A M (1992) *The Tourism System: An Introductory Text*, 2nd edn. Englewood Cliffs, New Jersey: Prentice-Hall.

Mintel (1992) British on holiday at home, *Leisure Intelligence*, vol. 1, pp. 1–30.

Myerscough, J (1988) *The Economic Importance of the Arts in Britain*. London: Policy Studies Institute.

Newman, D (1977) Subscribe Now! New York: Theatre Communications Group.

NOP Research (1989) *Survey of Visitors to Blackpool*. Blackpool: Blackpool Borough Council.

Norman, B (1989) Looking ahead to the 1990s, *Insights*, A3–11. London: English Tourist Board.

Norris, G (1994) Test your tolerance – to pain, *European*, 18–21 March.

Observer (1994) Time to make motoring tough, *Observer*, 16 October, p. 26.

Office of Arts and Libraries (1988) *Financing our Public Library Service: Four Subjects for Debate*. London: Her Majesty's Stationery Office.

Pearce, P L and Stringer, P F (1991) Psychology and Tourism, *Annals of Tourism Research*, vol. 18, pp. 136–54.

Pick, J (1988) *The Arts in a State*. Bristol: Bristol Classical Press.

Policy Studies Institute (1989) *Cultural Trends 1989*, vol. 2. London: Policy Studies Institute.

Proshansky W H *et al.* (eds.) (1976) *Environmental Psychology*, 2nd edn. New York: Holt, Rinehart and Winston.

Prospect Music & Art Tours Ltd (1992) *Prospect 1993*. London: Prospect Music & Art Tours Ltd.

Quest, M (ed.) (1990) *The Horwarth Book of Tourism*. London: Macmillan.

Raban, J (1974) *Soft City*. London: Hamish Hamilton.

Renfrew, A C (1973) *Before Civilisation*. London: Jonathan Cape.

Ritchie, J and Hawkins, D (eds.) (1991) *World Travel and Tourism Review*, vol. 1. Wallingford, Oxon: CAB International.

Ryan, C (1991) *Recreational Tourism: A Social Science Perspective*. London: Routledge.

Samuel, J (1994): Little and large show, *Guardian Weekend*, 17 December, p. 58.

Scott, J (1978) Now is the summer of York's discontent made inglorious by tourists, *Yorkshire Post*, 9 August, p. 1.

Sharrock, D (1994) Museum helps Irish to bear pain of famine, *Guardian*, 14 May.

Sherwood, C (1994) Bed, breakfast, burgers, boys – and banter, *Observer*, 19 July, p. 67.

Short, J R (1991) *Imagined Country*. London: Routledge.

Slingsby, H (1994) Advice squad, *Marketing Week*, 8 July.

Smithers, R (1992) Tourist board faces cut, *Guardian*, 14 November.

Sorensen, T C (1965) *Kennedy*. London: Hodder & Stoughton.

Stage and Television Today (1993) BARB ratings for week ending April 11 1993, *The Stage and Television Today*, 29 April, p. 25.

Taylor, N (1975) *The Old Town Conservation Area*. Hull: Hull City Council.

Thanet District Council (1991a) *Kent's Leisure Coast Holidaymaker Survey 1991*. Margate: Thanet District Council.

—— (1991b) *Kent's Leisure Coast Tourism: the Key Facts*, 1st edn., January 1991. Margate: Thanet District Council.

—— (1991c) *Foreign Students in Kent's Leisure Coast*. Margate: Thanet District Council.

—— (1991d) *Draft Marketing Plan Update – November 1991*. Margate: Thanet District Council.

Torkildsen, G (1986) Lord Forte of Ripley in conversation with George Torkildsen, *Leisure Management*, vol. 6, no. 7, July.

Tourism Society (1993) *The Profile of Tourism Degree Studies in the UK 1993*. London: The Tourism Society.

Travis, P (1992) The seaside fights back, *Insights*, vol. 4, C-9. London: English Tourist Board.

Travis Davis and Partners (1989) Advertising the English Riviera, *Insights*, 1989/90, C1–1. London: English Tourist Board.

Urry, J (1988) Cultural change and contemporary holiday-making, *Theory, Culture and Society*, vol. 5, pp. 35–55.

—— (1990) *The Tourist Gaze*. London: Sage.

Uzzell, D L (ed.) (1989) *Heritage Interpretation*, vol. 1. London: Belhaven.

Venter, M (compiler) (1992) *The Spirit of Place: an anthology of travel writing*. Oxford: Oxford University Press.

Vidal, J (1994) £7m green festival in doubt after second executive quits, *Guardian*, 24 July.

Voase, R N (1981) Sunny future, *Sheffield Star*, 5 October, p. 6.

—— (1992) *The Relaunch of the Kent's Leisure Coast Resorts of Ramsgate, Broadstairs and Margate as a Tourist Destination*. Unpublished paper produced for the Chartered Institute of Marketing.

—— (1994) Strategy or chance? A perspective on the cultural regeneration of our cities, *Regional Review*, vol. 4, no. 3. Leeds: Yorkshire & Humberside Regional Research Observatory.

Wainwright, M (1994) Bridge over which it can be better to travel than to arrive, *Guardian*, 15 November, p. 2.

Walmsley, D and Lewis, G (1993) *People and Environment: behavioural approaches to human geography*. Harlow, Essex: Longman.

Walsh-Heron, J (1988) Bradford: the Myth-Breakers? *Leisure Management*, February.

Ward, D (1994): Well-prepared middle classes rise to protect their back yards, *Guardian*, 18 June.

Ware, A and Goodin, R E (eds.) (1990) *Needs and Welfare*. London: Sage.

Waterson, M J (ed.) (1992) *The Marketing Pocketbook*. Henley-on-Thames, Oxfordshire: Advertising Association/NTC Publications.

Watts, C (1991) The New Listings Market – An Overview, *Insights*, A-33. London: English Tourist Board.

Wernick, A (1991) *Promotional Culture: advertising, ideology and symbolic expression*. London: Sage.

WGBH Educational Foundation (1981) *Enterprise: Not By Jeans Alone*. Video. Distributor: Gower TFI.

White, L A (1959) *The Evolution of Culture*. New York: McGraw-Hill.

Wickers, D (1987) Splashing out, *Guardian*, 20 June.

Williamson, P (1978) Industrial tonic top aim for heart of Hull, *Hull Daily Mail*, 4 October, p. 8.

Wilson, R M S and Gilligan, C, with Pearson, D J (1992) *Strategic Marketing Management*. Oxford: Butterworth-Heinemann.

Woodward, M (1993) Still my kind of town, *Huddersfield Daily Examiner*, 17 December, p. 15.

Wright, P (1994) Harvesting a future from rocky ground, *Guardian*, 14 May, p. 31.

WTTC (World Travel and Tourism Council) (1992) Travel & tourism: environment and development, *World Travel and Tourism Environment Review*, 1st edn. Brussels: WTTC.

Yorkshire Post (1978) Visitors to York. 9 August, p. 6.

—— (1994a) Holiday firms step up package price war, 4 August.

—— (1994b) Faltering city plans tourism campaign. 11 August.

Index